CRIMINAL INVESTIGATION

Consulting Editors for the Holbrook Press
Criminal Justice Series

VERN L. FOLLEY

Chief of Police
Bismarck, North Dakota

DONALD T. SHANAHAN

Associate Director, Southern Police Institute
and University of Louisville

WILLIAM J. BOPP

Director, Criminal Justice Program
Florida Atlantic University

George B. Mettler

CRIMINAL INVESTIGATION

HOLBROOK PRESS, INC.
BOSTON

Printed in the United States of America

Library of Congress Cataloging in Publication Data

Mettler, George B
    Criminal investigation.

    (Criminal justice series)
    Includes index.
    1. Criminal investigation. I. Title. II. Series:
Criminal justice series (Boston)
HV8073.M48   364.12   76–49649
ISBN 0–205–05761–6

To
Darlene
and
Jaime

There are some things which cannot be learned quickly,
and time, which is all we have,
must be paid heavily for their acquiring.
They are the very simplest things,
and because it takes a man's life to know them,
the little new that each man gets from life
is very costly and the only heritage he has to leave.

Ernest Hemingway

Contents

Preface

This book is the outgrowth of a series of lectures given in criminal justice at Macon Junior College in the fall of 1974 and 1975. I hope the lectures were interesting as well as informative. I hold the same hope for this book. It has been written as the lectures were given, with primarily the student-reader in mind. I trust, therefore, that any element of pedanticism that might still exist in the presentation of the material is slight and unobtrusive.

Though I have excised most of the personal anecdotes used in the lectures, I have endeavored to retain a bit of the humor in a subject matter that might easily become ponderous. I can see no valid reason why the learning process cannot be served in a palatable form without any measurable loss of substance.

The book is intended as an introduction to the fundamentals of criminal investigation, not as a definitive treatment of the subject. As such, it should serve the new student as a primer, the experienced investigator as a refresher exercise, and the general reader as a thought-provoking introduction to the phenomenon of crime and its investigation in our society.

In no way should the reader anticipate mastery of the specialty of criminal investigation upon completion of the book, no matter how carefully it is studied. He or she should, however, acquire a thorough familiarity with the basic principles of investigation and the technical specialized services available to the modern investigator, as well as a succinct introduction to the rules of the criminal law, which are of such importance to the successful investigation and prosecution of any criminal offense.

I have resisted the temptation to explore in detail the

marvels of modern criminalistics, not because this aspect of criminal investigation is unimportant, but rather because it is so vital to overall success in the prevention, control, and investigation of crime in a modern society. As such, it requires book-length treatment by a competent criminalist and, in my opinion, should be studied as a major subject in its own right. I have also eschewed comprehensive coverage of the major substantive crimes so commonly found in textbooks on the subject of criminal investigation. The fundamentals herein discussed are generally applicable to all crimes. The student-reader should be thoroughly exposed to these fundamentals prior to undertaking a more intensive study of specific criminal offenses.

Nor have I devoted the space deserved to such important functions as report writing and records administration that might more properly and effectively be handled in another book. In view of the limited time element of the quarter and semester systems, I have found the present division of the vast body of information applicable to the subject of criminal investigation to be not only appropriate but helpful to the ultimate learning process.

This book is not intended as a training manual. It should, however, lay a foundation that will assist the student-reader in acquiring more advanced knowledge and specialized expertise by further diligent study and/or practical experience in the field of law enforcement. Most importantly, it should be acknowledged that the book is designed to make the student-reader think for himself by provoking far more questions than it provides answers.

In addition, the book is especially presented in such a way as to allow the course instructor considerable opportunity to bring to bear upon the material his own special interests or expertise, and, indeed, his philosophical orientation as to the crucial issues concerning crime and its detection and control in a democratic society.

Acknowledgments

I would like to express my gratitude to the students of Macon Junior College who were exposed, in slightly different form, to most of the material included in this book. The use of the manuscript as a working classroom text and the student reaction, comment, and advice have proven most helpful in fusing the component parts into, hopefully, a coherent whole.

My thanks also to Linda James, who typed the lecture notes and the early drafts of the manuscript.

Final appreciation must be reserved for my wife Darlene whose editorial assistance, final typing, and unflagging encouragement made the project a reality.

G.B.M.

Forsyth, Georgia

"I think we could safely rule out suicide, Watson."

From *Penthouse* Magazine, copyright 1976. Reprinted with permission.

SHERLOCK HOLMES

1

• *Historical Notes*

"But how the deuce did you know it was the butler?"

"It was elementary, my dear Watson."

If the investigation of a criminal offense were truly as prosaic as the exploits of the legendary Sherlock Holmes would make it seem, then real-life detectives would be as famous and highly paid as many of their fictional counterparts in novels, films, and television programs.

However, there is nothing simple or elementary about the conduct of a criminal investigation.

To understand the system of law enforcement and criminal investigation as we know it in America today, one must look to English history (if not to the fictional exploits of Sir Arthur Conan Doyle's Sherlock Holmes) in order to examine most of the practices and procedures of our police services that we more or less take for granted. For modern police service in America is a direct extension of the experiments in social control initiated in seventeenth- and eighteenth-century England.

The entire system of criminal law may be said to be nothing more than the means devised by man by which to regulate the ebb and flow of human behavior. That man has by and large failed in his efforts to so regulate society is a thesis that is calculated to engender a heated (often emotional) response from opponents and proponents alike. That criminal law as we know it today works imperfectly, however, seems beyond dispute. That it succeeds at all is perhaps beyond the bounds of man's reasonable expectations in light of the history of man's behavioral development.

Human life is thought to have begun countless millennia ago in the tidal beaches of the Pleistocene age and to have

culminated in the upright, square-shouldered, handsome creatures that we presently know ourselves to be. Any attempt to
account for man's existence throughout the course of these
protean millennia is clearly beyond the scope of this book. Likewise, any effort to trace the origins of criminal investigation into
these swirling mists of aboriginal experience is perhaps a task
more suited to a masochistic archaeological historian, rather
than to a criminologist.

However, that a system of criminal justice existed during
mankind's ancient dawn of development, however rudimentary,
is not a particularly improbable concept. Since it has been said
that history is the story of mankind, may one not contend that
criminology is nothing but history's police blotter account of
man's folly? Nor is there much persuasive evidence that such
folly is primarily a latter-day development. Certainly by the
time of the first great civilizations along the Nile–Euphrates
river basins, man had clearly begun to exhibit this most durable
of human traits.

As man developed into a social being, he avidly evolved
the means by which to destroy his peace and, eventually, society itself. He has apparently also developed the inclination
toward such destruction. Year after year, decade after decade,
century after century, man has pursued his unending march
toward civilization. He has settled into cities; he has raided and
conquered; he has formed larger cities, conducted more violent
raids, and imposed harsher, longer conquests. He has littered
the pages of history with stories of greed, lust, and indescribable
brutality; with jealousy, deceit, and treachery; with folly; and
with crime.

ANCIENT ORIGINS
OF CRIMINAL INVESTIGATION

In the earliest times, man's social actions were regulated by a
utilitarian law of survival. It was not until some two thousand
years before the birth of Christ—rather late in the long skein of
man's development—that we find mankind having progressed

to the utilization of a specifically formulated code of law in an attempt to regulate social behavior. The Code of Hammurabi, the legendary king of Babylonia, is the first known code of conduct of which we possess archaeological proof.

The several sections of the code were found to contain laws relating to agricultural matters, personal property, real estate, business, domestic relations, labor, personal injuries, and criminal offenses.

In addition, Babylonia was clearly revealed to have been an agricultural society, a materialistic society, and a multiclass society. Indeed, there were separate laws for the separate classes: one for the small body of freemen, another for the serving class, and still another for the numerically predominant body of slaves. Criminal penalties varied greatly depending upon the class of the victim and the perpetrator. (There are many voices in our present-day society that are heard to register a similar complaint.)

By modern standards, many of the penalties of the ancient code are thought to have been cruel and excessive, based as they were upon the principle of *lex talionis,* or the law of the talon. Of course, this same "eye for an eye" approach to justice was to be found some two thousand years later in the more popularly regarded Mosaic law. This code of conduct also dealt with discriminatory comprehensiveness with such matters as property rights, slaves, crimes, and immorality.

The existence of such criminal codes requires but slight argument, it would seem, to support the contention that there must also have been a duly constituted body of officials charged with the responsibility of enforcing the law according to the provisions of the code. A bark without a bite is poor protection indeed against the trespasser. But in order to put a direct trace onto the development of criminal investigation as a device for social control, we must move forward in time to the period that saw the emergence of the Greek city-states and subsequently the ascendancy of the Roman Empire. To do this requires a chronological leap of some fifteen hundred years, no mean feat in historical broad jumping.

The turbulence that characterized the leadership of the Greek city-states, in which powerful groups rose and fell upon the tide of their own special interests, could only be controlled by the creation and use of military units specifically designed to carry out the domestic policies of whatever contending group was in power. As larger and still larger kingdoms developed, their rulers maintained tight control over the lives of the burgeoning masses of citizens by the continued use of military police units and a security guard system.

When the Romans finally conquered the entire Mediterranean world, they imposed their own law and administrative system upon the assimilated Greek culture and, in doing so, exercised a lasting influence on the evolution of law enforcement as we know it in the modern world.

Mankind's first known attempt to secure universal justice was reflected in the Roman body of law known as *the twelve tables.* This socially progressive code applied to such matters as judicial process, property rights, inheritance laws, personal injuries, and crimes. In its several parts, it was not unlike the earlier Code of Hammurabi; in its spirit of equality and justice it was light-years away.

We can now look back in history and conclude that Augustus (63 B.C.–14 A.D.), the grandnephew and heir of Julius Caesar, was one of the foremost contributors to the cause of law enforcement in his time and his influence was felt for many centuries thereafter. The *vigiles of Rome* was an integrated service comprised of civilian appointees with the dual responsibility of controlling fires and of exercising police powers. The creation of this force was a landmark in the evolution of a modern system of law enforcement.

Roman contribution to the system of criminal justice as we know it today did not end with the innovations of Augustus, however. Subsequently, Emperor Justinian summarized the whole body of Roman law in what is referred to as *Corpus Juris Civilis,* the world's most influential compilation of laws. Included are such modern concepts of jurisprudence as the right to a fair trial, conviction only upon a clear proof of guilt, the right of the accused to face his accuser, and many more precepts that we now more or less accept as inalienable, at least in principle.

But the collapse of the Roman Empire around 500 A.D. plunged the western world into a dark night of ignorance and savagery (two scourges of mankind that have historically been found to exist in tandem) that lasted many hundreds of years. Indeed, it is not until the sixteenth century that the nature of the English social order was transformed from the harsh rural predominance of the middle ages to increasing urbanization and technological advances that led man's way, however falteringly, out of the barbarism of the Dark Ages.

This is not to say that the medieval period was devoid of contribution to the system of criminal justice. The governmental structure and culture of its people evolved in England during this period, and in this respect, influences extending until this very day were experienced. In fact, the administrative structure of present-day American society, its states and towns and cities, and its judiciary and policing agencies can be directly traced to these early English antecedents.

During the reign of Henry II, for example, we have the origin of the trial by jury and of the indictment for a criminal offense by a jury. It was also during the reign of this Angevin king that judges began to maintain a record of their decisions and thus laid the foundation for the body of *common law* upon which modern American law so depends. And not least of the advances during the Middle Ages was the promulgation of the *Magna Carta* in 1215, which assured the concept of due process of law and trial by jury as a right of the people.

Then there were the enormous contributions of King Edward I, who seems to have influenced the course of law enforcement as much as did Augustus Caesar some one thousand years before him. To combat the shocking rise in crime within his kingdom and the apparent indifference of the citizenry, Edward issued the momentous Statute of Winchester, which placed responsibility for crime control and the administration of justice squarely upon the local citizenry. This requirement gave official sanction to the necessity of raising and maintaining local police units to carry out the royal edict and new impetus to the budding profession of law enforcement.

However, the development of the law and its enforcement

toward equity and justice was not an unbroken progression guided by wisdom and fair play. There were (and are) numerous pitfalls, setbacks, and "dead spaces" along the way. Such was the environment sponsored by the reign of Charles I (1625–1645).

In his continuing dispute with Parliament over who was to run the country, Charles used the Court of Star Chamber much as a bludgeon to coerce Parliament into acceding to his will. The court had been instituted by Henry II in 1487 as a special forum in which to adjudicate cases of official corruption, such as the bribing of sheriffs, constables, or jurymen. The members of the court were appointed by the king and served at his pleasure. It proved to be an infamous body in concept and deed.

The Court of Star Chamber assimilated all of the components of the criminal justice system unto itself. It issued criminal charges, caused persons so charged to be arrested and brought before the court, tried the case, and pronounced the sentence. In operation, the procedure was a simple one indeed; to be charged by the court was tantamount to conviction.

Although the decisions of the court were in most cases preconceived without application to any evidence supporting the charges, the court was much moved to favor the introduction of confessions into the record. Such confessions were routinely extracted from the accused by means of cruel tortures limited in variety only by the imagination of man. It is not surprising that the judgments of the Court of Star Chamber were more often than not supported by a high percentage of "confessions." One can only suppose that the investigators for the court developed the technique of interrogation to a degree of professionalism seldom surpassed in the evolution of the art and science of criminal investigation.

Finally, Charles and his henchmen on the Court carried their expertise to such inordinate excesses that the country was driven into a state of civil war. In 1649, Charles was defeated, tried in a court of law, convicted of treason, and beheaded.

A period of military rule followed in England, under the protectorate of Oliver Cromwell (1653–1658). Law and order descended upon the country with a vengeance, martial law replacing civil law in the belief that nothing short of total military control would prove successful in curtailing the rampant crime and disorder that followed the collapse of the royal succession.

After the death of Cromwell, Charles II was invited by Parliament in 1660 to resume the throne under strict democratic conditions, including the rule of *habeas corpus*. The king was to rule by the consent of the people, not by divine right. Parliament, as the instrument of the people, had emerged as the dominant body of government. The future governance of the United States was to be affected by this system.

With the coming of the industrial revolution, which began in England around 1760, we have an environment that all but dictates the next giant stride in the development of the rule of law and the profession of law enforcement. With the advent of this period we can now begin to examine some of the more pronounced advancements in the techniques of criminal investigation.

MODERN ORIGINS
OF CRIMINAL INVESTIGATION

In the first wave of the industrial revolution, the crime rate was rising in England to a degree never known before. Nowhere were social conditions more deplorable than in the great city of London itself, the first city of the world by every standard of evaluation. Citizens were literally unsafe on the streets and in their homes, day or night. Henry Fielding, a novelist and justice of the peace, was among the first to see the need for a formal police force to cope with the rampant crime rate. Most police historians consider the "Bow Street Runners," organized by Fielding in 1750, as the first civilian "detective" force. Although this unit never exceeded fifteen members, it served London with a modicum of success for nearly a century. (It also served as a linchpin of forensic science to modern society.)

Society was also bursting at its seams on the continent. In France, another innovative attempt to cope with the spiraling rate of crime was the formation of the Paris Sureté in 1810. This new investigative organization was characterized by the novel philosophy and background of its leader, Eugene Francois Vidocq.

A former French criminal of no small reputation, Vidocq convinced the authorities of his day that crime could only be successfully contested by detectives who had come by their knowledge of crime and criminals firsthand. He was selected to administer such a unit of investigators and in turn chose his men from the ranks of former criminals. In the twenty years that Vidocq supervised the Sureté, he achieved outstanding if controversial results. He was finally forced to step down, however, when the concept of an investigative force made up of former criminals fell into official disfavor.

Meanwhile, in England the Bow Street Runners had incurred a similar official disfavor (and for much the same reasons as the French Sureté). The passage of the Metropolitan Police Act in 1829 saw the creation of the first formal police service, rendering the Bow Street operations obsolete. Sir Robert Peel was named by Parliament to head the new organization. The astonishing success of the Metropolitan Police is still a high watermark in the history of law enforcement. The principles of professionalism laid down and scrupulously implemented by Peel are as applicable to modern police service as they were in 1829.

As early as 1842, the plainclothes division of the Metropolitan Police was established by assigning twelve policemen to what has become popularly known as Scotland Yard. The exploits of Scotland Yard are, of course, legendary. Author Charles Dickens is credited with the coinage of the word "detective" when his fictional Inspector Buckets introduced himself in the novel *Bleak House:* "I am Buckets of the detectives," he said. "I am a detective officer."

And from Buckets to Sherlock Holmes, to Sam Spade and Dick Tracy, the function of the specially trained criminal investigator has evolved in fact and fiction to the point that "detective" is now a household word.

The practice of officially sponsored "detecting," however,

FIG. 1.1   Sir Robert Peel (1788–1850)   (Historical Pictures Service, Chicago)

appears to have come into American police procedures in fits and starts. One of the earliest detective forces was a three-man unit established in Boston in 1846. It was not until 1857 that New York established an official unit of police officers designated as "detectives." Chicago established its first detective unit in 1860, followed by the city of Detroit in 1866. There is no doubt that corruption and malfeasance in office was endemic to police service in the early years of U.S. law enforcement; modern scandals are based on solid precedents. There are, in fact, police administrations in America today that could in no way measure up to the standards or the performance of Sir Robert Peel's "Bobbies" of 1829.

Still, the concept of specialization in the investigation of

Wyatt Earp (U.S. Signal Corps Photo Number 111–SC–94117 in the National Archives)

Pat Garrett (Collections in the Museum of New Mexico)

Allan Pinkerton (Courtesy Pinkerton's, Inc.)

FIG. 1.2 Famous U.S lawmen

Elliot Ness   (United Press International Photo)   J. Edgar Hoover   (FBI/ Washington, D.C.)

FIG. 1.2—*continued*

criminal offenses continued to make its impact upon American law enforcement. By the early 1900s, most of the major police services in the country—city, county, and state—included a detective force of one size or another, of one degree of effectiveness or another. In spite of chicanery and incompetence, the fledgling specialty of criminal investigation had come a long way toward professionalism since its inception. In addition, the federal government also employed criminal investigators in numerous departments throughout the national bureaucracy. The Justice Department, the Department of the Treasury, the Post Office Department, and the Departments of Defense and State were merely a few that maintained federal law enforcement agencies.

In 1924, federal law enforcement was given its greatest impetus toward professionalism in its history. President Calvin Coolidge appointed Harlan Fiske Stone—who was subsequently to become chief justice of the Supreme Court—as U.S. attorney general. Stone in turn appointed a young lawyer in the Department of Justice to be his director of the Bureau of Investigation. This agency later became known as the Federal Bureau of Investigation. The twenty-nine-year-old lawyer was J. Edgar Hoover. He served as director of the FBI for forty-three years, until his death in 1972.

The task of reorganization and professional leadership that Hoover faced in administering the inefficient and corrupt Bureau of Investigation beginning in 1924 was not unlike the challenge met and mastered by Sir Robert Peel in London slightly more than a century before. Legend has it that when Attorney General Stone offered him the position, Hoover replied that he would accept only upon the agreement of two conditions: 1) that appointment to the Bureau be based solely upon merit, and 2) that there be absolutely no politics involved in the administration of the Bureau.

Stone is said to have replied: "I wouldn't give you the job under any other circumstances."

• DISCUSSION QUESTIONS

1. *Why should the modern criminal investigator concern himself with the historical development of systems of law?*

2. *What does the Code of Hammurabi have in common with modern codes of law?*

3. *How influential was the Roman* Corpus Juris Civilis *upon western civilization?*

2

- **Contemporary
Observations**

Criminal law and criminal investigations, like every other aspect of society, are subject to the forces of social organization. The primary characteristic of the society in which we live is change. There has been more change in man's way of life in this century than in all the history of man before it. And those who survive the coming decade will in all likelihood see even further changes.

The issue of survival has always been uppermost on man's list of priorities. In a stable society, survival depends primarily upon adherence to the tactics for survival that have proved effective in the past. The old adage that "nothing succeeds like success itself" has long since proved its truth. In an unstable environment, however, in which drastic change is the rule and not the exception, it is necessary to discard many of the techniques of survival that succeeded in the past but which have little, if any, relevance to survival in the present or in the future.

This is a task far easier suggested than accomplished. For we have often paid a heavy price for the accumulation of such knowledge and have suffered and sacrificed greatly in order to retain it. Yet, if our customs no longer serve our needs, we must somehow find the courage to set them aside. We can honor the past, and of course we should do so when our past is deserving of honor. We can remember the past always. But we cannot live in the past—not if we wish to survive in the future.

Therefore we must develop new concepts, new techniques, new strategies for survival that will meet the challenges of our changing times. These developments, too, will be bought and paid for with pain, sacrifice, and suffering. But without such growth, we will surely pay the ultimate price—our extinction as a people with a viable role to play in the onward march of civilization.

In this regard, there is no aspect of society that can benefit more by accepting this challenge than the field of law enforcement. And the specialty of criminal investigations, while drawing upon the tried-and-proven fundamentals of its accumulated experience, must now move ahead into the realm of the future.

Not everything need be abandoned, of course, only that which no longer serves our needs. The frontiersmen could circle their wagons and draw in upon themselves when under attack. It was an effective technique at times. Today we cannot circle our wagons in the face of swarming crime. If we draw in upon ourselves and cling to the old strategies, we will be hopelessly overwhelmed. Mere population alone will trample our static defenses. Consider this prospect: by 1990, there will almost certainly be an additional billion people in the world!

Developments in science and technology will make it impossible to detect, control, and prevent crime by the use of outmoded techniques of criminal investigation. Indeed, it is already impossible. Law enforcement has lagged far behind its times in this respect. It dare not fall much further behind.

That professional police service is lacking in most jurisdictions today, especially in the field of scientific investigation, is incontestable. Most police agencies, including the biggest and most widely acclaimed, do not function anywhere near peak efficiency. It is axiomatic that most police officers are undereducated, undertrained, and grossly underpaid. The same holds true for most police administrators.

On the other hand, the educational and cultural level of the majority of our population—our youth—is consistently rising, increasing the separation between our police and the very people they are supposed to serve.

Everywhere the volume of crime increases as the primary causes of crime increase; such causes as overpopulation, environmental pollution (physical, spiritual, and cultural), and social intolerance. We live in a time when every value we once cherished has become suspect, and more often than not for good reason, a fact that only makes our prospects for survival all the more frightening.

This is not an inappropriate period in American history in which to undertake the study of criminal investigation. A criminal investigation in its simplest terms is a search for the truth concerning the facts surrounding the commission of a crime. A crime is, for all practical purposes, that which the most powerful voices in our society say it is. A criminal, in short, is one who violates the rules and regulations laid down by the powerful among us.

It seems rather safe to say that if we as a society sincerely wish to prevent and control criminal activity in the changing future, then our system of justice is going to be required to balance the scales a little more even-handedly than it has done heretofore. We will have to wield the cutting sword with a bit more discrimination.

THE MODERN CRIMINAL INVESTIGATOR

What role, then, does the modern criminal investigator play in accepting this challenge of the future? As a professional, he must study and analyze the methods of investigation used in the past, discarding those methods that no longer work, and improving upon the many methods that do still apply. It is reasonable to suggest that he will have no small opportunity to develop his expertise through the time-honored technique of trial-and-error, since crime—the raw material of his craft—is likely to be around in abundance for a considerable time to come.

The seeds of such a dour prediction might more readily be found in our national character than in an examination of the ever-spiraling crime statistics with which we are regularly confronted. For is there any nation of people with a more abiding fascination for crime and the perpetrators of crime than our own? One wonders if it is because we are so inundated with crime or whether crime is rampant as a more or less natural outgrowth of our collective obsession with it.

Most criminologists and social scientists probably agree

that Americans generally have an overwhelming sense of curiosity about crime; the more violent and grotesque, the more avid the curiosity.

We seem to be inordinately intrigued by successful crime and openly cheer the more flamboyant criminal in his exploits. We have made enduring folk heroes of the likes of Jesse James, Al Capone, John Dillinger, Eldridge Cleaver, and Charles Manson. Novels, TV, and movies are saturated with crime stories featuring detectives and private eyes only slightly more loyal to the precepts of the Constitution than the lawless criminals they pursue. Leading gangsters are portrayed by leading actors who make their subjects all the more appealing by adding to their criminal legend the power of the performer's own mystique, personality, and celluloid charm. A random sampling of such casting might include the following:

Jesse James	Tyrone Power
Frank James	Henry Fonda
Al Capone	Rod Steiger
Pretty-Boy Floyd	James Cagney
The Godfather	Marlon Brando
Butch Cassidy	Paul Newman
The Sundance Kid	Robert Redford
Bonnie & Clyde	Faye Dunaway & Warren Beatty

A casual examination of the records and photographs of such "heroes," however, gives the lie to the living legend. (Fig. 2.1.) For the most part, they were dirty, scruffy little punks, deformed physically, mentally, and socially. They had in common only a certain evil genius and a fierce animal amorality that permitted them to snarl their way through a world to which they could only relate in terms of dog-eat-dog. One of the young female killers of Sharon Tate could only respond to her victim's plea for mercy on behalf of her unborn child with the following revelation: "Look, bitch, I have no mercy for you."

And yet we Americans honor their memory and gild their legends with gold and glitter. The likes of Lee Harvey Oswald,

Sirhan Sirhan, James Earl Ray, and Squeaky Fromme are given national magazine cover treatment—not the victims but the assassins and would-be assassins. Why?

As a people, what so fascinates us about crime and criminals? Perhaps we are tottering on the cutting edge of a collective state of schizophrenia. On the one hand we profess an impeccable code of public and private morality; yet, on the other hand our society is infested with crime, and we glorify violence and immorality. It must tell us something fundamental about the American character. A criminal investigator ignores such implications at his professional and personal peril.

NATURE OF A CRIMINAL INVESTIGATION

Simply defined, a criminal investigation is nothing more or less than a search for the truth. The search is accomplished by a systematic examination of facts; the detection and collection of physical evidence; and the identification, location, interview, and interrogation of witnesses and suspects—all in an effort to reconstruct the physical and mental elements comprising a violation of the criminal law.

Although such a definition is simply put, the actual searching out of the truth concerning the commission of a crime is easier said than done. Mr. Shakespeare is guilty of oversimplification at the least, when he assures us that the "truth will out."

Criminal investigation is far from being a discipline with fixed rules and techniques that insure success. More often than not, the sum of two plus two does not equal four. There are some cases that practically solve themselves, others that are solved only as a result of hard work and heavy infusions of luck, and still others that are never solved at all. Criminal investigation is an art that numbers but few Picassos among its practitioners, a science that has yet to produce its Einstein.

It might be useful at this point to give a moment's attention to the exact nature of a criminal investigation. This perhaps

Jesse James (left) and Frank James (right) with their mother (The Bettman Archive)

Henry Fonda (left) as Frank James and Tyrone Power (right) as Jesse James (The Museum of Modern Art/Film Stills Archive)

Al Capone ("The News")

Rod Steiger as Al Capone (The Museum of Modern Art/Film Stills Archive)

FIG. 2.1 Notorious criminals and actors who portrayed them

Pretty Boy Floyd   (United Press International Photo)

James Cagney as Pretty Boy Floyd (The Museum of Modern Art/Film Stills Archive)

"The Godfather"   (Photo by Pat Torelli)

Marlon Brando as "The Godfather" (Paramount Pictures)

Butch Cassidy (extreme right) and Harry Longbaugh, "The Sundance Kid" (extreme left)   (Photo from Pinkerton's Archives)

Paul Newman as Butch Cassidy and Robert Redford as "The Sundance Kid"   (The Museum of Modern Art/Film Stills Archive)

FIG. 2.1—*continued*

26

Clyde Barrow   (The Bettman   Bonnie Parker   (United Press
Archive)   International Photo)

Warren Beatty as Clyde and Faye Dunaway as Bonnie
(Pictorial Parade)

might best be done by recognizing at the outset the difficulty of precisely defining a criminal investigation, notwithstanding the preceding attempt to do so. The procedure cannot in truth be called an artistic endeavor, nor a scientific pursuit. Nor is the socially sanctioned commission of investigating the occurrence of criminal offenses in the larger sense a profession. Perhaps the best that can be said is that a definition of the occupation of criminal investigation is comprised of aspects of all of the above considerations.

Generally, any field of inquiry that yields knowledge susceptible of exact formulation is called a science. Every science begins as philosophy, dealing in hypothesis, and develops into a science only upon the achievements of its formulations. Criminal investigation is a mode of inquiry not unlike the philosophical pursuit of knowledge that concerns itself with problems not often reducible to scientific certainty—matters such as good and evil, love and hate, chaos and order, repression and freedom, and, above all, life and death and the pursuit of happiness.

What, then, shall we call this undertaking, if not a profession, if not truly an art or science? Throughout this book, I shall refer to criminal investigation as a specialty, leaving to each reader the opportunity of ascribing a more precise definition according to the tendency of his own perception.

Criminal investigation, then, restated, is an activity, a specialty, that is based upon instinct and craftsmanship (art), that utilizes the stunning advances in science and technology that the twentieth century has placed at its disposal.

In practice, however, there is no aspect of law enforcement more open to just criticism than the gross neglect of police agencies in failing to utilize these technological advances in the exercise of crime detection. The potential in this regard has scarcely been tapped by our nation's police services.

If the end result of any criminal investigation is the discovery of truth, then it is axiomatic that whatever techniques and scientific aids are employed, an investigator never sets out on a case determined to establish guilt or innocence. He should endeavor to gather facts that tend to establish the truth, be that truth the guilt or innocence of a particular suspect or suspects.

The time-honored precept of American criminal law must pertain even in the investigatory phase of the criminal justice process: every accused person is presumed innocent until guilt has been established in a proper court of law. It is a principle too often taken for granted.

That the presumption applies to such offenders as mass murderers, child molesters, and sadistic rapists is often a bitter pill for a conscientious investigator to swallow. However, a truly conscientious investigator *will* swallow it, if not cheerfully, then dutifully. He might ameliorate the odious taste in his mouth by reminding himself that he might someday have occasion to be personally thankful for the protection offered by the presumption. That it applies to everyone and for everyone, police officers included, is the special strength of the concept.

A professional investigator, then, is one who arrives at the truth and accepts that truth, whether it be the establishment of guilt or innocence.

A criminal investigation need not be—indeed, it should not be—a static exercise in progressive routine. An investigation properly conducted is a creative activity with a goal as noble and socially desirable as any painting or work of music or literature. Through the discovery of Truth, it seeks to establish Justice. In point of fact, many artists have made the identical search the cornerstone of their work, for in the last analysis, there is no higher form of Ideal Beauty than the face and figure of Justice.

- **DISCUSSION QUESTIONS**

1. *What is the primary characteristic of modern society, and how does it affect our lives in both the present and the future?*

2. *What role will the criminal investigator play in the coming decades in view of the answer to the question above?*

3

• The Crime Scene

It is a quiet deep-starred moonless night. And it is hot. The deputy sheriff pulls his cruiser under the sagging canopy of a roadside grocery store and sits for a moment with the engine idling. It has been a slow, boring night and his lower back is aching from sitting too long in one position. Still, he hesitates before getting out of the car.

He has stopped at this store for coffee and cigarettes dozens of times in his three years with the department. He was later to contend that he'd known something was wrong the instant he'd pulled up in front of the store. At the moment though, he isn't sure why the hackles on the back of his neck are so cold and prickly.

The front door is partially open, but there's nothing particularly odd about that. The light is on, the radio is blaring country music as usual. But something is *wrong;* he can *feel* it in his guts.

He turns off the engine but leaves the headlights burning. As he climbs out of the cruiser, he can feel his pulse beginning to quicken and can taste the tension in his mouth. He unsnaps the safety over his .357 magnum and moves cautiously toward the door.

There is no need for a weapon. What he needs is a good strong stomach. Inside, the owner of the store, his teenaged daughter, and two men are lying face down on the floor. Their hands are tied behind their backs, and all but the girl's feet are bound with rope at the ankles.

All of them have had the backs of their heads blown off.

That the above narrative is a blend of fact and fiction does not make it any the less useful to our purpose in the study of the fundamentals of criminal investigation. What we must do is examine the crime scene in systematic detail, using as our guide certain principles of investigation that have proven effective in the past.

Of course, not all investigators in fact utilize all of these fundamentals. Some, alas, use few if any. But there is no set routine that an investigation must follow, no check list of techniques that will insure success. Intuition, imagination, and improvisation all play an important part.

And yet creativity of the highest order is generally unproductive unless it is based upon a solid foundation of fundamental knowledge. It is almost certain that the investigator who is known in his field as a great improviser is likewise a master of the fundamentals of his craft. Long before Picasso assaulted the world of imagination, he had made the reality of nature his ABCs.

What, then, are the ABCs of criminal investigation, and how should they be applied to the above case?

First, let's further develop the factual statement of the case.

After vomiting beside the fender of the cruiser, the deputy recovers his poise and instantly gets on the car radio for assistance. There is no dispatcher on duty at the sheriff's department after midnight, so he is forced to contact the nearest State Patrol station and request that they telephone the sheriff at his home. The deputy is more than a little relieved when the dispatcher says he will send a state trooper directly to the scene to assist him until the sheriff can arrive.

There is nothing to do but wait. Suddenly he notices the silence, broken only by the rasping sound of his own irregular breathing. Certainly the others are no longer breathing. Like shattered clocks, they have ceased keeping time. But is there anyone else on the premises?

His scalp begins to burn, there is a terrible itching at the base of his spine. He wishes now that he'd gone to the bathroom at his last stop. As he moves around behind the cruiser, his grip tightens on his revolver, and he strains his eyes to see in the shadows, his ears to catch any sound other than his own heartbeat.

He is later to admit that had a cat moved suddenly in the darkness he would have blasted it into a sodden ball of fur. When asked what he would have done had a human walked around the corner of the building, he could only shake his head and reply: "God only knows. I don't."

He finds himself pressed as close as possible to the side of the building. The killer might be lurking behind any of those darkened windows upstairs. And suppose there was more than one. Somebody might be over in those bushes or behind that big oak tree, sighting down the barrel of a shotgun right this very moment.

He drops to one knee and cocks the hammer of his revolver. The sound is like a mallet striking against an anvil. In his mind's eye he can still see the gruesome sight on the floor inside. And then, in a split flash of precognition, he visualizes his own body sprawled in the dew-wet grass beneath his feet.

The deputy has never known anything like the sensation that now washes over him. He has never knowingly faced death before, never killed anyone, never seen a dead body. Now there are four corpses on the floor inside, and the stench of his own death is vile in his nostrils. He wonders what he will do if . . . Thoughts begin racing through his mind. Why had he ever taken such a job in the first place? Suppose something should happen to him. What about his wife and kids? Would it be worth it to lose his life in such a job as this? Would anyone care?

He is more than a little relieved when the State Patrol car arrives. He greets the trooper and relates the few facts in his possession, then waits as the trooper goes inside the store. When the trooper returns, grim-faced, the two officers continue a search of the grounds with their guns drawn.

Moments later, the sheriff, followed by his chief deputy, wheel their cars into the gravel drive with blue lights flashing and both sirens blaring.

The sheriff rushes directly inside the store, followed closely by his chief assistant. The trooper and the deputy remain out-side where a crowd is beginning to gather. Neighbors drawn by the sound of sirens, flashing lights and general commotion; passing motorists stopping along the shoulders of the roadway to see what the excitement is all about; and the editor of the local weekly newspaper, who has left his car just behind the state trooper's vehicle and is busily snapping photographs through the windows with his Polaroid land camera.

The trooper goes out to the road and attempts to keep the traffic moving while the sheriff's deputy attempts to handle the milling crowd. Wide-eyed children, barefooted and in pajamas, are climbing in and out of the patrol cruisers, while the adults bob and weave about in an effort to catch a glimpse of what is going on inside.

Suddenly a collective gasp sweeps through the crowd like a hot wind up in the pine trees. They watch in stunned fascina-tion as the chief deputy pushes open the screened door and scrapes his highly polished boot back and forth across the old fieldstone step, leaving a swath of blood that looks like smeared paint on the stone.

Just then another official vehicle arrives, containing a driver and the county coroner. They leave the car in the drive-way and proceed directly inside the store. While the door is still open, the sheriff comes over and tells the young deputy to come inside and make a search of the upstairs living quarters.

Someone in the crowd remarks that the old coroner looked like he was three sheets in the wind again, and their laughter coincides with the slamming of the screened door.

Just inside the door, the young deputy pauses before what appears to be a wide patch of smeared blood. He looks around for a clear path over to the stairs, finds one and takes it. He is about half way upstairs when the sheriff exclaims in an excited voice: "Here it is fellas!"

He is standing behind the store counter with a double-barreled shotgun clutched in both hands and a grin that seems to split his face from ear to ear.

The deputy shakes his head and proceeds upstairs to com-plete his assignment. He wishes the sheriff hadn't sent him up here alone. It would be good to have a back-up man, just in case. It certainly wouldn't *hurt* anything. Even if that is the murder weapon downstairs, there might be others. The murderers probably wouldn't still be around, but you never could tell.

He opens the bedroom door and his heart nearly leaps out of his mouth.

It is dark inside, but sufficient light from the hall has spilled into the room to reveal the storekeeper's wife sitting on the side of the bed in some sort of trance. Later, he remembered thinking that she looked like a cold marble statue. She just sat there, he testified in court, staring at a spot on the floor in front of her. She didn't even look up when he entered the room. She was wearing her nightgown, her hair was up in curlers as if she was ready for bed, and there was dried blood all over the front of her gown and on her hands and bare feet.

He takes her downstairs. She offers no resistance, gives no sign of recognition. She moves like a sleepwalker, totally unaware of her surroundings. She has not said a word.

The sheriff is obviously relieved. They are no longer searching for a killer, nor even for physical clues. They have the murder weapon and the perpetrator; what they want now is a motive. Why in the world has she done it? Why would she kill her own husband and daughter; not to mention the other two men, whoever they are?

The sheriff enters into a discussion with his chief deputy, both men considering the worst possible motive they can think of. The daughter is an awfully pretty little thing they agree, or used to be. They'd heard she'd always been something of a flirt, real grown-up for her age and all. And everyone knew her father was no better than he ought to be. There had been stories about them being seen together, drinking together, running around with a pretty wild crowd. It was possible. It was certainly reason enough, a thing like that between a man and his own flesh, to cause a woman to commit murder.

They wondered who the other two men were though. They'd never seen either one before, and neither man had a scrap of identification in his pockets. The sheriff wondered too why the girl's feet hadn't been tied up like all the others had been?

The chief deputy said he couldn't find any shotgun casings, and the sheriff wondered about that too. Maybe they should have asked the woman some questions before sending her off to the hospital with that young deputy. She'd seemed to be in pretty bad shape though, and he didn't suppose she would tell them much until she'd gotten over the shock.

"What we have to do right now," reminds the chief deputy, "is try to identify these dead men."

Three neighbors are called inside for a look. The coroner has already turned the bodies over and had them placed side by side for easier handling. No one recognizes the two dead men. Both are poorly dressed; neither man has a billfold or any other identification on his person.

The sheriff goes over and counts the money in the cash register. Fifty-two dollars and some change. Robbery certainly wasn't the motive, and this fact served to reinforce his theory of the case: it was a crime of passion, an act of revenge. The woman was the murderess. He writes out a penciled receipt and puts it in the cash register and then puts the money in his pocket.

Meanwhile, at least six more witnesses have come in to view the bodies. Everybody identifies the man and his daughter, but no one has ever seen the other two men before.

The sheriff looks at his watch. It is after two o'clock. He says that that about wraps it up. It's pretty late, so they might as well get the bodies over to the morgue. They'll lock the place up real good and then come back in the daytime and make a more careful check of things.

INVESTIGATIVE IMPLICATIONS OF THE HYPOTHETICAL CASE

Clearly there are any number of inadequacies in the investigative technique in the above narrative. Mistakes at this point in an investigation may very well prove fatal. Though many texts on criminal investigation will contend that this or that phase of an investigation is the most important, in fact, there is no such phase. They are all equally important. Certainly none is more vital to the overall investigation, however, than the handling of the crime scene itself.

The first consideration at this point might very well be to effect a definition of the crime scene. Exactly what is it? Where is it? How can an investigator recognize it?

The obvious definition is that it is the place where the crime was committed. But is the location where the crime was committed always, in fact, so obvious?

In the strict topographical sense, many criminal offenses do not have a crime "scene" at all. For example, it doesn't much matter "where" the crime of forgery actually took place, nor is the actual "location" of the crime of official bribery controlling concerning the commission of the crime itself. These acts are crimes irrespective of where they occurred, and the fact of a person's presence in a given location is not of much evidentiary value in determining if he is the perpetrator of such a crime.

The act of forging a commercial document may take place in a warehouse, an armchair, or a bathtub without affecting the nature of the offense itself. Likewise, an official may allow himself to be bribed at the dinner table, in the boudoir of a lady of the night, or in a rowboat in the middle of the ocean. The offender may come and go without secrecy or stealth, leaving clear traces of his presence and identity.

A quite different situation is presented, however, in cases in which the surroundings themselves may have a bearing on the commission of the crime and on the identity of its perpetrator. In such cases, to know exactly "where" an act occurred, when and under what circumstances, and to know who has been at the scene and when, may also be to know who perpetrated the crime as well.

This is particularly so in property crimes and in crimes of violence. It would be rather difficult to establish a case of arson without knowing the exact location of the burned building. And the actual spot in which a homicide took place might very well be controlling in the determination of whether the death was a result of an accident or of premeditated design. In such cases, the crime scene itself must be considered a vital part of the investigation.

For example, taking shoe impressions or dusting for latent fingerprints in the bookkeeping department of a bank in which an embezzlement has recently taken place may very well be omitted. Failure to do so in the case of a homicide having occurred in the same room might well constitute criminal negligence on the part of the investigators.

Such investigative oversights are not merely imagined by inexperienced novelists or TV script writers. By way of practical example, in the case popularly referred to as the Manson–Sharon Tate murders, out of forty-five samples of blood types taken from the gory scene, only a mere twenty-four examinations of subtypes were ever run by the criminalistics experts. (There are thirty known blood subtypes. If blood is already dry, however, only three of these may be determined.) The actual crime scene was a veritable fountain of evidentiary information bearing directly upon the perpetration of the offenses. Such an investigative oversight as that previously mentioned by one of the leading police agencies in the country can only prompt one to speculate upon the performance of lesser-endowed departments.

DEFINING THE CRIME SCENE

It is no simple task, however, to specify the crime scene of a particular case, let alone to work it. What is its perimeter; where does it begin and end?

The answer can be given quite succinctly: there are no set boundaries of a crime scene. It may extend from a room to a few hundred yards, to a mile or more, or even span an ocean. The criminal act itself may begin in one location and be concluded in another jurisdiction entirely. A homicide scene may be confined to one room or, again, as in the Manson-Tate-LaBianca cases, it may embrace an entire building and its surrounding grounds.

An alert investigator must never accept the barrier of a closed door or a precipitous height to scale and must always avoid painting himself into that proverbial corner of no escape. He should bear in mind at all times the possibility that a corpse on the living room floor may very well have begun its journey into death in a waterbed on the second story.

Some years ago, author Ralph Ellison wrote a novel entitled *The Invisible Man.* He was speaking metaphorically of course. In reality there is no such animal as the invisible man. In the course of his journey through life, man always leaves his mark in one form or another. So does the criminal. The Bible says: "And by your deeds shall ye be known." You shall also be known by your fingerprints, palmar surfaces, blood type, voiceprint, laundry markings, and so on.

And not only does a criminal more often than not leave his own mark at the scene of the crime, he is likewise apt to carry away with him evidentiary traces of where he has been. For the locus of a crime is very often a movable scene. Rape committed on a sandy beach may very well be traced to the perpetrator by an examination of the sand particles in a pair of tennis shoes in his bedroom closet.

The scene of the crime, then, is a veritable Pandora's box of evidentiary goodies. More is required of the criminal investigator, however, than merely opening the lid.

• DISCUSSION QUESTIONS

1. *Is the hypothetical case nothing more than TV melodrama, or does it have a more relevant application to modern police work?*

2. *What is the relationship between fear and courage, and how does such a relationship apply to police work?*

3. *What are the generally accepted boundaries of a crime scene?*

4. *Name two primary means by which an individual might be connected with any crime scene.*

4

• *Types of Investigations*

There are two primary types of criminal investigations that, depending upon the nature of the case, may more or less overlap in their execution. These are the *preliminary investigation* and the *continuing investigation.*

The focus of the preliminary investigation is the crime scene itself. It should first establish whether or not a crime exists in fact and in law. It should then determine, if possible, the identity of the perpetrator(s) of the crime, the victim(s), the existence or absence of witnesses and physical evidence closely related to the crime scene; and it should insure the integrity of the crime scene itself.

The continuing investigation is simply that phase of the investigation that follows the preliminary phase. The line of demarcation between the two, however, is not an easy one to draw in every case. The preliminary phase generally should be concluded prior to pursuing investigative leads produced thereby. The nature of the crime itself is generally controlling in determining whether or not the investigation must continue in depth from the moment the first officer arrives upon the scene.

If, by way of example, the suspected perpetrator of a previously reported homicide should fire a greeting shot through the windshield of the patrol vehicle as the investigating officer first approaches the scene, then it is not unreasonable for the officer to decide on the spot to press his preliminary investigation to the point of disarming and apprehending the suspect. (It is also hoped that the officer will have the training and presence of mind to radio for assistance before attempting any major action alone.) Both phases of the investigation are of necessity fused.

On the other hand, there are many cases in which the continuing investigation might follow only after a period of hours, or even days, has elapsed since the conclusion of the preliminary phase of the investigation.

THE PRELIMINARY INVESTIGATION

The arrest of the perpetrator of the crime is the ultimate goal of any criminal investigation. If the identification and arrest cannot be accomplished upon the officer's arrival at the scene of the crime, however, then the preliminary investigation is primarily responsible for developing the following three aspects of the case: the protecting and searching of the crime scene; the collection, marking, and preservation of physical evidence; and the location and interviewing of witnesses.

Arrival at the Crime Scene

A police investigation of a suspected criminal offense generally begins either when a crime is reported by a concerned citizen or is detected by the police agency itself. Typically, uniformed, noninvestigative personnel are the first officers to respond to such reports.

The first obligation of the initial officer arriving at the scene of the crime is to determine whether or not the perpetrator is still present and, if he is, whether or not he is likely to be dangerous. If the suspect is present, and if it is feasible to do so, the officer should arrest him. If a one-man arrest is impractical or too dangerous under the circumstances, the officer should immediately radio for assistance and then maintain surveillance on the scene until the appropriate back-up support arrives.

Assuming the officer has satisfied himself that the perpetrator is no longer present, he should then render whatever emergency assistance is required to any injured or frightened persons on the scene and again radio for whatever medical assistance is necessary.

After determining the exact nature of the crime and the

time it occurred as nearly as possible, if eye witnesses are available, the officer should obtain a description of the perpetrator and of the manner and direction of his flight. He should then relay any such information to the dispatcher for appropriate action.

More detailed on-the-spot interviews might well follow at this point. Such interviews should include the victim (physical, mental, and emotional condition permitting), as well as any interested or seemingly disinterested witnesses. At this stage of the investigation, no potential witness should be overlooked. Witnesses may often know a good deal more about the details of a crime than they themselves realize. The identity and addresses of all such witnesses should be obtained and accurately recorded in the officer's notebook, as well as all information and statements elicited by questioning.

The officer must exercise great care in noting such material. Evidence that may seem unimportant or irrelevant at the time it is obtained may in fact provide the linchpin upon which the entire investigation subsequently hinges. How helpful it would have been to the preparation of the prosecutor's case had the detectives in the Tate-LaBianca murders only realized what evidence they actually possessed.

Protecting the Crime Scene

One of the primary duties of the first officer on the scene is that of protecting the crime scene itself. That the suspect has left every conceivable piece of identification other than his calling card is of no benefit to the development of the case if the evidence is lost, damaged, or otherwise contaminated. Any physical evidence found at the scene must be protected from the moment of its discovery until its appearance as an exhibit in court.

The officer must therefore safeguard the scene by issuing whatever orders are necessary to accomplish this purpose, and by physically isolating the scene itself. In addition to insuring that evidence at the scene is neither moved, contaminated, nor destroyed, the officer must also make certain that nothing is either added to the scene or removed. A subsequent crime scene search that reveals little more than fingerprints and shoe impressions belonging to participating police officers is embarrassing as well as nonproductive. An expensive pair of sunshades that a spectator fancies as a souvenir of the crime scene might well prove to be the primary connecting link between the crime and its perpetrator.

The methods by which a crime scene is actually secured are limited only by the ingenuity of the individual police officer. Most police agencies provide such aids as posting signs (customarily reading *Keep Out—Crime Scene Search In Progress,* or *Authorized Personnel Only,* or simply *Stop*), ropes, wooden or metal barriers, and the like. In addition, an officer on the scene might utilize materials actually present in the nearby vicinity, such as a neighbor's wooden sawhorse, items of yard furniture, indeed, even motor vehicles.

The goal is to seal off all routine entrance and exit passages to the crime scene as securely as possible without causing any disturbance to the scene itself. If the officer is alone for a time, the task is increasingly difficult. Circumstances might even arise in which he finds it necessary to utilize the survices of a witness on the scene in order to block a passage while the officer sends a radio call for assistance. Obviously, all unauthorized persons must be excluded without exception—including spectators, members of the news media, and even friends and relatives of the victim.

However, all persons present at the scene upon the officer's arrival, as well as anyone appearing subsequently who indicates some connection with the crime, should be detained for questioning whenever possible. Witnesses should always be interviewed separately in order to obtain independent statements.

In most instances, depending upon the size of the police agency involved, the first officer upon the scene is unlikely to be the one who will ultimately be in charge of the investigation. It would therefore be inappropriate for this officer to actually commence the formal search of the crime scene. In fact, he should not move or even touch any object save under circumstances of the utmost necessity. He should also direct other officers of similar rank as they arrive, until such time as a superior with appropriate authority appears and assumes control of the investigation. At this point, the initial phase of the police response merges into the investigative procedure.

Most police agencies of medium size and larger will dispatch a specially trained investigative team to work the scene of a major crime. As a matter of practical experience, however, it must be admitted that most cases neither warrant nor receive such thorough treatment due to such factors as the relevant importance of the offense, the allocation of manpower, the case load of the investigative personnel, and so forth. In such a situation, the initial officer upon the scene may very well find his duties and responsibilities considerably enlarged.

It therefore becomes abundantly evident that the procedures and techniques used at a crime scene are of the utmost importance, not only to investigative specialists but to all law enforcement officers.

The Officer in Charge

Assuming that a search team is employed, for maximum effectiveness it is absolutely essential that one man be in charge. He must direct the search, assign each officer his respective duties, supervise and coordinate every phase of the search, and, of course, he must bear responsibility for the completion of the search.

In short, the blame is his alone for incompetency and inefficiency, and praise for success must be equally shared with the members of his team.

Plan of Search

Experience has shown that prior to beginning the actual search itself, the investigator in charge should pause long enough to survey the scene, to review in his mind whatever facts he already possesses, and to lay his plans for implementing the search for physical evidence. He should determine the method to be employed, decide upon a convenient location from which to direct the operation, assemble the necessary men and material, and then take a long breath and metaphorically rub the rabbit's foot buried deep in the pocket of his experience.

Next, he should reduce this mental and visual survey of the scene to a photographic record. In an important case, this phase of the preliminary investigation should be managed with the technical assurance of a Hollywood director filming a scene in the *Godfather III* or *IV*, or whatever. The actual specifics of such a procedure and the photographic techniques will be discussed in chapter 6. Suffice it to say at this point that even if the investigator is not himself an accomplished artist with the camera, he must know how to direct a competent photographer in such a way as to obtain the desired results.

After the photographs have been taken and duly marked for identification, the search for physical evidence may begin. In a homicide investigation, of course, the body or bodies should not be moved or disturbed (unless otherwise dictated by the particular circumstances of the case) until the medical examiner has arrived and completed his initial examination.

In this second phase of the preliminary investigation, all physical evidence must be noted, collected, marked for identification, and properly preserved. At this point *nothing* can be justifiably overlooked; anything of any possible evidentiary value must be considered.

The methods of searching a crime scene and the techniques for handling physical evidence will be examined in detail in subsequent chapters.

We are left then with the third and last phase of a preliminary investigation to be merely mentioned at this point. And that is the location and interviewing of witnesses, a matter that also will be discussed at length in a later chapter.

Recapitulation

Where the perpetrator of a crime has fled the scene and is not immediately susceptible of arrest, a preliminary investigation consists of three distinct phases: 1) protecting and searching the crime scene; 2) the collection, marking, and preservation of physical evidence; and 3) the location and interviewing of witnesses, including the victim whenever practicable.

We will now consider these three phases of a preliminary investigation in relation to the previous narrative statement of facts in chapter 3 concerning the multiple rural homicides.

INVESTIGATIVE IMPLICATIONS OF THE HYPOTHETICAL CASE

We must first acknowledge that the deputy who initially arrived at the scene of the crime did so without benefit of having received a complaint or any other reason to believe that he would soon be involved in a major crime of violence. With this qualification in mind, we must nevertheless assess his performance.

Initially the young deputy sheriff had only his intuition to guide him. He didn't know *why* he thought something was wrong; he simply *felt* it in his guts. Any experienced investigator will verify that a hunch based upon accumulated experience is as good a reason as any to give pause and pay heed to any such "messages" from the "inner man."

Call it ESP, clairvoyance, precognition or what have you, the professional investigator must use every means at his disposal in his quest to solve crime. The fact that such "hunches" cannot be identified, measured, and explained by any of the physical sciences is insufficient reason for ignoring the utility of such "information." Such evidence might be the keystone to the speedy solution of a crime; it might very well be the decisive factor in saving a police officer's life.

In any case, the deputy was well advised to proceed with caution. And upon the discovery of the grisly fact of the multiple deaths, his immediate call for assistance was clearly indicated. Such a situation was far too complex for any one officer to contend with.

At this point, the young deputy's human responses must be dealt with. Was his reaction to the blood and gore of the scene unrealistic as well as unprofessional? The author would submit that such human responses do occasionally occur in the course of a police officer's duties and should in no way cast doubt upon the individual's manhood or professionalism. Intelligence, discipline, and training are the desired traits of a professional police officer, not the macho super-coolness of a modern celluloid hero.

Obviously the test is whether or not such responses continually occur and whether or not they impede the officer's performance of his duties, or create a hazard for his police associates and innocent bystanders. It goes without saying that not every person is cut out for police work. However, it is never too late to reassess one's nature and capacities for such employment. Psychological counseling should be made available to all personnel in modern police agencies, and there should certainly be no stigma attached to any officer who voluntarily seeks such assistance in an effort to better understand his own nature. Such understanding is to the individual's benefit as well as to the police and to society generally.

Of course the pressure of aloneness instantly assailed the deputy. Even the most case-hardened investigator experiences such fleeting moments of alienation. Suddenly he is alone against the forces of darkness that he can neither see, hear, nor apprehend. He is in many ways nothing more than Primitive Man again, standing in the mouth of his cave with his puny little weapon in his hand, listening to the soundlessness that confronts him, straining with every fiber of his being to know the unknowable, asking in all too evident humanness: "What is out there; why am I here?" So the deputy faced those darkened windows, the trees and bushes in the encircling shadows, and realized that at any moment the killer whom he sought might very well find him. In the grip of his fear, the hunter had now become the hunted.

This flash of insight may last only an instant, or one may become so immobilized by the confrontation with his own vulnerability that he is powerless to function without external stimulation. Has one, under such circumstances, behaved cowardly, unmanly, unprofessionally? Not at all. Such behavior is quite human under the circumstances. Nowhere in the police code of conduct is it required that the officer exchange his humanity for a badge and a gun. Only a fool or a psychotic fails to experience fear in the face of frightening events. One who experiences fear yet deals with it functionally behaves with a mature rationality that is psychological armor as important as the badge and gun that afford him physical support.

In the case presented, the deputy's power to act was immediately reinvested upon the arrival of the state trooper. (One can imagine how Peter Pithecanthropus must have breathed a sigh of relief when his burly neighbor strode out of the menacing shadows to stand guard with him at his cave against the lurking dangers of the night.)

Although it is debatable whether or not the trooper had any valid reason for entering the store for a look at the death scene, the search of the grounds that followed was certainly warranted by the circumstances. There was no indication of how long the victims had been dead. It was entirely possible that the deputy had arrived at the scene only moments after the last killing, that the assailant(s) had not had time to effect an escape and was even at that moment in hiding on the premises. (During a predawn raid on the Barker Ranch, police, who at that time were investigating the Manson family for auto theft, discovered Charlie Manson concealed in a wooden cabinet under the kitchen sink. The cabinet measured a mere 3 by 1½ by 1½ feet.)

But where should the officers have begun their search? Should they have proceeded at once into the grocery store to conduct a search inside, rather than confining their search to the grounds, as they did in the statement of facts? Absolutely not. They are only two men, the building is large and dark, and assistance is already on the way. It was quite in order to make a cautious inspection tour of the grounds while keeping the building under surveillance until such time as reinforcements might arrive.

Even had they known the perpetrator to have been inside

the building, the best course of conduct under the circumstances would have been a holding action. The ultimate goal at that point would have been the arrest of the suspect. It would have been more likely accomplished without bloodshed by the presence of more arresting officers.

It might well be mentioned here that a successful arrest is one in which the suspect is taken into custody by the use of the minimum amount of force necessary, with as little personal injury and loss of life as is possible under the circumstances. An arrest at any price, regardless of the cost, should be accepted (if ever) only as a last resort. If one police officer is injured or killed unnecessarily, the cause of law enforcement suffers. If one suspect is injured or killed unnecessarily, the cause of justice suffers.

In the case in point, with the noisy arrival of the sheriff and his chief assistant in their separate vehicles, authority for the conduct of the investigation passed to the senior law enforcement officer in whose jurisdiction the crime was committed.

The decision whether or not to make a personal appearance at the scene of a crime is an important one for all ranking officers, including agency heads themselves. If the ranking officer at the scene is not actually directing the investigation, an awkward situation arises in that the chain of command is being circumvented. No one quite knows what role is expected of him. Will the superior officer countermand orders given by the officer in charge? Who will assume responsibility for mistakes and oversights? In short, unless the ranking officer intends to assume command of the investigation, he should stay away from the actual scene of the crime.

In our case, the sheriff emphatically assumed command of the investigation. How well did he handle his duties? Not nearly as well as might be desired. In the first place, he was much too impulsive in his actions, quite likely as a result of his own lack of knowledge and experience of such cases. It would be surprising to most citizens to learn how many elected law enforcement officials throughout the country have never received the benefit of any training or formal education in the area of criminal investigation.

Certainly the sheriff should have paused before rushing

inside the store, at least long enough to have conferred with his deputy as to the particulars he then possessed. Surely the deputy would have had *something* beneficial to tell him.

For example, the deputy might have informed him that the suspect was barricaded inside the building with a loaded shotgun, having sworn to kill the first person who came through the door. Such information might very well have had a bearing on the sheriff's course of action.

Or the deputy might have wanted to warn him of the location of the puddles of blood and gore just inside the doorway that would best be left uncontaminated by walking around rather than through them.

And so on.

But the sheriff had work to do and wanted to get on with it. So he proceeded at once inside the store, followed closely by his chief assistant. This of course left the trooper and the young deputy outside without instructions as to their duties. On his own initiative, the trooper began directing the increasing volume of vehicular traffic. Spectators were beginning to gather too. But before the deputy could do anything about blocking off the area, he was summoned inside by the sheriff and instructed to go upstairs and search the living quarters.

This, of course, left the neighbors and curiosity seekers to mill about at random, tromping back and forth over any physical evidence that might have been left at the scene by the perpetrator of the crime. And in order to completely insure that nothing of value would be left for the investigators, two more vehicles were allowed to contaminate the ground immediately adjacent to the entrance to the store. Certainly there would be scant opportunity to make note of any pertinent tire tracks or footprints for evidentiary purposes.

One of the latter arrivals, the local newspaper editor, commenced taking photographs of the outside and then snapped a series of pictures of the murder scene itself through a side window. No one in the sheriff's office knew how to use a speed graphic camera. In fact, the only photographic equipment that the department owned was a Polaroid camera, and it was in the shop for repairs. There was a bill before the state legislature to authorize and equip every state patrol vehicle with photographic equipment, especially for use at the scene of traffic accident investigations, but this bill had not as yet been voted out of committee.

However, even had a police photographer been available, his product would not have been of much use in a court of law. The crime scene had already been so distorted and abused that it would be difficult to reconstruct the scene in its original state.

For example, the bodies of the four victims had been turned over and moved to facilitate their examination by the coroner. The chief deputy sheriff, at the least, had tramped through the blood on the floor and attempted to clean his boot on the front step. In all likelihood, others had likewise stepped into the prospective blood samples. And, of course, the suspected murder weapon had been moved from the spot in which it was found by the sheriff himself. It will be remembered that he handled the shotgun with no particular effort to protect the integrity of any latent fingerprints that might have been on the weapon. It is quite likely under the circumstances that the only prints that would ever be lifted from the suspected murder weapon would belong to the sheriff in charge of the investigation.

Nor was the remainder of the preliminary investigation to afford much improvement.

Identifications of two of the victims—the storekeeper and his daughter—had been immediately effected. The identities of the other two male victims were unknown. The sheriff therefore invited a few of the neighbors inside the store in an effort to obtain on-the-spot visual identifications.

After some nine or ten spectators had been herded in and out of the store, the two victims were still unknown. The exact quantity of the victims' blood that had been carried away on the shoes of so many transients was unknown too.

It should be noted that all of this coming and going and bustling about has taken place at the scene of a particularly violent multiple murder in which it has not yet been established who the perpetrator is and whether or not he is still on the premises! No search has been organized by the sheriff, either of the building itself or of the surrounding area. A number of additional victims might very well have joined the four corpses on the floor of the immediate crime scene.

Needless to say, when the sheriff did decide to initiate at least a partial search, it was not a very wise procedure to send the deputy upstairs by himself. He might very well have found more than he could handle alone. As it turned out, he found only the storekeeper's wife. And with this discovery, the sheriff, in effect, wrapped up his case.

True, there were a few questions still unanswered. They hadn't yet found any of the spent shotgun casings; they didn't know the identity of two of the victims; they didn't know the motives for any of the homicides. Yet it seemed apparent to the sheriff that the woman was the perpetrator of the crime. Her dazed condition, the blood and viscera on her nightgown, her presence in the room upstairs, and those stories the sheriff had heard about the storekeeper and his daughter. He didn't know exactly *why* she had done such an awful thing, but he was certain in his own mind that she was the killer. It didn't shock him. He'd learned long ago not to be surprised by any aspect of police work. A lifelong deacon of the church could go just as beserk as the next fellow with no reason at all to put your finger on.

No, the sheriff was pretty well satisfied with the way things were shaping up in the investigation. But the factual statement of the case has not yet been fully stated.

FURTHER DEVELOPMENT
OF THE HYPOTHETICAL CASE

The sheriff is watching the last ambulance pull away with the victims when a call comes in over the patrol radio. There are still a good many spectators milling about, shaking their heads and clucking their tongues, laughing and exulting in all the excitement. A slew of kids are dodging in between the parked fleet of police cruisers, playing cops and robbers. The sheriff knows most everyone by name, including the kids who are still some ten or twelve years shy of casting their first votes. He lets a few of the older boys go inside for a quick look around the crime scene. Then he excuses himself to a group of his constituents and takes the call on the radio.

It is the young deputy who has accompanied the storekeeper's wife to the hospital under police arrest. An interview with the suspect just before she succumbed to sedation has produced the distinct possibility that things really aren't as cut and dried as they'd seemed to be. The woman, he says, kept muttering something incoherent about "masks . . . terrible things . . . hiding in the bushes."

Perhaps the sheriff ought to continue the investigation at the crime scene after all.

The Crime Scene

Unfortunately, protection of the crime scene had been grossly neglected after the sheriff's arrival. The bodies had already been moved, several times, without any floor markings as to original locations and positions. The suspected murder weapon had been moved and carelessly handled. There had been no dusting for latent prints, inside or outside the building, and no blood samples taken. There were no police photographs nor field sketches made.

The preliminary investigation would have to be assessed as a failure.

If any one glaring error or deficiency can be singled out, perhaps it was the tendency of all the police officers involved— particularly the sheriff—to take entirely too many facts for granted. Assumptions such as were made in this case are the quicksand of a criminal investigation.

It should be noted that this narrative of a composite case history and the foregoing analysis of the investigatory procedures employed is in no way intended to reflect upon the reputation of any particular police agency or police officers in general. However, it is not such an exceptional description of modern police work that it is without utilitarian benefit to the study of the fundamentals of criminal investigation.

If there were no need for impersonal criticism and impartial suggestions for improved techniques in the field of criminal investigation, it would mean that the methods presently employed are perfect. It would mean that there is little or no unsolved crime in our society. Unfortunately, this is not the case.

Reference has previously been made to one of the nation's most highly respected police departments—the LAPD (Los Angeles Police Department)—and the investigation conducted by that agency in the Manson-Tate-LaBianca cases. In addition to the aforementioned failure of the investigators to collect sufficient blood samples for testing type and sub-type, important latent prints were negligently destroyed and/or contaminated; blood stains and other tracing materials were entirely overlooked; physical evidence was misplaced, mislabeled, and misunderstood; numerous investigative leads were not followed. Finally, and most significantly, the investigating officers often showed an unwillingness to be enlightened in regard to investigative oversights that would have appalled even the slovenly sheriff of the above-narrated case study.

And all of these deficiencies, mind you, occurred in one of the most spectacularly lurid cases of violence and bestiality in the annals of American criminal law.

But let us now return to the analysis of the investigative procedure—or lack thereof—in our case at hand.

THE CONTINUING INVESTIGATION

Up to this point our hypothetical investigation has been a classic of forensic bumbling. Can the investigation be salvaged? Absolutely. With hard work and more than a little luck, the loose ends of the case may still be pulled together into a successful conclusion in the phase known as the continuing investigation.

This phase is by no means secondary in importance because it is second in point of time. Many an investigation all but rendered hopeless in its initial phase is salvaged by a competently executed follow-up.

Although most crime scenes contribute *something* useful by way of physical evidence, it is by no means the general rule that this preliminary phase holds *all* of the keys to the successful conclusion of the case. More often than not there is considerable work of importance yet to be accomplished by the investigators who participate in the ongoing process of identifying and apprehending the perpetrator of the offense.

After all, the primary goal of the investigation is the identification and apprehension of the guilty person(s) and the exoneration of all innocent suspects.

So after the initial phase of the investigation has been concluded—that is, the crime scene search, the collection of physical evidence at the scene, and the identification and interview of witnesses—it is the duty of the investigator(s) to whom the case is assigned to press the investigation on to a successful conclusion.

Review of Work Product

The first task is to review the work product of the preliminary investigation, slight as it may upon occasion be. The investigator should study the assembled facts; analyze the theory of the case (and revise it if necessary) in light of whatever physical evidence is on hand; and review the statements and observations (if any) of witnesses, as well as of the victim of the crime and of any suspect that might have been developed.

One ready source of such information is the investigative reports previously prepared by all officers who have worked on the case. Not only should such reports be reviewed at the outset of the continuing investigation, but also throughout the remainder of the investigation, right up to the trial of the case. Although a detailed discussion of report writing is beyond the scope of this book, the subject is deserving of more than passing reference.

Reports

Investigative reports are designed to serve as a permanent official record of the case history, to provide the basis for further investigative leads, and to furnish the prosecutor with sufficient information upon which to base a decision to proceed with criminal charges or to withhold or temporarily delay legal action.

The writer W. Somerset Maugham insisted upon the self-imposed standards of simplicity, lucidity (clarity), and euphony (melody) for his own work. Certainly such self-imposed standards as the first two would benefit the criminal investigator in his report-writing duties, and the third would unlikely be detrimental to an informed reading of the material.

In order to insure completeness, the investigator might do well to adopt the journalistic method of answering the questions who, what, when, where, and why? Accordingly, the report should develop logically and should include all relevant information, favorable and unfavorable, positive and negative, supportive or antagonistic to the developing theory of the case. Surely the necessity for accuracy as opposed to conjecture need not be stressed.

There are three self-explanatory primary types of investigative reports: 1) the initial report, 2) supplemental or progress reports, and 3) the closing report.

It should be remembered that whatever style is used in writing such reports, the ultimate goal is to convey information to others and to serve as a review of the case for the writer. Completeness and accuracy are empty virtues if the material is for any reason unreadable or incomprehensible.

Developing a Theory of the Case

A criminal investigation is an effort to reconstruct the events of a crime in such a way as to understand exactly how the crime occurred, perhaps why it occurred, and by whom it was committed. As the process of reconstruction builds, a theory of the case, or logical pattern of events, begins to develop. More often than not, the investigation then begins to focus upon a suspect or group of suspects.

This is a critical stage of the investigation, and much can be won or lost by the reasoning employed and the decisions taken thereon. In reconstructing the crime, the investigator attempts to develop a rational theory based upon deductive or inductive reasoning, or a combination of both, whichever pertains to the evidentiary information on hand.

Clearly such reasoning is an ongoing process. At no one moment can the investigator assume that he possess *all* of the information that exists concerning the case. Such an attitude would foreclose all future investigative accomplishments. Therefore, although he may be tending toward a theory of the case based upon the information then possessed, he must be willing to continually test that theory, to revise it according to the suasive evidence of new information, and to discard it wholly in the light of contrary logic.

The investigator must never allow himself to become so personally involved in the developing theory of a case that he is unable to perform objectively. He should not adopt such a theory as "his" view. Rather, he is simply reading a set of facts that taken together present any objective person with a logical conclusion as to the meaning of those facts.

For example, if the evidence shows that a homicide victim purchased a quantity of poison from a druggist and was discovered dead a few hours later, and the autopsy report indicates death by poisoning, then it is logical to conclude that the victim died either as a result of poisoning by suicide, negligence, or accident. Such is an acceptable theory of the case. It is not, however, a conclusive theory.

New evidence might change the reading of the facts. Perhaps the victim purchased the poison at the request of his wife. Perhaps the wife has been involved in an affair with another man who wants to marry her and evidence establishes the fact that the lover has given the woman an ultimatum to either divorce her husband or terminate the affair. Might not one or two or more alternate theories of the case then be suggested to the investigator?

Personal prejudice is another factor that the criminal investigator must carefully consider. History seems to indicate that there has been only one perfect man and that the rest of us have fallen far short of His example. It seems fair to say that all men are prejudiced against something or someone. One may dislike spinach, pornographic films, or evangelical crusades; one may distrust blacks, Republicans, Baptists, or all three. The point is that prejudice does exist, we all share in its cancer, and we ought simply to admit the fact and then proceed from there. Certainly the police officer ought to recognize and admit to his own prejudices.

Perhaps it is debatable as to whether or not the existence of prejudice is immoral in itself or unethical; it is not, however, criminal. What is important is what one does about one's prejudices. It is legally acceptable to dislike Hottentots as long as one does discriminate against them. A police investigator can dislike blacks, hippies, bankers, or business executives—as long as he does not discriminate against them in the performance of his duties.

Developing a rational theory of a case, then, is a process whereby the investigator arrives at a reasoned conclusion based entirely upon the unprejudiced examination of the information he possesses, while retaining at all times the option and the willingness to alter his conclusion should new information logically call for such revision.

But just as the role of the reasoning process in a criminal investigation cannot be overstated, neither should a reference to the elements of chance and intuition be omitted. Reasoning alone does not solve crime; reasoning is not exercised in a vacuum. The reasoning process is based upon facts, information, and insights derived from the use of an investigator's total mental and sensory equipment. An open, energetic mind is the passage through which chance and intuition often inform the reason.

Thus reasoning, it is the task of the investigator to assemble the facts, construct hypotheses or theories, and derive conclusions from them. No one method of reasoning, however, can be said to be the correct one. The correct one is the one that works.

What are some of the methods actually used by investigators? First, let's restate in simple terms the investigator's task. It is his function to reconstruct the past, to determine what happened, to whom, by whom, how it happened, and perhaps why it happened. In many respects, an investigator is much like an archeologist; he must locate and dig up evidence from the past. But how can he know what to look for? And where does he begin?

Well, he can rely on a confession, on eyewitness testimony, or on circumstantial evidence. He can rely on his imagination, ingenuity, intuition (more especially, perhaps, if the investigator is a woman), or even on luck. Or he may pray a good deal.

All of these methods, and others, work sometimes. They are not without shortcomings, however. Confessions are notoriously unreliable, eyewitnesses are as often as not mistaken in their observations, circumstantial evidence is misleading, and luck has a way of being bad as often as it is good.

Yet there *is* one technique that has proved remarkably successful for those investigators, intelligence agents, and courtroom attorneys who have experimented with its use. It has been called by the world-famous and extraordinarily successful attorney Louis Nizer the *rule of probability*.

The Rule of Probability

Properly utilized, this rule more often than not indicates to an investigator what facts to seek and exactly where to find them. It will tell you of the existence of physical evidence that you didn't know existed. It will tell you of the existence of witnesses that are determined not to be forthcoming. It will warn you of the likelihood that a particular witness will lie, and will even indicate to you a line of questioning to which a recalcitrant suspect will respond affirmatively. How does it work?

Through the sum of our experience, we are able to "see" or "know" how a person will behave under a given set of circumstances. This body of accumulated "knowledge" permits us to make highly informed judgments as to whether a particular act under investigation is probable, or whether the information sought probably exists, or whether a particular witness probably will lie and why he will likely do so, etc. The operation of this rule, it must be emphasized, is more than guesswork, and it is more often than not accurate.

To illustrate, a confidential informant once advised this author (who was acting as her control officer in a drug case involving an organized crime investigation) that she had participated in a number of drug parties as a guest but had never herself indulged in drug use. The informant was a nineteen-year-old college student with two known arrests for casual acts of prostitution and a circle of friends closely allied to the youthful counterculture of the early 1960s. It was improbable that the girl was not herself a user of drugs or marijuana. Inquiries of a discreet nature led to the statements of more than a dozen members of her peer group to the effect that the girl was an habitual drug user bordering on the edge of addiction. When subsequently confronted with such anonymous character appraisals, the girl admitted the truthfulness of the statements and agreed that her motivation for informing on her friends was to earn the funds to support her habit. The probability of the girl's involvement in the drug scene was simply too great to be discounted.

It should be stressed that the rule of probability is not a secret device available only to the select among us. In fact, it is used to some extent by almost everyone, however unconsciously. We believe a thing to be so if it is plausible, or someone's statement if what he says is plausible. Certainly the criminal justice system relies heavily upon the rule. A jury uses it when it decides to accept one witness's contradictory testimony over another (e.g., Patty Hearst *vis-à-vis* Emily and Bill Harris). A judge certainly employs the rule when weighing conflicting testimony. Even our political process relies heavily upon the rule. The voter uses it when deciding which politicians are telling fewer lies than the others. (Remember the wit who once remarked that it is harder for a politician to tell the truth than for a hound dog to pass a tree without stopping?)

Might not the rule of probability have been successfully applied to the Watergate saga from start to finish?

Was it *plausible* to believe that the plumbers acted on their own authority?

Was it *plausible* to believe that an Attorney General of the United States would listen to a proposed scheme of illegal acts in his own office if he was not at least willing to consider the implementation of such a scheme?

Was it *plausible* that eighteen minutes of controversial dialogue was erased from the Watergate tapes by some outside nonhuman sinister force?

Was it *plausible* that the President of the United States was unaware of the activities of his closest associates within the government in their efforts to effect his reelection to office?

And so on.

The rule of probability is not magic, though in some situations it evinces magical qualities. In the final analysis, it is perhaps nothing more than common sense. And the investigator who seeks to use the rule should bear in mind that it is not evidence in itself, but the means by which evidence is obtained.

Investigative Leads

Only after thoroughly digesting and correlating the work product in hand should the officer in charge commence the continuing phase of the investigation. He should then vigorously pursue all leads as they are indicated.

Obviously any and all leads indicating the identity and whereabouts of the perpetrator of the crime should be expeditiously followed up. Likewise, a continued search for witnesses to the crime should be pressed at this time; interviews with newly discovered witnesses should be conducted, as well as re-interviews with witnesses and/or victims previously questioned. This phase of the investigation, for obvious reasons, is referred to in police lingo as "hitting the streets" or "beating the bushes."

Investigative techniques of an administrative nature may be every bit as productive as footwork and are certainly not to be slighted.

For example, laboratory technicians must be consulted for

advice and reports concerning their analysis of physical evidence already submitted for examination. Such results can be invaluable, whether positive or negative in character. A murder weapon may be positively identified by a routine ballistics test, a blood sample may be determined to be animal rather than human, a suspected quantity of heroin may be nothing more lethal than a packet of sugar.

Possession of such information greatly assists the investigator in the continuing reexamination of the theory of the case, in assigning leads, and in the handling of status reports with members of the news media.

The investigator in charge might also find himself at this point supervising the preparation of wanted flyers if a suspect has emerged, vehicle APBs, or even polygraph examinations for witnesses, suspects, and/or victims alike. One thing he can certainly anticipate in a major case investigation is that he will not be spending much time at home with his family and friends. Meals will be missed, children will go to sleep without a bedtime romp with Daddy (or Mommy), and spouses or sweethearts will spend restless hours alone.

Hopefully, the investigative leads in the case will prove productive. If the physical evidence is such as to support the witness information, and if the investigation has indeed focused upon a suspect, then the investigator will be responsible for affecting the arrest of the perpetrator, for preparing the case for trial and for conferring with the prosecuting attorney.

Of course, not all cases are susceptible to a successful conclusion. In some instances a suspect is never developed; in others there is merely circumstantial evidence that the prosecutor feels is too slight to warrant prosecution; and in still other cases a valid suspect, in spite of exhaustive investigation, remains at large and his eventual arrest seems highly unlikely.

In such cases as the latter it is entirely within the prerogative of the investigator in charge to recommend that no further action be taken and that the case be closed. Of course, there is no statute of limitations as far as murder cases are concerned. In 1976, Alabama authorities arrested three white men for the murder of a young black some nineteen years before. All members of the Ku Klux Klan, the three men were accused of forcing the black youth at gunpoint to jump to his death from a bridge spanning the Alabama River. He was killed because the men thought he had "smiled" at a white woman. There is considerable evidence that the youth's death was a case of mistaken identity.

CONCLUDING FACTUAL STATEMENT OF THE HYPOTHETICAL CASE

In the case under examination, an arrest was made in spite of the many deficiencies of the investigation. When the store-keeper's wife recovered from her trauma, she gave a graphic description of the two young males who had robbed the store, raped and killed her daughter, and murdered her husband and two unfortunate hitchhikers who had stopped in at the store to make a minor purchase.

The woman had survived, she explained, only by the intervention of the Almighty. The assailants had not tied her feet, possibly because she too was going to be raped in the course of their bloody rampage. In all of the confusion, however, she was able to escape out the door and hide in the surrounding woods until the men gave up searching for her and drove away in a high-powered sports car.

She went on to describe the car and the first three digits of its out-of-state license number. Police in the continuing investigation subsequently discovered the car at a motel on the other side of the county. A check with the motel clerk revealed that two young white males had used the room for more than a week. He said they had paid in advance, had come and gone at all hours of the day and night, and would not allow a cleaning woman to enter their room.

A joint raid was hastily organized between the sheriff's department and the state patrol. The trooper in command of the state unit cautioned a pause to consider the legalities of the situation. The sheriff was insistent that there was ample cause for moving without a warrant and did not want to lose any time. A pass key was used, a swarm of law enforcement officers rushed into the room, and the two men were in handcuffs before they could rouse themselves from a drunken sleep.

The motel room was a warehouse for stolen merchandise; TV sets, small appliances of all kinds, silverware, jewelry, clothing, and assorted items of yard furniture. Nearly a thousand dollars was found in cash in a dresser drawer, along with the wallets and identification papers of the two itinerant hitchhikers. A sawed-off shotgun, wrapped in a blanket, was on a shelf in the closet. There were no spent cartridge cases, but the gun had been recently fired. The cartridge cases were never found, nor was there any explanation of why the assailants had overlooked the fifty dollars in the cash register.

In the glove compartment of the sports car, a crumpled and bloody pair of women's lace panties was found. A souvenir that, after the mother's identification of the panties as a Christmas gift to her daughter, proved to be the last nail used by the local prosecutor in hammering together a solid case comprised of enough life sentences to keep the two convicted murderers behind bars for the remainder of their natural lives.

Or until they were paroled.

• DISCUSSION QUESTIONS

1. *What is the ultimate goal of any criminal investigation? Why?*

2. *What role does the use of force play in a criminal investigation?*

3. *Should the highest-ranking police officer of the agency investigating a crime appear personally at the scene of the crime?*

4. *How fixed or flexible must an investigator's theory of the case be?*

5. *How might the existence of prejudice affect a criminal investigation?*

6. *What is the rule of probability, and how does it operate?*

7. *What are the three primary purposes of investigative reports?*

5

- *Methods of Search*

We have previously examined a statement of facts and engaged in considerable discussion of what not to do in a criminal investigation in view of those particular facts. Now let us turn our attention to a discussion of more positive matters concerning the investigation of a criminal offense.

We have seen that there are two types of criminal investigations, the preliminary investigation and the continuing investigation. In addition, every criminal investigation is comprised of a series of components, the execution of which is spread throughout the duration of the investigation as a whole. Our discussion will continue now with an examination of the methods of a crime scene search and an application of some of the principles to be discussed to our hypothetical case.

The primary purpose of a crime scene search is to gather evidence of what occurred during the commission of a crime. It seeks to answer the questions what, who, how, where, and why.

The search for physical evidence at the scene of a crime is not a game played in the manner of a children's Easter egg hunt. It is a serious business, the end result of which often encompasses matters of life and death. It plays a vital part in the determination of whether or not a criminal suspect is found innocent or guilty of the charges brought against him. Many a guilty soul has walked out of a courtroom scot-free because of the unprofessionalism of police investigators during the crime scene search many weeks or months before. On the other hand, more innocent citizens than we shall ever know of have spent countless years behind cold prison bars, or paid the maximum forfeiture, as a result of the investigative incompetence of police officers at the scene of the crime.

To illustrate, how helpful it would have been to the clarity of justice had the police successfully located the murder weapon with which the late Dr. Sam Sheppard was alleged to have killed his wife in 1954. No weapon was ever linked to the murder save only through the legally insufficient expedient of conjecture and wish-fulfillment. Indeed, this lack of credible evidence concerning the murder weapon was one of the primary weaknesses of the prosecution's retrial of Dr. Sheppard after one of his numerous appeals finally succeeded in a reversal of his original conviction. Although he had served some ten years in prison on the original conviction, he was acquitted of all charges by the jury in his second trial.

In either case, justice aborted or justice misapplied, it is a penalty that the American citizen need not have to pay in such alarming proportions as has been our heritage. Investigative professionalism is the best means by which the bill may be reduced.

How should the experienced professional investigator approach the task of searching a crime scene? With fear and trembling? No, with confidence based upon awareness of his experience and training. Since he is well-versed in such matters, he is undismayed by the responsibility of recognizing, recording, collecting, marking, packaging, and preserving physical evidence incidental to a crime scene search.

What, then, is the best method for searching a crime scene?

There is no one answer. The nature of each particular case, the type of evidence sought and likely to be found, and even the physical topography of the scene itself will dictate the method of search to be used. The goal, however, is always the same: a systematic search for the discovery of physical evidence, conducted by as few police officers as the circumstances of the case will permit.

Such physical evidence may include evidence left by the perpetrator of the crime at the scene, such as fingerprints, tool marks, blood, semen, foot impressions, tire marks, hairs, and fibers, etc. Or it may include evidence carried away from the scene by the criminal, such as personal property belonging to the victim (weapons, tools, jewelry, money, etc.), tracing material from the victim's body (blood, tissue, hair, etc.), or from the victim's home, place of business, or motor vehicle. Or physical evidence may be of the sort that will have some bearing upon the motive for the crime, such as love letters, legal documents, bank statements revealing disastrously declining assets, and the like.

By way of example, it is unlikely that Britain's Great Train Robbery of 1963 would ever have been solved had it not been for the variety of physical evidence recovered in the course of the investigation, which spanned from 1963 to 1968. (Fig. 5.1.) In fact, although the last suspect was arrested in 1968, the investigation is still continuing in that the bulk of the $7,145,600 in English bank notes is still unaccounted for.

The crime, one of the world's largest robberies, was craftily planned and executed by individuals obviously in possession of inside information. The target train was stopped near the village of Cheddington by the ruse of covering a green light on the track with a glove and activating a red light by the use of flashlight batteries. When the engineer responded to the red light,

FIG. 5.1   Investigators at the scene of the Great Train Robbery (*Paris Match*)

FIG. 5.2 Detectives stepping across the rails to pick up a crowbar
(*London Daily Express*)

FIG. 5.3 The farm of Leatherslade, the hideout of the robbers
(*London Daily Express*)

the robbers seized the engine and uncoupled all but the two mail cars from the rest of the train and then proceeded to a predesignated spot some one half mile distant, where they unloaded the mail sacks into a waiting Land-Rover and sped away. The entire caper employed all of fifteen minutes.

The solution of the crime was almost as brilliant and painstakingly executed as the robbery itself. It was based heavily upon connecting physical evidence with the perpetrators of the crime. At first, Scotland Yard's sole clue (Fig. 5.2.) was a crowbar left on the tracks at the scene of disembarkation. But the subsequent discovery of empty mailbags at an isolated farm (Fig. 5.3.) established that it had been the robbers' hideout. Still later, in a seaside resort on the English Channel, police dug up several cases of the stolen bank notes (Fig. 5.4.) and made their first identifications and arrests of some of the robbers. (Fig. 5.5.) Ultimately, fifteen suspects were arrested. Unfortunately, the "Cheddington caper" is still an open case, however, since most of the stolen money is still missing.

Search Personnel

Why the stipulation concerning the number of officers participating in the search? The rules of court regulating the proffer of evidence in a criminal trial (which will subsequently be discussed at length) are as binding upon the investigator during the search of the crime scene as upon the prosecutor in his attempt to introduce the material into evidence. The integrity of physical evidence is maintained by keeping it as far as possible in its original state. Obviously, the fewer the number of investigators having handled the evidence, the better.

Even if an investigative team is utilized, it is the better practice whenever possible to limit the actual search to only one man. Other members of such a team are then used as assistants, as note takers, sketch artists, interviewers, etc., but do not actually touch or collect evidence. This is particularly advisable when the evidence is of such a nature as can be perceived and collected by nontechnical means.

Depending upon the type of case, however, technical assistance may very well be required. Availability of such assist-

FIG. 5.4 The £100,000 found buried in the wood at Dorking, transferred to a case, being loaded by police to be taken to the Aylesbury Police Station, headquarters of the investigation (*London Daily Express*)

ance is of course controlled by such elements as manpower variables and the extent of modernity of the police agency involved. Circumstances permitting, extensively equipped mobile labs staffed by the new breed of field evidence technicians are often dispatched to the crime scene. (Fig. 5.6.) In such situations these evidence technicians will generally examine the crime scene for fingerprints, footprints, tool marks, tire marks, and other impressions prior to the general search team going into operation. (Fig. 5.7.) Technicians should also photograph the scene prior to a general search. A more detailed discussion of the capabilities of such technicians will be discussed in a subsequent chapter.

FIG. 5.5   Two hooded women leaving Linslade court after being charged
in the robbery   (*London Daily Express*)

After the investigator in charge has either arrested the
perpetrator of the crime or satisfied himself that no suspect is
available, he must then secure the crime scene by appropriate
orders and instructions, signs, and physical barriers. He must
then survey the scene with a view toward determining the
extent of the area to be searched, the method of search to be
utilized, and the number and kind of personnel that will be
required.

A plan of search is then formed sufficient to the task of
systematically covering the entire scene, the dimensions of
which have been previously decided upon. The search plan
must be scrupulously followed, with the knowledge uppermost

FIG. 5.6   Mobile crime laboratory   (Public Safety Department Metropolitan-Dade County, Florida)

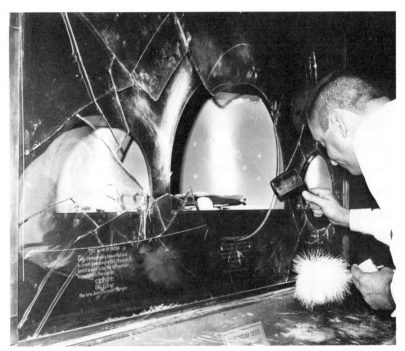

FIG. 5.7   A detective dusts for fingerprints on the case from which the Star of India, the world's largest star sapphire, was stolen. The Star of India, among other precious gems, was taken from the Museum of Natural History on October 30, 1964.   (United Press International Photo)

in mind that the success or failure of the case may very well rest on what is done at this point.

Obviously, not every crime scene is searched in anything like so thorough a fashion. As we have noted, some crimes do not even have a "scene" in the sense of a place-location in which physical evidence bearing upon the perpetration of the crime itself might yield to a search. Embezzlement, political graft, and forgery are such crimes, to name only a few.

On the other hand, there are certain crimes that in and of themselves demand a detailed search of the crime scene. The nature of such a crime makes the scene a reservoir of potentially vital physical evidence. Certainly most crimes of violence fall within this category, as do many burglaries and auto thefts. Such crimes more often than not involve either a struggle with the victim, property damage, or both. As previously remarked, in such offenses, vital physical evidence may not only have been left at the scene, but traces of the scene itself may very well have been carried away with the offender.

To cite merely one example, eight Chicago student nurses were brutally murdered in 1966 by a killer who either stabbed or strangled each girl to death. In less than three days, Chicago police arrested Richard Benjamin Speck and charged him with the multiple murders. The arrest was based primarily upon fingerprints found at the scene of the crime. Speck was subsequently tried, convicted, and electrocuted.

How easily the Chicago murders cited above might have gone unsolved, as did the death of the young daughter of U.S. Senator Charles Percy, who was murdered in her bed in a Chicago suburb the very same year of the nurse killings. She was stabbed numerous times in the face and body and bludgeoned with a still unidentified object, yet her grisly murder scene yielded no tangible evidence other than her own mutilated body. Or if the linking evidence was there, it was never found. A fingerprint, a piece of a knife handle, an item of clothing, a single hair or fiber. Such is often the difference between success or failure in a criminal investigation. It is therefore impossible to exaggerate the importance of the crime scene search.

But there are so many different kinds of crime scenes that it is impractical, and perhaps counterproductive, to attempt to explain the exact procedure that should be used in each situation. There are, however, certain common techniques that experience has shown to be useful in the task of searching most any type of crime scene. Such methods of search have been variously designated, more or less by way of describing the technique used in the performance of the act. The name given to the method is unimportant and in some ways not very useful. It can lead to confusion on the witness stand, for example, through a preoccupation with the technique itself rather than an examination of the end results.

Searches may be divided into two basic categories: indoor and outdoor. Physical characteristics of each category will dictate the method of search to be used. (Fig. 5.8.) There are three general methods of searching a crime scene: 1) a point-to-point progression, 2) a circular flow, and 3) a sector system.

After the crime scene has been photographed, sketched, and dusted for latent prints, one of the above methods of search may then be applied.

Point-to-Point

Just as a pool hustler begins with the number-one ball and progressively makes his way toward the last number on the table, so an investigator using this type of search method moves from the first piece of physical evidence discovered to the next logical item at the scene.

For example: An investigator has a three-room apartment with which to work. A scantily clad body of a young woman is sprawled in the center of the living room floor; a number of raw, bloody gashes are visible about her neck and shoulders; a pool of blood has trickled out from beneath her head; and trailing away from the body in a chain-link affair is a series of blood patches leading into the connecting bedroom, on the floor of which there appears to be a bloody object some nine or ten inches in length. Now even our fictional country sheriff could proceed rather rapidly from the body, to the wounds, to the

CIRCULAR FLOW

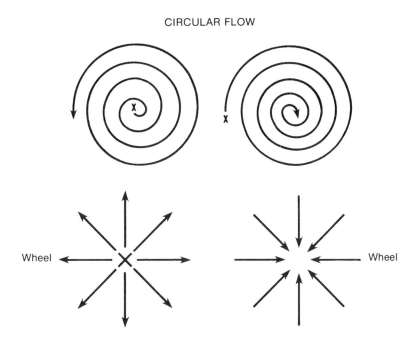

Wheel

Wheel

SECTOR SYSTEM

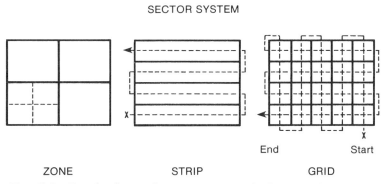

End

Start

ZONE

STRIP

GRID

FIG. 5.8 Circular flow and sector system methods of search

blood trailing into the bedroom, to the spot where the suspected murder weapon lay on the bloody carpet. A point-by-point progression must be followed from one evidentiary item to the next until the scene has been covered in its entirety.

Great care should be observed when using this method. The tendency is to follow each clue in the excitement of discovery without exercising the calm deliberative judgment that is called for. Since there is nothing to indicate that crimes are committed with a concern for logic, aesthetic balance, or forensic niceties, there is every likelihood that such clues will have been deposited in a most haphazard manner. The potential for destroying as yet undetected evidence is to some extent built into this method of search.

Circular Flow

This type of search finds the investigator standing in the center of the crime scene and searching outward in a clockwise (or counterclockwise) direction until the entire scene is covered. Or he may begin at the outer edge of the scene and carefully work his way inward toward the center in a spiral fashion.

When a number of searchers have been utilized for one reason or another, a variation of this method is called the *wheel* or *spoke search*. The investigators gather at the center and proceed outward in straight lines or spokes until they reach the fringes of the scene. Clearly, the greater the distance from the center, the greater the area to be covered. A major consideration in determining whether to employ this particular method is the wisdom of having a number of officers trampling over potential evidence while getting into their starting positions at the focal point of the scene.

Sector System

In many respects, this is the most effective and thorough method of search, as well as the safest. The scene is simply subdivided into segments that are searched as individual units. The division of the scene may be either a zone, a strip, or a grid variation.

The area to be searched is plotted like a rectangle. In the zone method, designated areas are searched completely one section at a time. Zones may even be subdivided. In the strip method, the searchers move from one side to the other and back in parallel lines until the entire rectangle has been covered. In the grid method, the rectangle is simply searched strip fashion parallel to the base and then again parallel to a side. Outdoor searches, due to the enlarged dimensions, often utilize stakes and cords with which to control the lanes of search.

APPLICATION TO THE HYPOTHETICAL CASE

Quite clearly, the crime scene in our hypothetical rural murder case was unprotected, and the search for physical evidence was haphazard and undirected. Although the sheriff was nominally in charge of the investigation, he himself was directly responsible for most of the mistakes that occurred at the scene.

How might the crime scene search have best been conducted?

Upon the sheriff's arrival, he might have halted his vehicle near the highway exit rather than pulling into the driveway with the other two vehicles already on the scene. Then he might have instructed the trooper and the deputy to move their cars so that the exit onto the highway at the other end of the drive was also blocked. Vehicular approach to the crime scene would then have been blocked. And since it was obvious that the commotion would soon draw a crowd of curious spectators, the sheriff might have assigned the trooper the task of keeping all vehicular traffic on the highway moving. He might then have profitably conferred with the deputy as to what information the young officer had already accumulated. Which, in fact, was no small amount.

The deputy could have told him that there were four dead bodies on the floor inside the grocery store, that they had obviously been killed by successive shotgun blasts to the head, execution style, with their hands bound behind their backs. He could have advised the sheriff that a large amount of blood and gore was splashed about the storeroom and that movement would have to be carefully restricted.

Most importantly perhaps, the deputy would have told the sheriff of the extent of the perimeter search that had been accomplished and of the possibility, if the unlikelihood, of the perpetrator's still being on the premises or inside the two-story building.

At this point, the sheriff might well have realized that he was faced with a major crime scene investigation. All crimes of violence generally require a careful crime scene examination. No case necessitates more care than a questionable death or a homicide—except for a multiple homicide.

So, after assigning the young deputy the task of denying all unauthorized personnel access to the scene, the sheriff might have begun to coordinate the investigation with his chief deputy. The tasks now were to make certain that the perpetrator was not still on the premises, to protect the scene, and to make a thorough search of the scene for incriminating physical evidence. The sheriff might logically have instructed the chief deputy to get on the car radio and begin to assemble the necessary personnel.

Prior to moving any closer to the actual scene, a general perimeter search might be made, including the use of flashlights (search lights if necessary) to illuminate the darkened areas around the building. Since there was no indication that the perpetrator was inside, the decision might now be made to enter the store.

The sheriff would have wanted a systematic approach, of course. Part of the crime scene, it should be remembered, would be the immediate vicinity around the store as well as its interior. At the very least, a careful examination of the ground just outside the door might have been made by a designated officer. What kind of evidence might he have been expected to find?—tire tracks, footprints, a spent cartridge case, or perhaps even the murder weapon. There might have been blood-smeared shoe prints on the step or blooded fingerprints on the door jamb. There *might* have been *anything*.

After searching the grounds, the sheriff might have decided it was time to move inside. Having assembled his search team by now, and having already made their assignments, he would now begin the interior search.

What does this mean? Would the entire search team now rush inside? Not at all. One officer would be assigned to take photographs, another to sketch the scene, another to search for latent fingerprints, and still another to collect blood samples, all of this prior to a general search. Of course, a couple of officers would have been assigned the task of carefully searching the building for the presence of other victims or perhaps of the suspected criminal.

One very important stipulation that the sheriff might have made to all the officers involved: do not touch or move the bodies until the medical officer has completed his examination. After this has been done, and the scene has been photographed, sketched, searched for latent prints, and sufficient blood samples have been taken, the general search might commence.

The members of the general search team would still function within the restrictions of their specific roles. The photographer would make pictures of individual items of evidence as they are discovered; the sketcher would continue to work on his rough sketches, noting each piece of evidence and its location; the evidence officer would collect, preserve, and tag each article of evidence; the measuring officer would work on the general measurements of the scene and work out the coordinates for every item of evidence discovered; and the sheriff would have continued to function as the search leader.

As for the actual search, any one of the aforementioned techniques might have been utilized, or even a combination of some or all of the techniques. The best that can be said for the sheriff in the hypothetical case, however, is that he played a pretty good game of hopscotch, and that, in this instance, luck was for the most part on his side.

Regardless of the method used in searching a crime scene, however, the investigator must have a feel, as well as a professional's knowledge, of what kind of evidence he is looking for and what he can reasonably expect to find under the circumstances of the case. The search must be organized and methodical, and it must be thorough.

Simply stated, only in direct proportion to his experience,

training, education, and professional attitude will the criminal investigator know how to conduct a crime scene search with a view toward locating and preserving pertinent physical evidence.

Searching a crime scene, of course, is not an end in itself. The scene must be adequately recorded for future investigative and evidentiary purposes.

• DISCUSSION QUESTIONS

1. *What is the primary purpose of a crime scene search?*

2. *What is the best method of searching a crime scene?*

3. *What method of search did the investigators employ in the hypothetical case of the rural multiple murders?*

6

- *Recording the Crime Scene*

We have noted that the purpose of a crime scene search is to gather physical evidence that will support a conviction of a guilty person or exonerate an innocent citizen in a court of law. It will serve little or no purpose in this regard if the investigator handles the evidence discovered at the scene in such a way as to preclude its use or its effectiveness in the subsequent trial.

The investigator to whom the case is assigned is the individual primarily responsible for assembling all the loose ends of the investigation into a coherent whole. He constructs a graphic picture of the case in much the same way one fits together the pieces in a jigsaw puzzle. The more systematically he works, the more complete in detail his final picture will be. Although a professional investigator may correctly view himself as something of a creative artist, his final product must conform to the principles of reality; there is no room for surrealism or abstract-expressionism in the discipline of criminal investigation.

The final picture of an investigation is fashioned more or less by a combination of the following elements: field notes, photographs, and sketches and diagrams.

FIELD NOTES

This is the basic record of the facts of the crime and the evidence developed as a result of its investigation. Field notes should be begun practically at the moment the investigator is assigned to the case. All intermediate reports, the final report, and the investigator's testimony in court will be based on the material accumulated in his field notes. If his notes are faulty, incomplete, or otherwise inadequate, the outcome of the investigation may be hopelessly jeopardized.

Obviously no investigator, however experienced or intelligent, should attempt to rely upon his unaided memory in reducing the details of an investigation to a permanent record. Only an inexperienced investigator would try. The mass of detail of a major case investigation would overwhelm even the prodigious mnemonic capacity of a John Dean.

A notebook should be employed, containing notes pertinent to only one investigation. Considerations of economy of operation, always important in police administration, are not controlling in this regard. Notes of more than one investigation contained in a single notebook are a practice that invites mistake and confusion. There is also the very real possibility of improper disclosure of information. Credibility of field notes is further enhanced by the use of ink and a bound notebook, as opposed to the impermanence of pencil and a looseleaf binder.

The use of language, symbols, abbreviations, style, and other like matters should be of such clarity and simplicity that anyone else having to read the author's notes would encounter no difficulty in understanding their meaning. The need for such concern is one of practical necessity. It is entirely possible that the investigator who begins the case will not, for one reason or another, complete the investigation. He must then turn his field notes over to the officer assuming responsibility for completion of the case. If the notes are illegible for any reason whatever, the case may be irreparably damaged.

Field notes may also be read on occasion by the prosecutor's office, the defense counsel, the judge, and the jury. This is a sufficient reason to induce an investigator to take adequate pains with his notes of the investigation from the very outset. Errors may perhaps be corrected, but they cannot be obliterated.

What are the contents of an investigator's field notes? Such notes are nothing more than a continuing memoranda of an investigation, commencing with the officer's assignment to the case and concluding when the case is officially closed. During that phase of the investigation involving the crime scene search, the following is an indication of the sort of material that would be found in an investigator's notebook:

1. date the assignment was initiated
2. brief classification of the type of case
3. name of victim(s) and suspect(s), if known
4. time search began
5. names of personnel comprising search team
6. weather and light condition
7. description of any special equipment used
8. general description of the area searched
9. detailed description of every item of physical evidence discovered; what, where, when, found by whom, etc.
10. measurements concerning the discovery of such evidence and the description of each item
11. sketches and diagrams drawn of the scene
12. notes concerning the details of each photograph taken of the scene and of all physical evidence

Such entries must be noted with such detail and specificity as the nature and the seriousness of the case dictate. Although it is unwise to clutter one's notes with nonessentials, it is often no simple matter, even for an experienced investigator, to determine on-the-spot those matters that will obviously prove significant at later stages of the investigation. In short, thoroughness is preferable to omission.

For example, negative information, such as the failure to locate physical evidence that might reasonably be expected to be present at the scene of a particular crime, should always be mentioned in the field notes. Such absence, among other things, may be important in itself as a clue, or may directly affect the investigator's ultimate theory of the case. At this stage of the investigation nothing can prudently be overlooked as having a relevant bearing on the outcome of the case.

The notebook itself must of course be carefully preserved. It will be less than impressive to contend on the witness stand that your secretary mistakenly set fire to your notes while attempting to answer the phone and to light her cigarette at the same time. Nor will it be very persuasive to the court and jury to claim that "the devil made her do it."

Resisting the urge to play around with a series of more or less humorous Watergate-isms, we should take note, however, that the day must surely come when all notes and reporting data will be recorded by use of small pocket-sized and desk-sized tape recorders. The tape will be transcribed in the typing pool and maintained by the investigator in manuscript form for all the same purposes of keeping a handwritten notebook, including its use in court. Accuracy will thus be greatly enhanced, and certainly more information can be retained.

One word of caution in this regard: presidential language may have upon occasion blistered a pious ear; investigatory language has a tendency to peel the paint off the walls.

PHOTOGRAPHS

Photography is but one method by which the investigator attempts to make a permanent record of the crime scene in order that such facts may be subsequently used in reconstructing the scene and, perhaps, even the very method (*modus operandi*) in which the crime was perpetrated. For example, photographs of tool mark striations on the door jamb of an otherwise secure office building would indicate the method of entry upon the discovery that the building had recently been burgled.

Photographs supplement an investigator's field notes; they do not replace such notes. Just as sketches and diagrams are said to be a part of the investigator's field notes, photographs may also be viewed in this regard without stretching the point too much. Pictures, after all, serve the same purpose as field notes, diagrams, and sketches; that is, they aid in arriving at a clearer understanding of the detailed facts of which a crime consists.

Just as the foot, the horse, and the buggy preceded man's use of the automobile, so maps, models, diagrams, and sketches preceded the use of photographs in criminal investigations. All that modern investigators were waiting for, however, was the discovery of the camera. Photographs have now become an indispensable factor of police work.

No longer need an investigator be intimidated by the complexity of the picture-taking process. Today the end product is no farther away than a ten-second Polaroid pause. With a few moments' instruction, the investigator will be sufficiently versed in the art of basic crime scene photography.

Not that such work begins and ends with the Polaroid system by any means. Today there are such photographic marvels to be considered as split-image rangefinders, behind-the-lens exposure meters, strobe lights, depth-of-field calibrations, fixed-focus cameras (especially useful for crime scene photography), and many other innovations in this continually developing field of scientific endeavor. Although an investigator will rarely, if ever, be called upon to display any knowledge of such matters as photomicrography, radiography, gammagraphs and the like, he should at least make himself aware of the existence and potentialities of such skills, as well as the procedure for their availability in the jurisdiction in which he operates.

In actual practice, however, the investigator need only develop his own skill in the use of the Polaroid, or speed graphic camera, and the fingerprint camera for use at the crime scene. (Fig. 6.1.) Photographic specialists usually must be looked to for anything more advanced.

At the outset of a criminal investigation, the officer in charge of the case must insure that nothing about the crime scene is disturbed in any way prior to being photographed; always excepting, of course, any emergency first-aid assistance that must be rendered to an injured party. Even such assistance, however, must be furnished with due caution to avoid any unnecessary disturbance or contamination of physical evidence.

But how does one preserve the scene of the crime in its original condition by the use of photographs? Certainly not by one overall picture of the crime scene. Depending upon the circumstances of the case, three, four, or a dozen or more photographs may be required. In the Tate-LaBianca murder cases,

FIG. 6.1 Hand-held pistol grip fingerprint and evidence camera (From Sirchie Finger Print Laboratories. Reprinted with permission)

countless photographs were taken at the grisly crime scenes.

The test is to provide a pictorial representation of the scene, including the location and position of every object. This can only be done by a series of expertly directed "shots," beginning with a general overall view and working downward in a variety of specifically detailed pictures that, taken together, will graphically support the investigator's subsequent oral and written accounts of what he found at the scene.

The series of photographs, then, must serve to pull the entire scene together, so that anyone examining the pictures will understand how the crime was committed. Occasionally such photographs even tell *why* a crime was committed.

Obviously the entire crime scene should be photographed before any objects are moved or otherwise disturbed. Small objects should be photographed at close range and at long range in relation to other objects to show the proper perspective. A pocket knife isolated on the floor from a straight overhead position may approximate the dimensions of a Samaurai sword to an observer who has not seen the actual object. A picture of the same object on the floor in close proximity to a child's shoe (or a ruler) will show it for what it is: a penknife somewhat less than three inches long.

It bears repeating at this point that in spite of the inflationary times in which he might be operating, the investigator should not be unduly cost-conscious regarding the expenditure of film. His determination of the boundaries of the crime must often include such long-range views as the approach route, all possible avenues of ingress and egress to the immediate scene, hallways, connecting buildings and the like. The circumstances of each case will determine how much should be photographed.

For example, a theft of jewels from a safe in a downstairs den might have been initiated by the thief when he forced his way into a locked window in the upstairs bedroom. He may have left more traces of the crime in the bedroom and in the flower bed below the window than in the den itself.

Certainly in a murder case the body (or bodies) must be photographed before and after removal. And if the victim was clothed at the time of the homicide, clearly the body must be photographed nude upon removal to the coroner's office. It is of no use to plead with your supervisor that you didn't photograph the body at the scene because it was too gruesome, so you waited until the undertaker had tidied it up a little.

Not only must the body itself be photographed, but the actual wounds on the body as well. Such pictures, however, must be done with as much good taste as is possible considering the nature of the offense. There must be no indication of an attempt to inflame the minds of viewers against the suspected criminal. In days past, for example, it has not been uncommon to find such inflammatory pictures in cases in which a black man was accused of having raped and/or murdered a white woman. This kind of investigative photography is absolutely intolerable in a society that espouses the equality of man and the color blindness of justice.

Five people, including Sharon Tate, were murdered at the Bel-Air home she shared with husband Roman Polanski. One body is under the sheet in front of the house at upper left. Another is in the automobile at lower right. A third was found near the swimming pool at the top, and two others were found in the house.   (Associated Press Wirephoto)

Actress Sharon Tate (United Press International Photo)

The body of Sharon Tate, eight months pregnant, being taken from her home (Wide World Photos)

Fig. 6.2   Scene of the Tate murders

100

A trail of blood on the porch of the Tate residence (Associated Press Wirephoto)

The blood-stained couch in the living room of the Tate/Polanski residence where Sharon Tate's body was found (Associated Press Wirephoto)

Los Angeles County Coroner Thomas Nogouchi (left) taking notes as assistants pick up the sheet covering one of the two bodies found on the lawn of the Tate/Polanski home (United Press International Photo)

A complete record of each photograph should be maintained in the investigator's notebook. Such record should at least include the following:

1. identification of the photos with the case under investigation
2. identification of the photographer
3. date and time each photo was taken
4. light and weather conditions
5. camera angles of each photo, distance and direction
6. technical information regarding the type of camera, film, and equipment
7. notation as to any special techniques used or suggested
8. complete information regarding the chain of custody

Motion Pictures

It should be noted here that all that has been said above applies equally well to the use of the motion picture camera. The operation of such a camera is no more complicated than the others that have previously been mentioned. As with the still cameras, to operate it is within the capability of the average police investigator.

The use of motion pictures (as well as videotape) can produce dramatic results in the investigation of criminal violations. The filmed record of a bank robbery in progress, an exchange of heroin in return for a sum of money, or a politician brownbagging it for lunch with a character of unsavory criminal reputation would be of considerable evidentiary value in a court of law, if such cases should ever advance beyond a hasty guilty plea. Motion pictures have become so common in bank robbery investigations, as a matter of fact, that criminals who engage in this specialty as their major source of income may soon be claiming the right to be compensated at scale for their work before the cameras. If they don't realize a profit in the robbery, they will earn a decent living from their acting chores. Today, Bonnie and Clyde might expect to win mutual Academy Awards.

Motion pictures have also been used with particular success in cases involving driving under the influence. Such cases are won more often than not before going to court simply by showing the film to the accused and allowing him the benefit of previewing his starring role, as it were. By the time he falls into the gutter for the third or fourth time, or sticks the wrong end of a lighted cigarette into his ear, he is usually quite eager to admit his guilt and get the whole thing over with.

Nor should the use of motion picture film be discouraged merely because of occasional abuse of the technique. Where investigators appear more inclined to perform their camera work in secluded lovers' lanes or park rest rooms with a view toward private beer-and-pretzel screenings for stag night at a local civic club, reassignments to the noonday traffic detail might then be well advised.

Staged Photographs

It is often of considerable value to reconstruct a crime scene by means of "staged" or "posed" photographs or motion pictures. Witnesses at the scene are used to recreate the crime as they recall it. Often, depending on how many versions there are, a number of "recreations" will be necessary. Such photos may serve also to identify persons and physical evidence at the scene that would otherwise have been overlooked. It often develops that the perpetrator of the crime participates in the mock action, thereby contributing to his ultimate identification.

Evidentiary Considerations

Photographs and motion pictures are next to useless if they cannot be used in court in order to illustrate all of the essential elements of the crime. To meet the stringent rules of admissibility, the photos must be material and relevant, must not unduly incite prejudice and sympathy, and must be accurate representations free of distortion.

It is of no legal consequence to have a portfolio full of

scintillating photographs revealing a married government official in compromising positions *vis-à-vis* a variety of lovely ladies
when the case under investigation concerns the issue of whether
or not the official was guilty of an assault to commit bodily harm
when he punched another official with whom he disagreed in a
committee hearing. Photographs of the actual blow or of its
aftermath would be much more material and relevant to the
charge than those illuminating his sex life.

Likewise, it takes little imagination to apprehend the reaction of a jury in a case like the Edelin abortion trial in Boston
to the submission of a sheaf of glossy color photographs of the
fetus that the doctor allegedly killed as a result of his operation.
The use of photographs at all, and particularly color photography, in such a sensitive and highly emotional case is to be carefully scrutinized. The problem of inflammatory incitation is one
that should be uppermost in the photographer's mind in such a
case. Thus, in homicide cases and other crimes of violence and
bodily injury, it behooves the police photographer to make his
pictures with both color and black and white film.

Obviously, any photograph intended to be utilized as evidence in a criminal trial should not misrepresent the scene of
the crime or any object or person sought to be connected with
the offense. Distortion, of course, is not generally of an intentional nature. In most instances, the photographs are defective
due to technical errors, such as faulty perspective and tonal
imbalances.

Nevertheless, crime photography is storytelling by way of
visual composition, and graphic exposition of the full story cannot be avoided or neglected merely because the scene it repre-
sents is repulsive. The end result of most crime is unattractive.
Certainly the *corpus delicti* of a crime (the body of the offense,
the basic element of the crime) is of major importance to the
development of the case and its ultimate presentation in court.
As such, it must be adequately photographed.

By way of example, *corpus delicti* material would include
photographs of the wounded victim of a homicide, the point of
origin of the fire in a suspected arson case, the sacks of money
stolen in an armored car holdup, and the place of forced entry

in a burglary. *Corpus delicti* evidence will be more fully discussed in a subsequent chapter. Suffice it to say at this point that it is nothing more complex than proof of the fact that a particular crime was committed. It is absolutely necessary to the successful prosecution of a criminal case.

In addition to such proof regarding *corpus delicti* evidence, photographs may also assist the investigator in establishing certain facts regarding the identity of the perpetrator of the crime and his *modus operandi*, which, taken together, constitute the elements of the offense that must be proved in court in order to sustain a conviction.

For example, in the hypothetical case of the multiple murders in the rural grocery store, the elements of the offense are: 1) the felonious killing, 2) of a human being, 3) by another, 4) with malice aforethought. Evidence photography (in this case, pictures of the dead bodies) would be most helpful in establishing the *corpus delicti* (the fact that a crime has been committed.) Photographs might also tend to help prove the above-stated elements of the crime.

SKETCHES AND DIAGRAMS

The crime scene sketch is the first permanent visual record of the investigation. The ultimate purpose of such a sketch is the graphic presentation of the facts of a crime with such clarity and precision that the crime itself may be reconstructed from the details of the sketch. In this regard, sketches are supplemental to written reports and photographs. There are basically two types of sketches: rough sketches and finished drawings.

Every sketch should include the same kind of identifying data as previously noted for photographs.

Initially, the investigator will make a rough sketch of the crime scene as part of his field notes. Though it need not be drawn to scale, it should be an accurate portrayal of the scene with the proportions approximated and the appropriate measurements indicated. The investigator should make his own

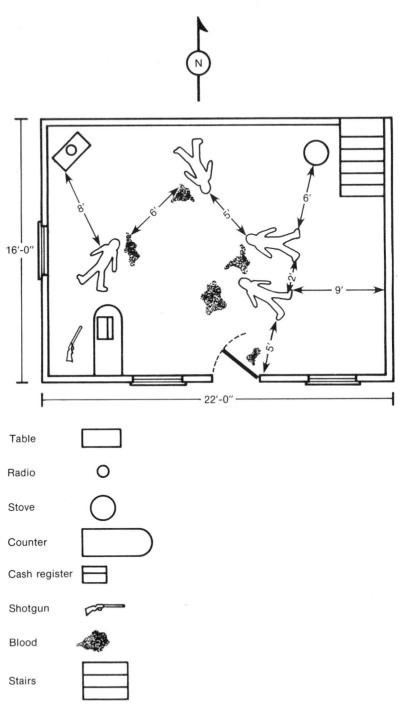

FIG. 6.3 A rough sketch of the downstairs of a hypothetical murder scene, with legend

Table

Radio

Stove

Counter

Cash register

Shotgun

Blood

Stairs

measurements, using such instruments as a steel tape, a wheel-type measure, and a compass with which to orient his sketch with a "magnetic north" arrow. (Fig. 6.3.)

In the case of large outdoor areas, of course, it is quite possible that the assigned investigator will require the assistance of a skilled surveyor. It can only be hoped that such assistance is within the budgetary and philosophical capability of the police agency involved.

In the rough sketch, architectural detail is not required. Simplicity is the controlling virtue. The rough sketch is little more than a diagram of the essential elements of a crime scene and their relationship to each other; unnecessary details should not be included. The use of standard symbols should be employed in order to further simplify the sketch by reducing as much clutter as possible.

In taking the measurements for a crime scene sketch, it is axiomatic that absolutely nothing about the scene should be altered in any way save under the most exceptional circumstances. The rough sketch is generally used as the basis for the finished scale drawing. And the purpose of the final scaled drawing is for use in a court of law. It is clear, therefore, that the original sketch or diagram must be beyond reproach in its execution. It must be a faithful, accurate presentation of the crime scene as it actually was. Hence, no item must be moved prior to completion of the rough sketch in the investigator's field notes; the sketch, once completed, must never be altered by anyone, not even by the investigator who executed the sketch; and the sketch must by all means be preserved in good condition for later scrutiny by investigators, prosecutor, court, jury, and defense counsel.

The final scaled sketch is usually prepared by a specialist using the rough sketch as a starting point, but drawing also upon the investigator's notes and observations, information supplied by victims and/or witnesses, and from his own examination of the crime scene. Since the primary purpose of the final drawing is its use in court, it is often not prepared until the case actually progresses to the point of trial.

• DISCUSSION QUESTIONS

1. *What are the three primary methods of recording a crime scene?*

2. *What constitutes the basic record of the facts and evidence of a crime and its investigation?*

3. *What are the three primary criteria for the admission of photographs into evidence in a court of law?*

7

• *Physical Evidence*

What is meant by the term *physical evidence?* The term embraces any and all objects whether animate or inanimate, solids or gases, that have a bearing on the solution of a crime. As such, any material that tends to establish the *corpus delicti* of a crime (proof that a crime has in fact occurred); or the identity and/or location of the victim, suspect, or witnesses; or that indicates the circumstances concerning the perpetration of the crime, the precise means of committing the crime, or the motive for the crime, must be collected, recorded, marked for identification, and preserved for subsequent use. No item, large or small, is too insignificant to be considered by the investigator; certainly no item can be taken for granted.

Although the primary source of physical evidence is generally the crime scene itself, it is by no means the only source. Many crimes have moving or multiple scenes; many criminals carry physical evidence away from the actual scene in addition to leaving evidence behind. Witnesses, as well as participants in the crime, are often major sources of physical evidence, as indeed is the victim himself. In addition, there are many types of evidence that are not susceptible to discovery by normal investigative measures and require scientific treatment beyond the capability of the investigator. Scientific examination under laboratory conditions is required of this kind of evidence. The investigator must be aware of such need and of the availability of such technical aid.

Of course, an abundance of physical evidence might exist right under an investigator's nose and yet not be recognized as such. A wide range of general knowledge concerning life and the affairs of man will best aid the investigator in spotting significant, relevant evidence.

In addition, certain knowledge specifically pertaining to the investigator's craft must be mastered through on-the-job experience and continuing education. For example, an investigator must develop an informed awareness of the law, in particular that substantive law relating to specific criminal offenses, criminal procedure, and the rules of evidence. He should, of course, also know something about the theory of law and the history of the development of legal systems. He should have sufficient imagination to be able to understand the operation of the criminal mind to recognize *modus operandi* evidence when he sees it.

All evidence must be carefully protected—scientifically and legally—after it is gathered. If through carelessness or willfulness it is damaged to the extent that laboratory analysis is inconclusive, or if legal procedures are violated to the point that it is unacceptable in court, then the evidence is all but useless.

To use physical evidence in court, the article sought to be introduced must be properly identified, the chain of custody must be established, and the evidence must be relevant to the issue at trial. (More on such matters subsequently.) The investigator insures the integrity of physical evidence by adhering to the procedure immediately following.

PROCEDURE

Generally, the procedure for handling physical evidence includes the discovery and recognition of the material; the protection of the material; the making of a record by the use of field notes, photographs, and rough sketches; the collection of the evidence; and the transportation of the evidence either to an authorized place of storage or to the laboratory for scientific examination.

It should be repeated here that the search for physical evidence, at the crime scene or elsewhere, must be planned and methodical. The handling of the crime scene itself is the phase of an investigation in which the most damaging mistakes are usually made. The fact that few, if any, crime scenes are perfectly handled should not deter the investigator from striving for perfection.

A case in point might well be the 1975 Joan Little–Alligood murder case in North Carolina. The handling of evidence at the crime scene—the jail cell in which the deceased was stabbed to death with an ice pick—left a great deal to be desired. The scene was not well protected, and physical evidence was incompetently handled and safeguarded. Expert testimony in the trial indicated that some of the blood stains on the deceased jailer's shirt appeared to have been wiped on after he was stabbed; the stains were found to contain more water than blood and the water seemed to have been added externally. In addition, only one blood sample retrieved from the crime scene was forwarded to the laboratory for examination; the sample was then lost, destroyed, or, conceivably, intentionally concealed.

Furthermore, wads of bloody tissue, the bloody sheet that was found beneath the deceased's body, a blanket, and a pack of cigarettes containing two different brands of tobacco were all destroyed by police officials. Finally, at the scene of the crime, a detective picked up the ice pick that appeared to have been the murder weapon and stuck it in his hip pocket, saying: "Oh well, it doesn't have any prints on it anyhow." It is difficult to imagine how evidence at a crime scene could have been more improperly handled. Needless to say, Miss Little was subsequently acquitted of all charges.

Although statistically not as important as many other types of violent crime, homicide (especially murder) is still the single crime that most consistently absorbs public and official attention. It is also the one crime that requires the most careful attention to detail in the handling of the crime scene, including the location, collection, and preservation of physical evidence.

Homicide Investigations

A thorough discussion of homicide investigation (as indeed, all substantive crimes) is beyond the scope of this book. Even so,

there are certain vital principles that ought at least to be enumerated so that the reader can obtain a clear understanding of
the extent and complexity of such investigations.

Criminal homicide is the killing of another without legal
excuse or justification. The category may be further divided into
murder, manslaughter, and negligent death. Individual state
statutes must be consulted for the precise categories and definitions in each jurisdiction.

In order to prove the crime of murder, the investigator
must establish the elements of the offense; to do so he must be
intimately familiar with the criminal code in his jurisdiction.
The elements of the crime of murder are:

1. The victim is in fact dead.
2. Death resulted from an act of the accused.
3. The accused had a premeditated design to kill; or intended
   to kill or inflict serious personal injury; or acted with such
   wanton disregard of human life that intent to kill is presumed; or the wrongful death occurred while the accused
   was engaged in the act of committing another felony, such
   as burglary, rape, robbery, etc.

Perhaps it should be mentioned here that proof of motive
(the reason why the crime was committed) is not a necessary
element in establishing murder or any other crime. The nature
and utility of motive evidence will be discussed further in a
subsequent chapter.

What, then, are some of the aspects of homicide investigations that a criminal investigator must keep always in mind? He
must establish the fact of death, the mode of death, and the
time of death. He must identify the victim, family members,
associates, and witnesses to the crime. He must discover and
collect physical evidence—blood, hair, fibers, weapons, clothing, etc.—that will establish the elements of the offense. He must
develop a theory of the case, the mode of operation, and logical
suspects. Finally, he must consider alibis, exonerate innocent
suspects, and focus upon a prime suspect as evidence and leads
indicate.

In order to properly perform any crime scene search for physical evidence, the investigator must have the necessary tools and equipment at his disposal. Although it is the province of the police agency for whom he works to provide such material, it behooves the individual investigator to maintain rather close supervision of the contents of the evidence kit. (Fig. 7.1.)

The search of every scene will of course be governed by the special circumstances of the scene itself and of the type of crime under investigation. The use of a bulldozer might well be required in order to retrieve a body or an item of physical evi-

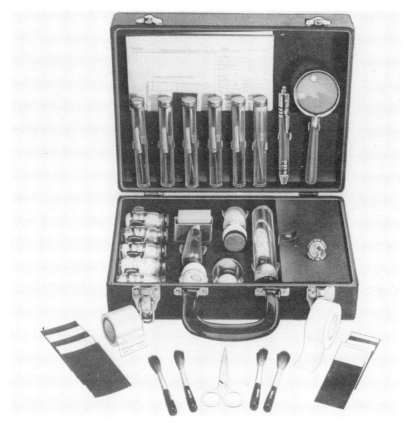

FIG. 7.1   All-purpose police field kit   (From Sirchie Finger Print Laboratories. Reprinted with permission)

dence from a swampy bog. Of course, it is a rare evidence kit that contains a bulldozer, certainly it is not standard police issue. However, experience has shown that certain items are more or less standard and should always be on hand and properly maintained. Included are such items as:

1. photographic equipment
2. fingerprint materials
3. flashlights and flood lamps
4. recording materials—i.e., notebooks, paper, pens, pencils, etc.
5. measuring instruments, including a compass
6. magnifying glass and mirror
7. tools—i.e., hammer, pliers, shovel, crowbar, etc.
8. evidence storage containers—i.e., envelopes, plastic bags, pill boxes, bottles, etc.
9. narcotics field test kit and casting material
10. incidental items—i.e., tweezers, scissors, rubber gloves, paper toweling, etc.

Of course, each investigator's personal experience and idiosyncracies will also have a bearing on the content of the evidence kit. Considerations of funding aside, each criminal investigator (or each team of investigators) should have an evidence kit specifically assigned and maintained.

PROTECTION

Physical evidence must be handled carefully to prevent its contamination, alteration, or destruction. The ultimate use of such evidence is its presentation in court. To be admissible as evidence in a criminal trial, the material sought to be introduced must be in a condition similar to when it was first retrieved by the discovering investigator.

The composition of physical evidence may be altered by natural causes (e.g., rain and wind), by accident, by negligence, by intentional act, or by theft. Although special precautions must occasionally be taken, the use of reasonable care and common sense in handling evidence will normally suffice. No further elaboration is required to understand why it is so important that the crime scene be immediately carefully sealed off and protected by the initial police officer on the scene. The potential for damaging crucial evidence during the actual crime scene search is readily apparent; fingerprints might easily be blurred or destroyed, blood specimens ruined, tire tracks obliterated, etc.

Nor does the need to protect the evidence terminate once it is taken from the crime scene or the place of acquisition. It is quite possible that an investigator might obtain physical evidence to a crime under circumstances in which he is less prepared than he would wish to handle such material. He will simply have to improvise. He will use a handkerchief, or perhaps a plastic drinking cup, a mason jar, a chewing gum wrapper, his hat, or possibly even his shoe. Better yet, his junior partner's hat or shoe.

Evidence may be damaged, destroyed, or lost at the scene of the crime, upon receiving the evidence, while transporting the evidence, and even after it has been stored in an authorized location. It is not uncommon for evidentiary materials to simply disappear (reference the Little-Alligood case mentioned above). Some law enforcement officers have been known to supplement their unspectacular salaries by the black marketing of confiscated weapons, drugs, liquor, and electrical appliances. Though this is certainly not the rule, such a possibility cannot be taken lightly.

Of course, not all material can be stored as is. Special handling is required for items such as food, blood, tissue, semen, and the like. Special preservatives may have to be added in order to maintain their evidentiary integrity. In other instances, nothing more complex than refrigeration is required. Most of these techniques will be beyond the case investigator's capabilities; they should not, however, be beyond his comprehension.

Sex Crimes

For example, the examination of a crime scene and the handling of physical evidence in connection with a sex offense presents certain specific difficulties of which the investigator must be aware. Proof of rape, in particular, is an extremely difficult charge to substantiate. Rape is generally defined as unlawful carnal knowledge of a female by force against her will. What manner of physical evidence must the investigator look for?

He must first establish that the offense did, in fact, occur. He must therefore prove that an act of carnal knowledge took place. Carnal knowledge is the legal term for sexual intercourse. Sexual intercourse, according to law, is the penetration of the female vagina by the male penis. The investigator must establish the fact of such penetration. How?

Although penetration, however slight, is sufficient to complete the offense, it must be shown beyond a reasonable doubt that the male penis entered at least to some extent into the vagina of the female. In addition to the victim's own testimony as to penetration, such fact can be established by witness testimony in the unlikely event there was a witness to the act, or by circumstantial evidence in the nature of expert medicolegal testimony.

The value of such expert testimony, then, would rest to a large extent upon the length of time that had elapsed between the alleged rape and the medical examination of the victim. Insofar as this decision is within the investigator's control, he must encourage the victim (delicately) to submit to a medical examination without delay.

The object of such examination, of course, is to determine the existence of signs of rape and of the actual penetration itself. Often such visible signs as wounds, bruises, scratches, lacerations and contusions will appear on the victim's body. And the vagina itself may reveal signs of recent use and abuse beyond that which is normally extant as a result of ordinary sexual activity.

The author once participated in a case in which a woman claimed to have been sexually assaulted in a parked automobile on a government reservation. Local police officers requested

FBI assistance due to the location of the alleged offense, and the author responded to the call. At the police station an attractive middle-aged woman, well-dressed and soft-spoken, asked to register the details of her complaint in privacy rather than amid the general disorder of the station house. The woman didn't appear to have been the victim of a recent sexual assault, as she had claimed, nor did she appear to be laboring under any particular distress, physical or emotional. The author, realizing it was best not to discuss her complaint alone with her, invited one of the local police officers to join them as a witness to the woman's statement. No sooner had the three of us entered the private office than the woman pulled her skirt up above her waist, revealing two raw bites implanted on the insides of her upper thighs that appeared to have been deposited there by a raucous man-of-war. In addition, her clitoris had been savagely chewed to the extent that corrective surgery was clearly indicated. To make the case even more sensational, the woman finally broke down and wept and admitted that the culprit was her own husband!

What can the medical examination expect to produce in a normal case, however? Proof of penetration, evidence of emission (though this is not necessary to the proof of rape), the presence of male pubic hairs, traces of pollen granules, etc. In addition to examinations of the victim's private parts, the victim's clothing should also be examined for signs of struggle, blood, sperm stains, and the like. And of considerable importance is the examination of fingernail scrapings for traces of blood, hair, human tissue, and clothing fibers that may have been acquired by the victim while resisting the attack.

It should be unnecessary to remind the criminal investigator that of all criminal offenses he is called upon to investigate, those classified as sex crimes are among the most sensitive. Unfortunately, such a reminder is necessary. Most police officers, like most citizens, are appallingly ignorant concerning sexual behavior in general and sexual deviancy in particular. There are far more police officers on active duty today than police executives would care to admit who have no understanding whatever of what is meant by such terms as fornication, sodomy, fellatio, cunnilingus, and bestiality, to name only a few. Many police officers can neither define nor comprehend the variety of sexual activity implicit in such preferences as homosexuality and lesbianism. Terms such as sadism, masochism, fetishism, and transvestitism are totally beyond their competency due to lack of training and education.

Is it any wonder that criminal investigations involving such activities are often less than successful? Without an understanding of the terms themselves, how can police adequately and justly enforce the law? What sort of behavior constitutes unlawful conduct? Is unusual (even abnormal) behavior in itself unlawful? By whose standards—those of the police?

What sort of purely legal questions present themselves for police consideration prior to making arrests and filing charges? Some such as the following might occur. Can a man be guilty of raping his own wife; can a husband be a party to the crime of rape in which his wife is the victim; can anal penetration constitute the crime of rape; can a female commit rape; can a man be raped by another man or by a female; can a woman who was once a man be the victim of rape; can a man who was once a woman be a rapist?

And so on.

Protecting the crime scene and the physical evidence in a sex crime investigation, then, often determines whether or not sufficient circumstantial evidence is collected that will serve to corroborate the victim's allegations. The actual methods by which such physical evidence is collected (and indeed, physical evidence in any type of criminal investigation), is the next important aspect to be considered.

COLLECTION

Physical evidence sought to be introduced in a criminal trial is not admitted as a matter of routine. It must conform to certain rigid legal standards. Physical evidence that is ruled inadmissible in court is usually evidence that has been irrevocably tainted by police handling at or near the scene of the crime or the place in which the evidence was taken into police custody.

As previously mentioned concerning the Little-Alligood

case, an officer picked up the murder weapon—an ice pick—handled it without regard to evidentiary integrity, and eventually stuck it in the back pocket of his trousers. Needless to say, fingerprint testimony played no part (or only a negative part) in the conduct of the trial. In the Manson-Tate murders, a police officer noted that there was a patch of blood on the gate-control button that opened and closed the gate to the house in which the murder victims had been discovered. This was the first officer upon the scene of the crime. As such, he was charged with the responsibility of protecting the scene and all of the potential evidence. Bloodstain notwithstanding, he pressed the button in order to open the gate, destroying any print that may have been subject to retrieval.

The crucial importance of this phase of a criminal investigation justifies the repetition of the exhortation to adhere to a standard procedure in protecting the crime scene and collecting the physical evidence. An investigator must bear in mind that nothing more than a reasonable doubt in the mind of one juror can jeopardize an entire case. The processing of physical evidence must be done strictly according to established procedures.

Experience has shown that, in addition to failure to secure the crime scene and protect the physical evidence that is on hand, errors made in the collection of evidentiary samples is a quite common cause of the inadmissibility of evidence in court.

In most instances, investigators simply fail to take a sufficient amount of the desired material as a sample for laboratory examination. With many (if not most) materials, a portion of the substance itself is consumed or otherwise destroyed in the process of chemical analysis. If an insufficient quantity has been furnished to the criminalistic expert, it is quite possible that the entire amount will be used up. Obviously, such an examination would be of slight value in a courtroom. If a person is accused of possessing a certain amount of marijuana, for example, the substance confiscated must prove to be marijuana. It cannot be so established if there was not enough of the substance on hand to analyze.

In addition, a portion of the substance should be retained after analysis for further tests of confirmation, as well as for comparison purposes in court. The judge and jury should be given the opportunity to examine the evidence in its natural state as well as after chemical analysis.

The importance of supplying sufficient samples for laboratory analysis can be further exemplified by considering the matter of blood specimens in light of modern technological breakthroughs. Recent scientific claims have indicated that it will soon be possible to identify a person's sex, race, and drug habits from a dried blood stain no larger than a half dollar and of several months' duration. Obviously, such a capability would be of considerable importance to investigators in their efforts to identify criminals from blood stains collected at crime scenes— but not unless sufficient samples are collected to insure an adequate supply of the substance for laboratory analysis.

Another common error is the failure of the investigator to provide, along with the clue sample, similar material in its natural state. For example, in the case of the rural murders to which we have previously referred, it is apparent that the investigators should have supplied a number of pieces of the blood-stained flooring on which the victims were lying. Perhaps it is not so obvious that unstained portions of the flooring should also be furnished to the lab technician as a control sample.

Control samples should be as nearly like the clue sample as possible, excepting only the extra clue ingredient itself. The substance upon which the clue is attached may or may not affect the analysis. Only through a familiarity with the properties of the material in its natural state can the lab technician make this determination.

The guiding rule for an investigator should be that of insuring the purity of his collected sample. The lab analyst can be of little assistance in the case if the integrity of the specimen furnished for analysis has already been contaminated by the police officer's negligence. Numerous items of physical evidence collected and transmitted in the same evidence bag share a general taint. A bullet dug from a wall at the scene of a crime by an investigator with a handy penknife is more likely to have been altered than had the investigator cut a portion of the wall loose and transmitted the entirety to the lab specialists for examination. Tactile comparisons of evidence specimens should never be made by the investigator on the scene, such as attempting to match a shoe that an investigator suspects fits a sand-print near the scene of a break-in. A plaster cast instead should be made of the print and forwarded along with the shoe to the laboratory for the proposed fitting. And certainly the laboratory specialists would prefer to make their own examination of a suspected marijuana cigarette rather than have an on-the-spot examination conducted by the discovering officer.

There is no limitation on the kind of evidence that an investigator can collect. These include fingerprints, firearms and other weapons, blood, semen and other stains, clothing, bullets and cartridge cases, paint, documents, dirt and soil deposits, to name only a few. The ability to determine what is material evidence and what is only matter is the quality that distinguishes an experienced professional investigator from a novice and/or an incompetent.

Physical evidence is either fixed or portable. (Figs. 7.2,

FIG. 7.2 A pair of prescription eyeglasses found at the home of slain actress Sharon Tate. The glasses are pictured on top of a notice describing them that was distributed to various optometric associations.   (United Press International Photo)

7.3.) Depending always on the importance of the case, the item should be moved whenever possible to the laboratory for examination. If it is impossible to remove the entire item, the investigator may wish to detach a piece of the item upon which the desired evidence is imprinted—the door of a burgled safe, for instance, that is thought to bear the suspects' fingerprints.

A special word of caution. An investigator should never attempt to lift a fingerprint at the scene of a crime. The print should be developed and photographed, and the object that bears the print should then be transported to the laboratory for processing.

In a situation involving physical evidence that is impossible or impractical to move, sketches, diagrams, photographs, plaster castings, and the like must be relied on.

Whatever the type of physical evidence collected, however, it must then be packaged in such a way as to avoid or at least minimize breakage, contamination, or loss while being transported to the laboratory or to a safe place of storage. The basic materials used in packaging physical evidence are clean, dry containers (boxes or bottles), wrapping paper, absorbent cotton, and sealing tape.

Some cases obviously present more difficulties than others in regard to the collection and care of physical evidence. For example, the handling of physical evidence in a suspected case of arson is generally more precarious than in other types of offenses, due primarily to the fragile condition of the material sought to be preserved.

Handling Physical Evidence in Arson Cases

The basic rule in collecting evidence in arson cases is never to move any object or substance thought to be of evidentiary significance prior to sketching and photographing the article in place.

FIG. 7.3   Deputy District Attorney Aaron H. Stovitz displaying a photograph of the 43-foot nylon cord found draped around the necks
of actress Sharon Tate and hair stylist Jay Sebring   (United
Press International Photo)

What sort of evidence might an investigator expect to find
at the scene of an arson? Arsonists have been commonly known
to utilize any container from tin cans to urine specimen jars in
which to place the combustible liquid to be used in the "plant."
The container itself and any residual liquid discovered therein
may, therefore, be vital to the investigation of the offense. The
liquid must be collected in a glass jar and tightly sealed, and
the container should be boxed and covered.

Ashes and debris are often ladened with clues indicative
of the nature of the fire and even pointing to the identification
of the arsonist. Traces of accelerant may be ascertained in the

ashes; remains of straw, excelsior, kindling or burned clothing may result from a careful sifting of the debris. Alarm clocks and other mechanical devices are often used to start fires, and such methods usually leave traces at the fire scene.

Perhaps the most crucial area of examination of a fire scene is the point of origin of the blaze. The exact point of origin can generally be determined by the intensity of the destruction in the area and by the relatively deeper extent of charring. The cause of the fire—whether accidental or incendiary—is most often determined at this point. Traces of combustible material are of utmost importance. The use of any liquid accelerant, such as gasoline, kerosene, or turpentine, may well be indicated by the burning pattern at the point of origin.

In any event, the primary consideration is always the safety and integrity of the evidence collected and packaged. In addition, the evidence must be properly marked or labeled for identification in order to be admissible in a court of law.

IDENTIFICATION

In order to identify evidence in court, the police witness will be called upon to state under oath the method by which he is able to identify an object that he discovered at the scene of a crime or pursuant to the investigation of a criminal offense. Such testimony is often not required until weeks, perhaps months, after the initial discovery of the evidence. Obviously, the investigator cannot recall such information from memory. He makes his identification by means of marks and/or labels (preferably both) that he affixed to the individual items of evidence at the moment of discovery or as shortly thereafter as practicable.

There is no particular method of marking or labeling to which an investigator must adhere. Most officers devise a system by trial and error (hopefully with not too many costly errors). The major concerns are for safety and legibility. Certainly the marking must in no way diminish the evidentiary value of the object, and the information must not be so obscure as to be meaningless to the investigator or to others attempting to refresh their memories at a later date. Shorthand is useful to a stenographer's employer only if the notes can be fully transcribed and expanded upon when needed; the same holds true of an investigator's ability to elaborate in court upon his notes concerning physical evidence.

Size and substance permitting, most investigators mark physical evidence with their initials, the date the object was discovered, and perhaps the name of the victim or suspect in the case. Obviously, the markings must be of a permanent nature. A carbide evidence scriber may be used, or pen and ink, depending upon the material to be marked.

The circumstances of the case and the object to be marked for identification are always the controlling elements in deciding upon the technique to be used. Objects of intrinsic value must be handled with more than routine care. The owner of an exquisite ruby-and-emerald pendant recovered in a police raid would be less than appreciative if the recovering officer monogrammed the face of the jewel with a penknife. Common sense is the factor to be desired.

Many objects cannot be marked at all. These may, however, be placed in containers or packages and then sealed and labeled with identifying data. Labels or tags should bear the following or similar data: identifying number or name of case, date and time of discovery of article, description of article, location of article at time of discovery, names of witnesses to discovery, and name and signature of investigator making discovery.

If the investigator is uncertain as to the method of marking or labeling in a particular instance, he should seek the advice and recommendation of the appropriate prosecuting attorney. The paramount consideration is always the usefulness of the object as evidence in court.

TRANSPORTATION

The investigator's responsibility in no way terminates upon discovering and marking physical evidence. It is generally his duty to attend to the transmittal of physical evidence to a laboratory, to a safe place of storage, to police headquarters, to the prosecutor's office, or to the courtroom in which the case is to be tried. Whenever practicable, the evidence should be delivered personally by the investigator. If appropriate, however, evidence may on occasion be delivered by mail, by parcel post, or by railway or air express, but always in conformance with governmental shipping regulations.

Ideally, each police agency would have its own laboratory facilities, and nothing other than personal delivery would ever be required. In reality, unfortunately, such is not the case. The FBI laboratory in Washington, D.C., therefore offers the most expeditious methods for local law enforcement agencies to obtain expert chemical analysis of physical evidence in criminal matters. Such examinations are provided free of charge by the Bureau, subject to the stipulation that the material has not and will not be analyzed by any other criminalistic expert. The FBI also furnishes expert witnesses for the trial, free of cost, unless testimony on the same technical subject in the same case is given by another expert for the prosecution.

In addition, evidence to be examined by the FBI must meet certain other requirements of which the conscientious criminal investigator would do well to be aware. The evidence must have been legally obtained; it must be properly described in a letter of transmittal; it must be initialed, labeled, and dated for purposes of identification; it must be properly handled, wrapped, and prepared for shipment; and, of final importance, the legal chain of custody must have been maintained.

CHAIN OF CUSTODY

This is nothing more than a record of the possession of the evidence from the moment of its discovery until it is offered as an exhibit for the prosecution in court. Each possessory link must be accounted for by way of written receipt and relinquishment. Obviously, evidence should change hands as infrequently as possible in order to minimize the danger of loss or destruction. The slightest irregularity in handling the evidence may very well be sufficient to raise a reasonable doubt in the mind of at least one juror, thus jeopardizing the value of the evidence and possibly affecting the outcome of the case.

By way of example, it might be recalled how such mishandling of potential legal evidence sent shock waves through the American political system in the fall of 1973. The nation was just beginning to adjust to the earlier discovery in the course of the Watergate controversy, that President Nixon had secretly installed a taping system in the Oval Office of the White House and had recorded every conversation that had occurred there. Obviously the fear was that such tapes might be doctored or manufactured in such a way as to exculpate the President and any of his associates who might be implicated in the Watergate affair. The care and security of such tapes, then, was of overriding concern to all persons involved. Then, on November 21, the President's attorney announced in federal court that one of the as yet undelivered tapes contained an unexplained eighteen-and-one-half-minute erasure, and two other tapes were "missing" entirely. Responding to the national shock some days later, the embattled President "testified" on national television, assuring the people that: "I am not a crook." The people, however, were not reassured. Juries can be expected to react with the same doubt and skepticism regarding courtroom testimony that clearly reveals mishandling of pertinent physical evidence.

It is axiomatic that physical evidence should never be maintained in an investigator's private possession. Even when correctly held in an authorized place of storage, access to the property room should be strictly limited to official need. Porno films should not be checked out for private stag screenings, marijuana or other hallucinogens should not be personally "analyzed" by nonlaboratory officials, and sums of hard currency should not be counted and recounted by anyone other than the investigator to whom the case is assigned and his reviewing superiors.

CRIMINALISTICS

On the night of November 1, 1955, one of the most heinous mass murders in the annals of American crime occurred some 5,000 feet above the scenic Colorado countryside. The crime was particularly shocking in that it did not involve sex or sadistic violence—save only in the broadest of psychological interpretations. The sole motive for the crime was money. Investigators eventually found a witness who told them he'd once heard the killer say: "I'd do anything for money."

At precisely 7:03 p.m., United Air Lines flight 629, eleven minutes after takeoff from Denver's Stapleton Airfield, was suddenly obliterated by an enormous explosion that seemed to ignite the peaceful nighttime sky. Witnesses said that the heavens appeared to have erupted and that for a moment it seemed as if all the stars were falling out of the sky. In fact, the celestial thermae was a ball of fire caused by a massive dynamite explosion, and the falling stars were streamers of flaming gasoline pouring down out of the sky.

Forty-four men, women, and children perished in the explosion.

The Civil Aeronautics Board (CAB) has primary jurisdiction over investigations involving plane crashes, and the Board requested FBI assistance in the examination of the wreckage. The FBI maintains a highly mobile air crash team that normally responds to such requests in a matter of hours. Bureau assistance was also requested by the airline in the task of identifying the victims.

Although the overriding investigative task was that of establishing the cause of the crash, first, the bodies of the victims had to be identified. A temporary morgue was improvised in a National Guard Armory near Denver. The bodies were fingerprinted and duly identified, mostly by way of comparison prints on file in the FBI Identification Division in Washington, D.C. Others were identified by fingerprints from such varied sources as the files and records of World War II defense plants, the armed forces, and the U.S. Immigration and Naturalization Service.

Next, the investigative teams of UAL, CAB, the FBI, and

the Douglas Aircraft Company went to work to discover whether the crash resulted from a mechanical failure, human error, an act of God, or sabotage.

Investigators were suspicious from the outset. Shredded bits of carpeting and upholstery, a greyish residue on bits and pieces of the plane, and an acrid smell around the wreckage, all indicated the presence of high explosives. Surveyors laid out a grid of numbered squares at the crash site; and evidence teams moved systematically over the ground, collecting, recording, and marking every item that had any connection with the fallen aircraft. Each item was carefully measured and recorded in relation to one another. (The tail assembly was located virtually intact more than a mile away from the original point of impact.)

Gradually, a recreation of the aircraft began to materialize. Each individual part found at the crash scene was removed to a large warehouse in Denver and placed on a scaled-down grid in a spot as closely proximate to its original point of discovery as was possible. A wooden mock-up of the crashed DC-6B was then fashioned in the warehouse, and the recovered pieces of the actual craft were carefully wired to it, somewhat in the manner of a toy model plane assembly kit.

In time, the fuselage was almost entirely reassembled, except for a large gaping hole on the right side near the tail section. A diagram of the plane showed that the hole was in the number 4 cargo pit.

Technicians soon determined that the metal at the point of the gaping side wound had been forced outward in a manner that could not have occurred as a result of the impact with the earth at the time of the crash. Pieces of the recovered fuselage were found to be smooth and clean on the outside but scorched severely on the inside. Items of wearing apparel and luggage produced instances of disfigurement that a normal crash was not likely to have caused. In addition, there were no fuel lines or tanks or electric wires in the vicinity of the damaged area that might have been the cause of an accidental explosion. It was soon clear to the experts, therefore, that an enormous explosion had occurred in the cargo pit prior to the crash. Now it was necessary to determine whether the blast was accidental or a deliberate act of sabotage. If it was deliberate, it would be the first known case of successful sabotage in the history of U.S. commercial aviation.

Soon, literally hundreds of FBI agents around the country and scores of state and local investigators were aiding in the investigation. Had there been any incendiary material illegally on board the plane that might have caused an accidental explosion? Did any of the crew members or passengers have any possible motive for sabotaging the plane? Gradually, the answer to the second query began to take ominous shape.

The FBI Laboratory reported that an analysis of the burned pieces of metal from the airplane showed traces of sodium carbonate, sodium nitrate, and sulphur-bearing compounds—all of which are customary residual aftereffects of dynamite explosions. The shredded bits of carpeting and upholstery also indicated high explosives, as did a cog from a clock that might have been used as a timing device. And the luggage of one of the female passengers was irretrievable save for tiny bits and fragments. The woman's son had a police record, including reports that he had once purposely stalled a vehicle at a railroad crossing in order to collect collision insurance, and had possibly caused a gas explosion in a family-owned business establishment, again for the purpose of collecting insurance. He had not been charged or convicted, however, in either instance.

Still more evidence began to focus the investigation upon this particular suspect. He had often fought violently with his mother over the management of their family business. His wife told investigators that she had seen him carrying a Christmas present for his mother—a tool set, he had said—that she supposed he gave to her just before takeoff. A neighbor said he had heard the suspect say that he'd bought his mother a Christmas surprise and slipped it into her suitcase. The suspect, however, denied any knowledge of the gift and further denied putting anything into his mother's suitcase.

However, he was cooperative and signed a waiver allowing agents to search his house without a search warrant. They found the shotgun shells and rifle ammunition that the suspect had said his mother had in her suitcase. They also discovered a cosmetic bag, personal articles of clothing, and some Christmas gifts that his mother was taking to her daughter in Alaska. And in one of the suspect's shirt pockets, agents found a small roll of wire of the kind used in detonating dynamite. Then, hidden in a cedar chest in the suspect's bedroom, agents discovered an insurance policy for $37,500 on his mother's life and payable to him as the beneficiary.

When faced with so much overwhelming evidence, the suspect broke down and confessed. He had sneaked a surprise Christmas present into his mother's suitcase all right, only it was not a drill for making costume jewelry from sea shells, as he'd told his wife. It was a fourteen-pound bundle of twenty-five sticks of dynamite, two electric blasting caps, and a timing device set for explosion after a ninety-minute interval.

Thirteen days after the crash, the suspect was arrested by federal agents for sabotage and was subsequently turned over to the state of Colorado on charges of murder. He was duly tried and convicted of murder in the first degree.

This case was a seminar in criminal investigative techniques and interagency cooperation, as well as in the utilization of scientific methods of evidentiary analysis. Even though the suspect confessed to the crime and furnished a great many details of how it was accomplished, he later recanted his confession. The physical evidence accumulated by the police investigators, however, coupled with the testimony of the laboratory experts, was so overwhelmingly conclusive of his guilt that he was convicted by the jury without resort to the use of his confession.

In past years, it may have been true that law enforcement could rely on little else but a solid well-documented confession in order to solve crimes. But that day is gone forever. Today there are few crime scenes that do not yield some usable clues to the trained criminal investigator and even fewer items of physical evidence that are not subject to scientific analysis.

It is not necessary, of course, that the criminal investigator should also function as a trained laboratory expert. But as otherwise noted, he should be aware of what the criminalistics experts can do for him and how he might assist them in successfully performing their duties. That it is a team effort is evident; one cannot operate without the other.

Not every police agency has access to an adequately staffed and funded laboratory, to be sure. Nor are funds the only impediment in this regard. Unanimity of opinion as to the benefits of criminalistics is not yet a reality. Still, the number of such facilities, local, state, and federal, is steadily growing, and as the personnel standards and qualifications improve, the service improves accordingly.

Ever since 1923, courts have accepted expert testimony pertaining to those scientific principles and observations generally accepted in the scientific field from which the principle or observation is deduced. Laboratory services in the United States have grown accordingly, from county coroners and medical examiners, to local, regional, and statewide law enforcement labs, to the nationwide facility operated by the FBI in Washington, D.C.

TECHNOLOGY AND
MODERN LAW ENFORCEMENT

There are no limits to the scope of the services provided by a properly staffed and equipped criminalistics laboratory. *Any* physical evidence is subject to scientific analysis. Yet it is precisely this area of technological potential that has been most neglected by our system of criminal justice. We have, in fact, only begun to take seriously the revolutionary role that science is capable of playing in the field of crime control and prevention.

It is the idea of scientific utility that must first be understood and accepted before the criminalistics laboratory can play any fundamental role in increasing the overall level of professionalism in the field of law enforcement. Only then can the laboratory, by utilizing the principles of the natural sciences, provide objective information to the criminal justice system generally and to criminal investigation in particular.

Though scientific discoveries and their application to modern society through technological advances have all but revolutionized most social institutions, the criminal justice system and the specialty of investigating crime have, for the most part, remained in the horse-and-buggy days of our national development. We know very little about the causes of crime, let alone the cure, and we are equally deficient in investigative techniques that prevent or control such behavior. It is a statistical fact beyond dispute that laboratory analysis is an infrequent factor in criminal prosecutions, in addition to which laboratory scientists rarely participate in searching crime scenes, nor assist in the training of police investigators in the techniques of recognizing and collecting potential physical evidence.

The scientific professionals among law enforcement are not entirely without blame for the lack of official and public acceptance of their discipline. With the primary exception of the FBI Laboratory, most crime labs have been unwilling or unable to object to the quality of the materials submitted to them by police agencies for analysis, let alone to refuse to examine such materials.

To properly justify the professional stature for which such laboratories have so long aspired, they must take the lead in demanding that physical evidence to be examined must be collected, screened, and handled by police according to strict scientific guidelines developed by the scientific community, and that comprehensive police training programs be devised and conducted for this purpose.

PHILOSOPHICAL AND LEGAL IMPLICATIONS

The scientific community has generally accepted as a definition of the term criminalistics, something similar to the following: That profession and scientific discipline that is engaged in the recognition, identification, individualization, and evaluation of physical evidence by application of the principles of the natural sciences in matters pertaining to law and science.

Crime is human behavior and should be understood as such. The study of the causes of man's criminal conduct, of course, is the proper concern of the medical and behavioral sciences. The scientific analysis of physical evidence that has a bearing on specific instances of man's criminal behavior, however, is the proper subject matter of the physical sciences and is therefore treated in the multidisciplinary field of criminalistics.

Though criminalistics as a profession dates back to the nineteenth century, it is only within the past decade that it has won popular notice. And to a large extent, such attention has resulted from the investigative deficiencies in a particularly lurid crime or series of such crimes, in the apparent hope that science applied to the investigative function might produce more successful results.

Even the U.S. Supreme Court decisions of later years have pointed to a greater reliance on scientific analysis of physical evidence as opposed to the traditional dependance upon confessions and witness testimony, which run a much greater risk of infringing upon the civil rights of persons rightly or wrongly accused of crime.

And the President's Crime Commission report of 1967 stated that: "More and more, the solution of major crime will hinge upon the discovery at crime scenes and subsequent scientific laboratory analysis of latent fingerprints, weapons, footprints, hairs, fibers, blood, and similar traces."

This is not to suggest that there are not some very crucial problems and deficiencies of operation and application within the field of criminalistics.

Socio-legal Considerations

Not the least problem to be considered in this regard is the socio-legal dilemma of adequately investigating crime while fully protecting the constitutional rights of citizens charged with crimes. It is a delicate balancing act that is only maintained in the modern criminal justice system by the nonjudicial expedient of wishful thinking.

The criminal court system in America functions only because of the widespread practice of plea bargaining and the resultant guilty pleas that eliminate the necessity of trials. And with the resources of scientific investigations available primarily to the prosecutorial component of the adversarial system, it is undeniable that the scales of justice are unequally weighted against the less-resourceful defense component.

The criminal justice system can only deliver justice when the defense enjoys equal access to the facts upon which the charges are based. As long as the police control the investigation of crime scenes and the discovery, collection, and handling of physical evidence that is to be scientifically analyzed in the criminalistics lab, it is not unreasonable to expect that the scales will remain weighted against the person charged with the crime.

The important question is how long will our courts, the administrators of our crime labs, and our citizens be content with a system that guarantees anything less than equality of legal rights under the Constitution?

THE FBI LABORATORY

A crime lab was officially established by the Bureau in 1932. It was comprised primarily of a borrowed microscope and an assortment of pickup equipment that might prove to be useful to the handful of scientific "experts" assigned the task of developing a capability of supporting investigators' findings in the field by conducting controlled experiments and analysis of physical evidence in the "laboratory." That it was a shoestring operation is probably an exaggeration in favor of the actual scope of its initial resources.

In less than a decade, not only was the laboratory making examinations for the FBI, but it was serving as a scientific clearinghouse for physical evidence and the analytical needs of law enforcement agencies throughout the country. And in less than twenty years, it was the largest and reputedly the most efficient criminal laboratory in the world.

Today the complex range of matters within the scope of the laboratory's capabilities is, in many instances, beyond the average criminal investigators' capacity to comprehend. The application of such scientific disciplines as chemistry, biology, electronics, physics, and metallurgy, to name only a few, are commonplace.

Experts in the laboratory, most of whom are trained special agents in addition to their scientific specialties in such fields as physics, chemistry, or electronics, may be assigned to examine blood stains, hairs, fibers; to compare markings on bullets, tools, or locks; to analyze handwriting specimens; and to conduct literally thousands of other examinations annually. They can determine whether or not the paint found on the clothing of a hit-and-run victim came from the fender of a particular vehicle, whether or not a surgical instrument was used as a weapon in a murder case, or whether or not a suspect was at the scene of a crime by an examination of the soil content on a pair of his shoes.

Not only does the FBI laboratory aid law enforcement in establishing the guilt of suspected criminals, it plays a vital role in helping to clear the innocent who are wrongly charged or suspected. Negative findings of the lab technicians, then, can be every bit as useful to the cause of justice. Imagine the relief of a suspected extortionist upon receipt of an FBI report that states without qualification that the suspect's handwriting is in no way similar to that used in the extortion letter.

Today, of course, FBI technicians and lab specialists have the newest and finest laboratory equipment available at their disposal, such as infrared and ultraviolet spectrophotometers, X-ray diffractometers, radioactive isotopes, differential thermal analyzers, gas chromatographs, neutron activation reactors, and so on. The laboratory has come a long way indeed from the borrowed microscope of 1932.

• DISCUSSION QUESTIONS

1. *What is meant by the term* physical evidence?

2. *What is the primary source of physical evidence?*

3. *How was the physical evidence in the Little-Alligood murder case handled?*

4. *It has been suggested that sex crimes are often less than competently investigated. What is a major contributing factor according to proponents of this contention?*

5. *What is meant by the term* chain of custody?

8

• Gathering Information

What is a criminal investigation? In its simplest terms, it is the accumulation of information. Where does such information come from? From complainants, victims, witnesses, informants, and suspects. And from records and physical evidence.

There is little romance or excitement involved in most police work. For the most part it is dull, tedious, and plodding. It can, however, be vitally important.

It is one thing to solve a crime when the identity and the whereabouts of the perpetrator are known to the police officer from the outset of the investigation. Having to determine the identity and whereabouts is quite another matter. If the offender is not caught in the act of the crime or while fleeing from the crime scene, the task is liable to be an arduous one.

Even should the identity of the perpetrator be provided by the victim or an eyewitness, if the offender's whereabouts are unknown, an extended investigation may be required in order to effect an apprehension. And even if the offender's identity and location are known, there may be insufficient evidence available to justify an arrest. It is up to the investigator to establish such evidence.

How does he go about it? By discovering and gathering information that will lead to the arrest of the offender and to his conviction in a court of law.

Initial Leads

Such leads are more often than not furnished by the victim of the crime or by an eyewitness. Statistics have shown that the perpetrators of most homicides as well as forcible rapes are at least casually known by their victims. Cases involving known suspects therefore constitute a high proportion of complaints to police that are cleared by arrest.

Many factors contribute to the development of the identity of unknown suspects and to their apprehension. Even if the victim is unable to identify the offender, he may possess (consciously or unconsciously) valuable information that will assist the investigator in establishing identity. Callous as it may at times appear to the layman, a careful examination of the background and recent activities of a rape victim, for example, may very well uncover information that leads directly to her assailant.

Let us consider a hypothetical case in point. A librarian was attacked and raped as she was locking up one night. She had no idea who her assailant was inasmuch as he waited until precisely the moment that she extinguished the lights before assulting her. She fought him, scratched his face, but finally was overcome by his superior strength. The investigator was tactful but thorough. The woman was married. Was she having marital difficulties? No. Did she ever encourage the attentions of other men? No, she certainly did not. Had anyone attempted to make a date with her recently, or tried to pick her up? No. Had anyone using the library recently offered to buy her a drink or a cup of coffee after work? No. Was she in the habit of stopping off at bars on her way home at night? Absolutely not. Had the library been crowded just prior to closing? Not particularly. Could she remember how many patrons had been present during the last hour before closing? Not really; people came and went; one or two of the regulars had been there. Men? Yes. Did she know their names? No, but she could check through her library cards.

Examination of the card file revealed that two men whose names and faces were known to the woman had been present. One man was almost seventy years old, was hard of hearing, and walked with the aid of a cane. He also customarily reeked of tobacco and the woman, now that she thought about it, had not detected any such distinctive scent during the attack. The other man was in his thirties, a loner who came to the library numerous times each week and often remained until closing time. Yes, he certainly would know her schedule and her particular closing habits. But she couldn't suspect him of doing such a thing. He was always quiet, polite, almost shy; he never said anything to her unless he was checking out a book. She was certain he could not have been her assailant.

The investigator took the man's address from the card file and went to his house. The man's wife answered the door. Her husband would be out in a moment; he was in the bathroom applying medication to a web of scratches and scrapings on his face which he'd received in a mugging on his way home from the library. She hadn't realized that her husband had already called the police; she hoped her husband's attacker would be caught and severely dealt with. It was getting so that no one was safe anymore, she said, and the public really ought to be better protected. When the man emerged from the bathroom, the investigator placed him under arrest.

Of course not all leads are so productive. In many cases there are more wrong turns and *cul-de-sacs* to contend with. Obviously the raw material that an investigator needs to work with is information. At times sufficient information to solve a particular crime is no further away from the investigator than his telephone book. Conversely, a warehouse crammed with facts and pertinent data may not be enough to identify the perpetrator or to determine his whereabouts. For example, despite tons of "information" gathered by state, local, and federal agencies, the question was still asked month after month: "Where is Patty Hearst?"

SOURCES OF INFORMATION

The proliferation in recent years of information gathering and storage technological advances has made the Orwellian nightmare of *1984* a cause for concern in millions of American homes. Potential for surveillance capability by computer is no longer a matter of science-fiction terror tactics. It is an inexorable force of our times that must soon be reckoned with if any hope for privacy and individual dignity is to survive.

It should not pass unremarked that but for the alertness of a night security guard at the Watergate Tower, a proposed scheme of government-sanctioned illegalities involving massive wiretapping, electronic bugging, break-ins, and mail interceptions might very well have become the established policy of the United States of America. Known as the "Huston Plan," it envisioned the cooperation, among others, of the CIA, FBI, NSA, Secret Service, IRS, and the re-election committee of an incumbent President. The scheme was considered and approved by the President, his closest aides, and the heads of all of the agencies to be involved in its operation—except the FBI. Only the disapproval of FBI Director J. Edgar Hoover prevailed upon President Nixon to postpone implementation of the plan. The Watergate discovery, of course, scuttled the administration altogether.

Be that as it may, political and ethical niceties aside, the criminal investigator, operating within the framework of statutory law and the Constitution, is aided in his task of identifying and locating criminal suspects by an almost bewildering array of official and unofficial sources.

Official Records

Federal, state, and local agencies compile cradle-to-grave data on millions of individuals that are available to criminal investigators on a more or less request-and-receive basis. Though by law and custom, some such information was once thought to be confidential, experiences of the sixties and seventies have proven that for the most part, no citizen's right of privacy supersedes the ability of government investigators (among others) to gain access even to the most historically protected information.

The various federal, state, and local agencies providing such information generally maintain current directories listing their governmental functions as well as the procedures by which to obtain desired information. An astute criminal investigator should be familiar with these listings.

Though not the only source of such information by any means, the Federal Bureau of Investigation is certainly a major repository of data in aid of the criminal investigator. Of primary assistance is the Fingerprint and Criminal Identification File at the Bureau, which serves as a national clearing house with over 200 million fingerprint cards on file. (Fig. 8.1.)

Fingerprint cards for each set of prints contain the name, physical description, occupation, reason for printing, and other like information concerning the citizens involved. And from these cards, identification records are developed containing information concerning the individual's personal and occupational background.

Information is furnished from these files by the FBI to authorized government officials ostensibly for official use only. Whether or not this stipulation proves to have been the case throughout the years will depend upon history and the vigilance of certain congressional investigating committees. The potential for serious abuse, however, should be apparent. Citizens of a concerned democracy dare not allow the perversion of technological advances to defile their cherished freedoms.

And if the FBI with its additional services such as the NCIC (National Crime Information Center), which is a computerized index containing information on wanted persons and stolen and/or missing property, and the Known Professional Check Passers' File did not constitute a sufficient threat to a free and open society, there is yet to be considered the CIA, NSA, IRS, BND & D, the Secret Service, the U.S. Postal Service, the VA, and almost as many other alphabetical combinations as

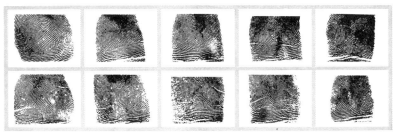

FIG. 8.1   FBI fingerprint card   (FBI/Washington D.C.)

one can imagine. All of these federal agencies and many more, including the military services, maintain information files numbering in the millions.

Nor can the criminal investigator overlook the numerous state and local repositories, such as law enforcement agencies, the courts, probation and parole offices, corrections facilities, motor vehicle bureaus, voter registration units, welfare and unemployment offices, and the like.

Unofficial Records

Such unofficial repositories of information are only slightly less thought-provoking. These sources are virtually unlimited and tend to multiply to the point of unaccountability. Public service companies, utilities, credit bureaus, financial institutions, educational facilities and the like often compile more complete dossiers on individuals than do some major police departments in the same locale. The National Auto Theft Bureau, administered out of New York City, for example, is more effective than many police agencies in the identification and location of stolen automobiles. And manufacturers of every sort of product can be of assistance in tracing stolen articles through the maintenance of serial number files and other identifying data. Obviously these outlets are primary sources of information pursuant to criminal investigations.

Tracing Sources

Still other sources available to the investigator in tracing operations are friends and relatives of suspects, witnesses, and missing persons, along with business associates, neighbors and other casual acquaintances. Of particular importance are spouses and lovers of the party sought. Criminals, like all citizens, are creatures of habit and private need. An otherwise professional criminal will often betray his whereabouts in a heart-weary effort to make an ill-advised contact with a sorely missed loved one. Of course the more information an investigator possesses about the suspect he is seeking, the more custom-tailored his tracing methods may then be.

INFORMANTS

A special source of information, without a thorough understanding of which an investigator could scarcely operate, is the category of confidential informants. Generally there are two kinds of criminal informants: voluntary (for a variety of reasons) and involuntary. The end result is the same in both instances: the obtaining of information.

To a considerable extent, the success of any law enforcement agency depends on the quality of its information-gathering apparatus. Every justified police success rests upon a foundation of solid information. Information is obviously gathered by the use of a variety of techniques. A criminal investigator's effectiveness depends almost exclusively upon his ability to obtain information. His ability to obtain information in turn depends to a considerable extent upon the effectiveness of his informant system.

It should be noted, however, that this evaluation of the informant system as it applies to police work is not subscribed to in all quarters. A 1976 report of the Rand Corporation regarding police detection said, in effect, that the image of the detective running a network of informants helping him to solve cases is a myth. The two-year survey of 156 U.S. police departments reported that the primary factor determining whether a case will be solved is whether or not the victim or a witness to the crime can furnish the initial patrol officer on the scene with immediate pertinent information. If not, so the report states, there is little that the police can do.

There is always the chance, of course, that the Rand investigators were operating with a deficient informant system of their own, and that they were remiss in adhering to one of the cardinal rules of information analysis: check and recheck your sources, and always verify information received by independent investigation.

An investigator (or any other student of police detection) who questions the value of cultivating and using informants would do well to study a page in the drama of the unmasking of a President of the United States, a President whose administration was so permeated by criminal and unethical behavior that the man and most of his associates had to be turned out of office lest the republic itself fail. How was such an all but impossible task to be achieved short of armed insurrection?

A situation existed during the Nixon administration in which the very institutions of government charged by law with the defense of our nation's liberties were themselves so corrupted, abused, and misused that they became the primary repositories of major criminal behavior in our society. Hindsight supports the contention that the misdeeds of so many persons in high places would surely have come to light by the force of their own proliferation. But would it have been in time? Thankfully, Americans will never have to know the answer.

The ultimate crisis was avoided by the overwhelming mass of incriminating information that was gathered and disseminated to the people of the republic. Information was gathered, significantly, not by the law enforcement officials charged with such responsibility, but rather by the news media (the print media primarily). And how was it managed? In large part by the resourceful utilization of the informant system.

In what has aptly been described as "the most devastating political detective story of the century," two *Washington Post* reporters broke the Watergate scandal in a flood of scalding information that swept the miscreants out of office like so much flotsom on a tidal wave. In this case, contrary to most, there was more than enough information upon which to base a solid case of wrongdoing. Indeed, there was almost too much information to be absorbed by the public and responsible officials alike. The body politic was all but inundated with information.

Woodward and Bernstein, the two reporters who perhaps did more to break the case than anyone else, faced a two-fold problem: they had to gather information concerning the nature of the break-in of the Democratic National Committee head-quarters itself, as well as information concerning a more threatening program conceived and operated by members, official and unofficial, of the President's administration, a program intended to crush and destroy by any means all those considered to be enemies of the administration and of the President's re-election.

How was such information obtained? By the use of informants, first and foremost. Informants in and out of governments, in high places and low, in the nation's capital, and elsewhere throughout the country and abroad. They elicited information, overtly and covertly, from cabinet members, party officials, law enforcement agents, Presidential aides, members of the Committee to Re-elect the President, secretaries, husbands, wives, other news reporters, taxi drivers, bellhops, and shoeshine boys, to name only a few sources.

Motivation for giving information to the reporters was as varied as the race, age, sex, political affiliation, and type of employment that distinguished the literally hundreds of informers who came forward or allowed themselves to be sought out. Money, patriotism, fear, stupidity, and malevolent intent were not lacking.

And so it is with informants generally. How to tap these undercurrents of individual psychic need is an ability that an investigator only develops through many years of trial-and-error, character analysis, and a more than casual familiarity with the principles of psychological motivation. Informant motivation is too complex to categorize here other than in the broadest of terms. Essentially there are two types of confidential informants—willing and unwilling.

The Voluntary Informant

An individual might be willing to provide information in return for money, either a one-time payment for specific information, or he may provide information of a general nature, often being himself unaware as to the value of the information being furnished.

Many a voluntary informant provides information simply

in order to curry favor with the law enforcement agency he is dealing with, or in an effort to have the agency intercede for him with the prosecutor or judge in a pending case or investigation. The criminal investigator's relationship with such an informer is a delicate one. He must work the informant according to the needs of the situation, but at no time must he make any promises or hold out any expectations that exceed his authorization on behalf of the prosecutor or judge.

As reflected in the Watergate case, information for pay or other personal gain is by no means the only medium of exchange to be appreciated by the criminal investigator. Patriotism and a sense of civic duty are not to be found wanting in the American public, though all too often such motivation is buried quite deep.

For example, there has been no indication that Deep Throat, the as-yet anonymous source of much crucial information in the Watergate revelations of Woodward and Bernstein, ever asked for or accepted remuneration of any kind in return for information furnished. Whether this individual received other personal gain or reward, or believed that he was being so rewarded, is open to conjecture. It is just as likely that his entire conscious motivation was one of civic duty. It is also quite likely that his motivation was so complex that he himself is not fully aware of why he acted as he did under the circumstances.

Still another case of more than passing interest is that of Sara Jane Moore, the alleged would-be assassin of President Ford. (Fig. 8.2.) Publicity surrounding her attempt to shoot the President has served to make her one of the most famous paid informers of the 1970s, if not of all time. Subsequent information has indicated that at the time of the shooting, Moore was working as a paid informer for the U.S. Bureau of Alcohol, Tobacco, and Firearms. She had previously been a paid informer of the FBI.

What did these government investigative agencies know about their employee that might have indicated a predisposition on her part to eventually perpetrate such a violent act? By exercise of hindsight, quite a lot perhaps. Upon the instant, very little.

Fig. 8.2   *Right:* Sara Jane Moore at home, June, 1975   (Janet Fries)
Left: Newspaper story of Moore's collapse in 1950   (*Washington Star*)

Moore was born in Charlestown, West Virginia, another famous resident of which was Charles Manson. She joined the WACs after high school, married and divorced four times, abandoned three children, and careened erratically from one vocation to another until she established an uneasy connection with the counterculture "movement" in the San Francisco Bay Area in the 1970s.

For a time, she worked as the bookkeeper for People In Need (PIN), the charity program sponsored by William Randolph Hearst in response to demands of the Symbionese Liberation Army, the group that was responsible for the kidnapping of his daughter Patty. Abrasive and unstable as she was, Moore managed at one point to interject herself into the bargaining process for Patty's release. It was in this way that she first established contact with the FBI, who subsequently came to believe that she might be of some usefulness to the Bureau as an informant.

Moore was hired by the FBI in the spring of 1974, assigned a code name and a control officer. Her assignment was to furnish information concerning radical groups in the Bay Area. Before she could be of much use to the Bureau, however, she was converted to Marxism, confessed her role as a government spy, and was thereafter ostracized by both her former radical companions and the FBI. Still unable to forsake the atmosphere of conspiracy and danger (she had come to believe that she was marked for assassination by the FBI and the radicals), she sold her services to the San Francisco P.D. and later to the U.S. Treasury Department's Bureau of Alcohol, Tobacco, and Firearms. And a few months thereafter, she attempted to shoot the President of the United States.

A sordid tale, but not particularly uncommon to the ancient profession of informing. It has been estimated that there are between twenty and forty thousand paid informers presently employed by law enforcement agencies in the United States. Such informants perform a vital role in police operations, and whatever the ethics of such employment, the realities are such as to insure their use for many years to come.

It is desirable for the investigator to be aware of the specific motivation of each individual informant whenever possible. Such knowledge might be quite useful in determining how the investigator will relate to the informant. Sara Jane Moore has partially explained her motivation in desiring to work as an informer. She had come to see her own life as unimportant, stagnant, and hopelessly unproductive. There was purpose and vitality in the radical movement. She felt that by aiding in their cause, she could find a purpose for her own life and contribute something useful to society. When she was welcomed with something less than enthusiasm by those in the movement, however, her need to be "involved" led her into still another underground ambiente—that of the government informer.

In her own words, Moore has written the following: "I had a raging curiosity and a kind of burning hunger to learn some more about things that were simply hinted at by members of the Movement. I frankly thought that participation with the Bureau might help me. I could use them to do some of the things that I wanted to do. Of course, they were using me to do some of the things they wanted to do."

Moore considered herself a religious woman, a devout Episcopalian. Her FBI contact officer was considered by her to be a devout Roman Catholic. Moore apparently believed that the religious nature of her "commitment" was the deciding factor in the Bureau's having relied upon her as a trustworthy potential informer.

Whatever the specifics of the Moore case, however, it is not at all necessary that an investigator should like or admire his informants. It is possible that such might be the case occasionally, but such a relationship is certainly the exception to the rule. Reliability, not affection, is the key factor in the investigator-informant relationship. The investigator must insure that he knows his informant well enough to predict within a reasonable certainty how trustworthy any forthcoming information is likely to be.

In this latter connection, the general rule must at all times be a healthy suspicion of any and all information received, whether from a voluntary or involuntary source. No matter how reliable an informant has been in the past, every new piece of information should be received and acted upon with caution. The investigator-informant relationship is an unnatural alliance resting on shifting sand. It should never be taken for granted.

The Involuntary Informant

Not every informant will supply information willingly. He may be a party to the crime and would not wish to implicate himself. He may be a professional criminal not involved in the particular crime under investigation but nevertheless would be unwilling to assist police authorities in any manner whatsoever. He may be a law-abiding citizen with a deep fear of involvement, or he may have been warned or threatened against divulging information in his possession. In other words, the motivation of an unwilling informant may be every bit as varied and complex as that of a voluntary informant. It is the investigator's task to obtain the desired information in spite of the individual's reluctance to cooperate.

How can this be accomplished? It is accomplished by a variety of methods actually, legal and illegal, ethical and unethical. Great care, however, should be exercised by the investigator to insure that only legal and ethical methods are employed. One might certainly attempt to persuade an individual to furnish information by appealing to his sense of justice, patriotism, citizenship, and so forth without raising questions of illegality or unethical behavior. One might enlist the aid of a reluctant individual's family or friends or employer in some instances. But when such pressure begins to constitute harassment, the investigator must make the difficult decision to suspend his efforts.

The judgment of what constitutes unjustifiable harassment is anything but clearly defined. Dropping criminal charges, interceding with a judge who is in the process of passing sentence, tapping telephone lines, bugging business offices, making open and close surveillance of a target's daily activities—all of these techniques and more raise serious questions concerning the violation of the civil liberties of all citizens. A good rule of thumb for a police investigator might very well be stated: *When in doubt, don't.*

Verification of Information

All informant information is suspect. Obviously any information obtained from a reluctant party, irrespective of the motivation for such reluctance, must be carefully analyzed and tested for reliability. What are some of the methods by which an investigator may test informant information?

One of the best techniques is to check the information against other information obtained from other informants. It is not unusual for more than one informant to be furnishing information concerning the same case. If informant A says that the subject of the investigation was seen gambling in a certain establishment the past Saturday night, the investigator might query a hat check girl at the establishment, a girl who has furnished bits and pieces of reliable information in the past. If informant B confirms the information, the investigator may proceed accordingly. In many instances, the investigator verifies

such information personally. If an informant says that lottery
chances are being illegally sold at a particular newsstand, the
investigator may bring the location under personal surveillance
and determine for himself if the information is accurate. Or an
investigator may on occasion devise a test assignment to determine the informant's general reliability.

Of course not all information received from informants
is subject to verification. Such unverified information, however, should always be so noted in the investigator's reports.
Unconfirmed information is often just as helpful as verified information. It may serve as the basis of important new leads, it
may influence the investigator to consider an alternative theory
of the case, and it may subsequently interact with new information developed from the same or another source. It may
even be important to the investigation of another case.

Running the Confidential Informant

Cultivating, acquiring, and managing a network of confidential
informants, then, is an indispensable phase of police work. The
specialist in criminal investigations might just as well fish without bait as attempt to function without the vigorous use of
informants.

And where will he find these eager, shy, greedy, self-
effacing, craven, patriotic bearers of good tidings? He will find
them everywhere: in bars, bistros, and banks; cabarets and
churches; schools, stables, and stores. They will come from all
walks of life: preachers and prostitutes; waiters and waitresses;
laborers and managers; husbands and wives.

The investigator must learn to exploit the unwilling informant and the unknowing informant, and he must above all
become adept at establishing a *modus vivendi* with the voluntary informant who has information to furnish, or the potential to do so, over a continuing period of time.

As previously stated, friendship is neither required nor
necessarily desired. The relationship in each situation must be
developed according to its own peculiar characteristics. Such

relationships are always fraught with danger and must be constantly assessed and re-evaluated for productivity or the likelihood of productivity. Relationships with prostitutes, narcotics junkies, members of organized criminal cartels, and the like are obviously incendiary in nature, and the investigator should use extra caution in handling such informants.

One guiding rule always to be kept in mind is that it is the investigator's task to obtain information, not to divulge it. An informant should be given only such information as is absolutely necessary in order for him to render the desired service to his contact officer.

It should be unnecessary to stress the fact that at no time should an investigator become involved in criminal activity himself. Unfortunately, experience has indicated that all too often an investigator has crossed over the line for reasons of obsession with his duties, a corrupt desire for personal gain, ignorance, poor judgment, and as many other motives as can be ascribed to the actions of the informers with whom he deals. A police officer's life is fraught with both the temptation and the opportunity to participate in criminal activities. There are ample reasons why it is desirable for such individuals to involve police officers in their actions. The law officer must at all times remain in control of such relationships.

Narcotics cases are especially delicate, and the investigator must conduct himself with scrupulous concern for his own behavior. In a 1973 decision of the U.S. Supreme Court (*U.S.* v. *Russell*, 411 U.S. 423), it was held that participation in an illegal act by an undercover agent did not constitute entrapment as a matter of law. The majority opinion held that a line should be drawn between a trap set for the unwary innocent and a trap for the unwary criminal. There are circumstances, the court said, when the use of deceit is the only practicable law enforcement technique available, and that it is only when the government's deception actually implants the criminal design in the mind of the defendant that the defense of entrapment is justified.

The investigator should note that four judges dissented with the above decision. The line between right and wrong in such cases is so fine that it behooves the investigator to proceed at all times as though he were walking a legal tightrope.

However, police involvement is not always so problematical. In one case, an FBI agent was accused of exploding more than a dozen bombs at homes, businesses, and in parked automobiles in an effort to cause internal confusion and warfare within certain reputed Mafia families. The agent was alleged to have employed informants to assist him in the bombings, leading them to believe they were acting in an official capacity. The agent's defense to the charges was based on the premise that the allegations were inspired by a desire to frame him and to discredit the FBI. Charges were subsequently dropped, but the agent was dismissed from the Bureau.

Precisely because of such cases, irrespective of the merits of the allegations against the particular police officers involved, sound policy dictates the tight supervision and control of the use of confidential informants, a scrupulous accounting of the funds available for the payment for information, and the absolute refusal to allow a police officer to engage in illegal or unethical behavior in an effort to obtain information for intelligence purposes or to use as evidence in court.

Administration and Anonymity

In spite of the personal relationship that exists between the investigator and the confidential informant, the informant in the final analysis is an employee of the police agency involved and does not belong solely to the investigator who manages him. The test of the informant's value is measured by his usefulness to the agency and not merely to the individual investigator.

Though many experienced investigators guard the sources of their information with such discretion that even the department does not know the identity of their most important informers, this is not the wisest policy to be pursued. Departmental procedure concerning the use of informants should be clear and detailed and scrupulously enforced.

Such procedures must ensure the anonymity of the informant; it is literally a matter of life and death in many instances. An FBI informer once known as Gary Rowe, Jr. appeared before a U.S. Senate committee in 1975 wearing a cloth mask to preserve a new identity adopted for self-protection, and then gave testimony that he had infiltrated the Ku Klux Klan for the FBI in the early 1960s. (Fig. 8.3.) The secrecy of a confidential informant may best be preserved by the use of code names, numbers, symbols, and the employment of such devices in all investigative reports in which the informant is referred to. Although the identity of an informant should only be made known on a need-to-know basis, each investigator must be supervised by a superior officer who is aware of the identity of each informant on the investigator's roster. Then, if the investigator should die or be otherwise incapacitated to act, the informant could be "assigned" to another officer for cultivating and handling. Otherwise a considerable fund of information might be lost to the agency.

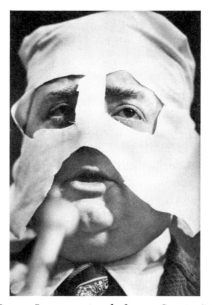

FIG. 8.3 Gary Rowe, Jr. appearing before a Senate Intelligence Committee on FBI Activities (Roddey Mims, *Time Magazine* © Time, Inc.)

Anonymity is also necessary in order for an investigator to successfully operate the informers that he has and to cultivate new recruits. All contacts with the informant, either written, oral, or in person should be covert in nature. Appropriate meeting places must be arranged, code names always used in telephonic communications, and the investigator's own identity and agency protected at all times. Paranoid for obvious reasons, most informants will accept nothing less than complete security precautions. Nothing dries up an investigator's sources of information like the loss of a few of his informants by way of violent reprisals. Word that an informant has been exposed and wasted spreads among the informant ranks like boll weevils in a field of cotton.

Disclosure

Of course there are instances when the disclosure of the identity of an informant is necessary in order to insure that a person charged with a crime receives a fair trial. If the testimony of the informant is essential to the vindication of the accused, then the court will compel disclosure of the informant's identity and require his testimony. The government then has no alternative but to produce the witness or dismiss the charges. It does, in fact, often dismiss the charges rather than divulge the identity of a particularly effective informant, which would destroy his future usefulness as well as endanger his life. In any case, the decision at this point has been effectively taken out of the investigator's hands.

Termination of Services

It often becomes necessary for a variety of reasons to terminate the services of an informant. Regardless of the reason, such termination should always be effected with as little rancor or animosity, personal and official, as is possible under the circumstances.

At no time should the informant's services be characterized with ridicule or scorn, no matter how trivial the information that has been forthcoming. Even if no information has been produced, the investigator should always bear in mind the possibility of productive service in the future. Information is too hard to come by to alienate any potential source.

Many informants, like many other people, are unreliable, incompetent, evil-minded, and self-centered. The investigator must fathom the strengths and weaknesses of his individual informants and learn to cut his losses whenever the liabilities outweigh the assets of the relationship. Although his eye is always on the future, he should not, however, burn his bridges behind him.

1. *Why is the advance in technical data storage capabilities a mixed blessing in regard to the modern criminal investigator and the quality of the society in which he functions?*

2. *How important is the informant system to the specialty of criminal investigation?*

3. *In what manner did the informant system serve to expose the Watergate derelictions?*

4. *What are some of the methods of verifying information obtained from informants?*

5. *Under what circumstances may an informant's identity be forcibly disclosed in a court of law?*

9

• Specialized Investigations

It should be obvious that many cases do not lend themselves to solution simply by the use of techniques such as checking routine sources of information (police records, telephone books, credit files, etc.), locating and interviewing witnesses, and the like. Nor is the information from confidential informants always forthcoming or adequate. Extraordinary measures are then required. Surveillance and undercover operations must be resorted to.

Such techniques are perhaps most frequently used in cases involving narcotics traffic, vice, organized crime, and radical militant group activities. Many knowledgeable communist-watchers of the fifties and sixties have estimated that two-thirds of the membership of the Communist Party USA were undercover agents of the FBI or paid Bureau confidential informants. Apocryphal or not, a member of the U.S. Senate Select Committee on Intelligence stated publicly in September of 1975 that in the year 1965, one in every five members of the Ku Klux Klan was a paid FBI agent.

There can be no question that such techniques are both effective and fraught with danger. In a democratic society, the uses of such measures cannot be taken lightly.

SURVEILLANCE

Surveillance is the observation of a person or place, usually by covert means. Generally, its purpose is to obtain information concerning the identity, whereabouts, and activities (past, present, and future) of a person or group, with a view toward the collection of intelligence, the construction of a criminal case, or the execution of an authorized arrest. The technique may also be used for such purposes as verifying a witness's statement, testing the loyalty of a confidential informant, or protecting a witness from harassment or a victim of a crime from further harm.

Whatever the reason for its use, this method of criminal investigation strikes directly at the heart of the meaning of democratic citizenship: the right of the individual to privacy in thought, deed, and conversation.

A telling fact of our times is that modern technological advancements have now made it feasible to completely destroy the privacy of not only designated individuals but of masses of people. Indeed, the predictions in Orwell's *1984* have descended upon us with a vengeance. Technology has made the possibility of audio-visual surveillance of every dark shadow of our society a reality. Individuality, as a result, is on the verge of extinction. Only a positive social commitment to privacy for all citizens as a good to be desired more than the control of crime will ensure the survival of privacy in the near future.

What are some of the surveillance techniques available to the trained law enforcement officer?

Types of Surveillance

Generally speaking, there are two types of surveillance: stationary and moving. The first is commonly known as a *plant* or *stakeout*, the second as a *tail* or *shadow*.

The character of the surveillance itself may also vary from one of close observation to loose observation, rough observation, or a progressive combination of the three.

Stationary Surveillance

An example of a stationary surveillance would be one in which a suspected gambling den is watched for activity around the clock by an alternating team of investigators using, say, a rented room in a hotel across the street from the suspect building. Binoculars, photographic equipment, and other such investigative aids may or may not be used.

A stakeout may also be conducted from an outside location, depending upon the particular needs of the case. Obviously the surveillant must blend in with his surroundings and in no way attract attention to himself or to his equipment. An unmarked sedan with a rear radio antenna and a two-way radio under the dashboard might just as well include the name of the police agency emblazoned on each door. The dress and behavior pattern of the surveillant(s) is just as important.

People are curious by nature. Entire neighborhoods as well as the subjects of investigation must be deceived by the techniques employed if a high rate of success is to be attained by the stakeout tactic. Members of a stakeout team must be inconspicuous in their appearance and activities. In this regard, the final place surveillance in the Patty Hearst–Harris–SLA manhunt has been described as something less than classic in certain of its details.

After having traced the fugitives to an apartment house in San Francisco, a stakeout was ordered by the FBI agent in charge of the investigation. For two days the apartment house was kept under close twenty-four-hour-a-day surveillance by teams of agents. (Fig. 9.1.) Using a camper van with Utah license plates, agents photographed everyone who went in or out of the apartment house. When agents were finally convinced that one of the couples using the apartment house was the SLA fugitives Bill and Emily Harris, they decided to make an arrest, hoping also that Patty Hearst would be discovered in the apartment. A team of some twenty-five agents and San Francisco policemen took up positions in the neighborhood.

In one late-modeled sedan parked on the street in front of the apartment house, four officers wearing sandals, beards, and beads waited for the fugitives to emerge. Three more members of the surveillance team waited down the block in a yellow-and-white camper. Such attempts to blend in with the inhabitants of the area apparently were not wholly successful. Many neigh-

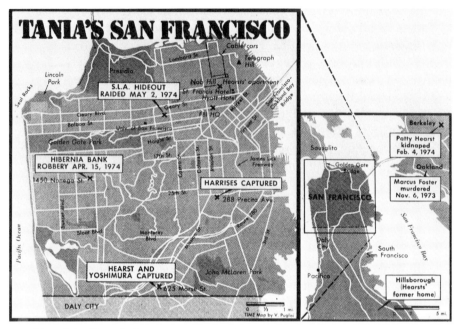

FIG. 9.1 Tania's San Francisco   (*Time Magazine*)

bors spotted the stakeout and watched with considerable curiosity as to exactly whom the police were after. Fortunately, Bill and Emily Harris were not so observant. The fugitive couple, returning from a jog in nearby Bernal Park, was arrested in front of the apartment house by the swarming, heavily armed agents. (Patty Hearst was not in the apartment house but was arrested later the same afternoon in another apartment a short distance away.)

Moving Surveillance

A moving surveillance would be one in which a subject is followed and his actions observed over a given period of time and distance. Such a surveillance might involve one or more investigators, might be entirely pedestrian, or might utilize official vehicles or public transport.

Generally speaking, a moving surveillance is best performed by a team approach rather than by one man or woman. The risk of discovery is obviously greater in the use of one surveillant, as is accidental and purposeful loss of contact.

Any number of tailing variations may be used, depending upon the number of surveillants employed in the operation. More often than not, a three-man team is used in most foot surveillances. Two men shadow the subject from behind, while a third man maintains visual contact from across the street. Through a set of prearranged signals, usually flashed from the operator across the street, the positions of the team members may be changed as a precaution against detection.

For example, the one closest to the subject can move on past and cross the street in a seemingly different direction. The next closest man then moves up and establishes the primary contact with the subject, and the third member of the team crosses the street and assumes the backup role in the extreme rear.

In fact, the agents should normally switch positions often, regardless of whether or not they suspect the subject of having become suspicious. Such alternations should generally occur at intersections and when the subject turns a corner or enters a building. Whether it is advisable to follow a subject into a building or not depends upon the kind of building involved and the peculiar circumstances of the case. There is no controlling rule of thumb. Certainly all exits must be covered and the subject must be kept in sight by at least one agent at all times.

A common problem in all such cases is the availability of private and public transport to the subject. If the subject has his own vehicle parked in the vicinity and is likely to use it, this fact should have been previously known by the surveillance team and necessary precautions taken. If public transport is used, the agents must be prepared by experience and training to handle the situation. It is both embarrassing and harmful to one's career and professional reputation to lose a subject who has suddenly hopped a city bus and left one standing on the corner hyperventilating for want of a bus token.

A moving surveillance need not be solely on foot, of course.

Tailing by automobile is even more difficult with the use of only one car, and night surveillances are especially hazardous. The team approach is generally much more effective. As in the technique of foot surveillance, the number of vehicles to be used in an operation is controlled by the peculiar features of the case, the manpower and material available, and the end results desired.

The three-car technique can be used much like the three-man technique previously discussed, depending upon the conditions of the road. Or a parallel auto surveillance might be employed, especially where traffic conditions are particularly heavy. A surveillance car parallels the subject car according to traffic lanes or city blocks. The surveillance autos should occasionally alternate positions to minimize detection.

It should be clear that the variety of vehicles used in auto surveillances should be as imaginative as the unit budget will allow. Standardization is out of the question where outstanding results are desired. An unmarked stereotypical radio equipped sedan of the Impala-Belair type, for example, is less than inspirational for a surveillance operation in the middle of a Kansas wheat field.

Loose Surveillance

A loose surveillance is one in which it is sought to obtain information concerning the subject's general activities and associates without taking the chance of having him discover he is under surveillance. If it becomes likely that discovery is imminent, it is generally best to break off the surveillance rather than take the risk, even if it means completely losing contact with the subject for the time being.

In such a situation, if enough general information has already been obtained by the surveillance team concerning the subject's habits and activities, he may very well be dropped at one point by an agent who is in danger of being "made" or discovered, and picked up again shortly thereafter by another agent acting upon an informed hunch as to where the subject would go next. This technique is especially effective in gambling investigations in which the bag man under surveillance is thoughtless enough, or secure enough, to resort to a more-or-less regular routine in his collection route.

Close Surveillance

A close surveillance is one in which the subject must be kept under close observation at all times regardless of the risk of discovery that may be involved. Suppose previously obtained information indicated the likelihood that the subject would soon commit a criminal act. Depending upon the nature of the act and the potential injury to other parties, the surveillance should obviously be so close that no opportunity is provided the subject to act unobserved.

Rough Surveillance

Rough surveillance is the technique of shadowing a suspect who knows he is being observed, and secrecy, therefore, is not a factor. This technique is often used in protecting material witnesses in a pending criminal case. It is also a common technique in the surveillance of known members of organized crime or foreign intelligence.

The author once participated in a high-speed multivehicle surveillance of a party of Soviet agents who knew they were being kept under strict observation. Their driver led us a not-so-merry chase across the western Bad Lands that would have caused Evil Kneival to withdraw from the race. The primary tactic-of-the-road was to see how close he could bring us to collision with an uninvolved vehicle. For almost an hour we endured more close calls than Charlie Coyote might expect to face upon the heels of the Road Runner. Finally we were saved from further terrorist tactics by the intervention of a dedicated State Trooper who was unaware of the federal road surveillance. He stopped us, he said, rather than the maniac in the lead vehicle because he realized the other car would be across the state line before he could catch it. He didn't know what to make of us when we thanked him profusely for the ticket.

Nevertheless, such rough surveillances are often necessary and much more productive than the one described. And while it is not illegal *per se* simply to observe a person's activities (so long as the laws against trespass are respected), any undue harassment of the subject may engender unfavorable publicity for law enforcement in the event the subject seeks legal redress by way of court injunction.

Surveillance by Combination of Techniques

Still another form of surveillance may be a combination of any or all of the above techniques. Certainly at one time or another in the search for Patty Hearst and other fugitive members of the SLA, all of the above techniques of surveillance of persons and places were utilized.

Counter-measures

Not all subjects of a police surveillance are unaware of their importance to law enforcement agencies. For one reason or another, they know they are potential subjects of surveillance operations and are ever on their guard. Many of their tactics, such as the high-speed shenanigans in the road surveillance described above, are more devious and ingenious than those employed by the official bloodhounds on their tails. The criminal investigator, then, must constantly be on the lookout for such tactics.

Primarily he must guard against being "made," or recognized, and must do everything he can to reduce the risk of being given the slip. Of course, he must not allow himself to become paranoid to the point that every time the subject looks at him, he believes he has been "made." If he is doing his work properly, the chances are that he has not, in fact, been discovered. There is nothing more heartwarming than for an agent to stand by undetected and watch as a particularly sadistic subject barges up to a startled citizen whom he has erroneously "made" and thumbs his nose in the innocent man's face.

It is all but trite to relate the much-used tactic of suspicious or obsessively cautious subjects who test whether or not they are being followed by jumping on and off buses, streetcars, or subway trains, or by using revolving doors and elevators in hotels and department stores in an effort to determine pursuit. It is not a bad practice with such a skittish character to allow him to "make" one member of the team and proceed to give him the slip, with contact being maintained all the while by other undetected members of the team.

Of course, subjects may often travel in units of two or more just like the team of surveillants. The investigator must always consider that the subject may have himself guarded or watched. If a tail is detected, the subject will then be alerted by a set of preconceived signals, operating along much the same lines as the surveillance team itself.

Especially in the case of investigations involving members of organized crime or foreign espionage networks, the investigator is liable to be confronted by such countermeasures and must be prepared to take evasive action. It is not uncommon that subjects of this ilk are possessed of considerable intelligence information relative to the law enforcement personnel in their immediate sphere of operation.

For example, Mafia types may very well know the faces, names, employers, automobiles, and license plate numbers (personal and official), home addresses, and telephone numbers of the various state, federal, and local police agents assigned to such duties. And foreign espionage agents often possess complete dossiers on their U.S. counterparts. The greatest mistake a law enforcement officer can make is to underrate the "enemy," so to speak.

Surveillance Preparation

A surveillance of any type is not a haphazard operation. It should be carefully planned in advance. The reason for the surveillance, the type of case to which it pertains, and the information already available should be thoroughly analyzed and digested. Alternative methods of obtaining the desired information should be explored and evaluated. Once the need for a surveillance is established and the type of surveillance to be employed is determined, it then becomes necessary to choose the personnel and select the equipment to be used.

The best officers available to perform the task should be chosen. Irrespective of questions of professional ability, certain requirements, advantages and disadvantages must be given priority consideration. For example, it would be an action in futility to assign an officer with the physical build of Karim Abdul Jabbar to a tailing operation in which it is imperative that the subject not realize that he is under observation. Seven-footers simply are not good surveillance material, unless the milieu of the operation is a National Basketball Association locker room.

Likewise, the choice of a male team of investigators assigned to maintain sight contact with a female subject is doomed to frustration and possible disaster outside the door of a room marked *Ladies*.

Therefore, it can readily be seen that certain basic considerations are indicated in any surveillance operation and that beyond these generalizations, each particular case must then be developed according to its own peculiar features. A strong dose of common sense is always the controlling factor.

Officers of average size, build, and general appearance are the most useful candidates for surveillance operations. Excessive beauty or handsomeness, as well as an uncommon degree of ugliness is every bit as disqualifying a characteristic as abnormal size. Possession of any physical characteristic that is likely to attract more than passing interest is cause for rejection of the officer for surveillance duty. Certainly personal traits indicating nervousness or self-consciousness cannot be exhibited, and an agent who is easily flustered by a sudden turn of events is of little use.

In the early days of the development of eastern block spy operations, an agent of an unfriendly foreign government was dispatched to New York City under orders to perform a variety of clandestine dirty deeds. In fact, the hapless agent's most pressing need was to develop a system of mundane stratagems that would get him safely from one day to the next. He spoke only rudimentary English, had no familiarity with the city, no understanding of such western conveniences as automats, laundromats, turnstiles, and taxi drivers. In short, he was at a total loss.

The FBI agent assigned to pick him up under surveillance when he disembarked at a Hoboken pier (the Bureau had broken the foreign government's secret code and was quite aware of the agent's assignment) also had his problems. He was more than a little taken aback when the burly spy turned and asked in fractured English if he could recommend a good hotel. Then the spy wanted to know how to get there, how much it would cost, where he could eat a cheap meal, and whether or not his luggage would be safe from robbers if he left it in his room while he searched for a place to wash his socks and dirty underwear.

Needless to say, the FBI man's partner was perplexed as he watched from across the street while the spy and the FBI agent hailed a taxi and sped off together, sitting in the back seat, hunched intently over a map of New York City.

Many surveillances, therefore, are a test of an investigator's wit and resourcefulness under pressure, as well as his vision, audio capacity, and physical stamina.

Another generalization that applies to any surveillance undertaking is the proscription against conspicuous wearing apparel. Obviously a business suit, tie, and a snap-brimmed hat in a nudist colony is calculated to attract undue attention.

In one case known to the author, an FBI agent was assigned to spend an entire day on the tail of a known member of organized crime. The subject was a health enthusiast and spent most every Saturday afternoon jogging in the city park. There was reason to believe that the subject was also conducting business while improving the state of his health, by passing bribe money to certain local public officials who contrived to cross his path at various predetermined locations. On the appointed day the agent was lurking outside the subject's apartment, wearing tennis shoes and a newly purchased sweatsuit, ready and eager to give chase. The subject emerged some moments later dressed impeccably in a tuxedo and top hat and proceeded by taxi to a midtown church wedding and champagne reception. The agent was left behind skipping rope and wondering if the subject was a friend of the bride or the groom.

A number of preliminary preparations must be accomplished prior to undertaking a surveillance, fixed or moving. Certainly the surveillant, or surveillants, must be thoroughly familiar with the appearance of the subject. Descriptions, photographs, and previous visual contact (or any combination thereof) are methods by which such familiarity may be attained.

The surveillant should also be as thoroughly conversant with the subject's habits and mode of conduct as is possible under the circumstances. What kind of family life does the subject have; what is his business or ostensible occupation; what are his hobbies and avocations; is he a high-liver or a miser; does he engage in extracurricular sexual activities—heterosexual or homosexual; are his activities generally predictable? These are merely a few questions that an investigator should seek to answer about the nature and activities of his subject prior to initiating the operation.

Equipment

Surveillance operations often break down after the operation has begun due to the impossibility of performing the job at hand. Quite often the failure lies in the lack of prior preparation. A surveillant with the tracking expertise of a Cherokee warrior-chief in his bloodline could not tail a subject through snow country if he were not properly equipped. Although every eventuality cannot be foreseen and planned for in advance, proper coordination and preparation may well reduce the likelihood of surprise and ineffectual response.

For example, a planned stationary plant should take into consideration the possibility that the subject might abandon the site under surveillance and move by automobile to another location. Even had the undercover team prudently kept a vehicle concealed nearby, it would have been to no avail if the subject made his move immediately after one of the team members had driven off in search of sandwiches and coffee.

There is no standard equipment necessary for all surveillances, of course. Each case must be equipped according to the factors peculiar to that case. The point to remember is that the equipment must be planned for in advance. Such plans may include items ranging anywhere from audiovisual materials to motor vehicles of every variety, fixed wing and rotary aircraft, seagoing vessels, and special clothing or camouflage materials.

Electronic Surveillance and Wiretapping

Ethical and legal considerations aside for the moment, technological advances in the field of electronic surveillance and wiretapping have afforded the criminal investigator an array of investigative techniques that would have given the legendary Dick Tracy cause for admiration.

Wiretapping, simply put, is the unauthorized interception of a telephone conversation. Traditionally, the telephone line is tapped and recorded by the police monitor. Such taps are most commonly made through connections in the telephone exchange, obviously the most secure method in which to go about such a potentially tricky business. Occasionally, however, the nature of the case will dictate an intercept somewhere between the exchange and the target phone. A variety of methods may be used. Small transmitters may be inserted in the telephone itself or may be attached to outside telephone wires for reception in a nearby listening post. A telephone mouthpiece may even be activated so that all conversation in a room may be picked up, even when the telephone is cradled.

Installation of such devices may at times require delicate penetration operations. An agent may have to enter a target room in person or perhaps drill his way through floors, walls, and ceilings. Such operations are not, however, routinely performed by ordinary undercover officers but rather by experienced, highly trained specialists. Even such specialists have been known to miscalculate.

The author was once involved in a bugging operation, the target of which was a suspected mafioso restaurant and lounge. An FBI technician was called in from another city to perform the wire job. The deserted building was entered surreptitiously in the early morning hours before any employees were on the scene. Entry was made on the second floor, above the target office, and while the author kept watch, the technician went to work.

Using one of his favorite drills with a newly issued diamond bit, the experienced, highly trained agent proceeded to drill a gaping hole all the way through the ceiling into the room below. Of course, it was absolutely necessary to enter the lower premises and perform a hasty patch-and-plaster job. Working frantically against the clock, the expert made Michelangelo seem like a laggard indeed, as he spread the quick-drying plaster and odorless paint across the ceiling and got us out of the building with about three minutes to spare before the first employees of the restaurant began to appear for the day's labor.

Today, however, by way of modern advances in technology, the same result (or better results) may be accomplished without the necessity of physical penetration in order to plant a bug or, indeed, even without the necessity of touching any of the telephone wires involved in order to effect a tap. For example, infrared beams may be bounced off window panes of target rooms, thereby capturing conversations in that room and recording them on a receiver in a nearby listening post. Cradled telephones may now be activated by electro magnetic or inductive wiretapping techniques that shoot a current down the line to the target phone without the necessity of any physical installation in the phone itself.

No definitive ruling of the U.S. Supreme Court has as yet settled the legal status of such procedures. Indeed, the entire body of wiretapping and electronic surveillance is as yet a muddy bog of swirling legal inconsistencies.

As early as 1934, Congress passed the Federal Communications Act in which Section 605 made it unlawful for *anyone* to intercept and divulge *any* communication without authority of the sender of the communication. Nevertheless, both state and federal agencies have conducted wiretaps ever since, and the courts, with persisting inconsistencies, have permitted the practice to survive.

There have been, however, numerous attempts by the courts to restrict such procedures and to clarify the existing laws—without notable success in either aim. Generally, wiretapping and electronic surveillance is illegal unless conducted by an authorized law enforcement agency with prior judicial consent. As a result of such rulings, police must now operate under much the same procedures as those relating to obtaining search warrants and warrants of arrest—minus the all-important requirement of showing probable cause.

Congress has further shown its desire to curb the potential for investigative excesses in this sensitive area by passage of the Omnibus Crime Control and Safe Streets Act of 1968. This act clearly indicates Congress' intention to vest the approval authority in a select few and clearly identifiable officials within state and federal enforcement agencies. Accordingly, only the U.S. attorney general or his designated assistant may apply to a federal judge of competent jurisdiction for an order authorizing the use of a wiretap or electronic surveillance device, and only for certain enumerated criminal offenses. (Sec. 18 U.S.C. Ch. 119 Sec. 2516 [1].) State authorization for such devices is also circumscribed by the act. (Sec. 18 U.S.C. Ch. 119 Sec. 2516 [2].) It is important to note that the act leaves untouched whatever constitutional power the President may have with or without a warrant, to eavesdrop electronically in national security cases.

The practice of "eavesdropping," then, whether by wiretapping or by electronically "bugging" an individual or a place, is as much a "dirty business" today as it was in 1928, when Supreme Court Justice Taft first coined the phrase in the case of *Olmstead* v. *United States*, 277 U.S. 438. Yet the practice continues. The high court has not as yet addressed itself to the fundamental issue raised by the Federal Communications Act of 1934. Is eavesdropping without the authority of the sender illegal *per se?*

It is an ethical as well as a legal question that every American citizen ought to consider carefully. Technology has the capability of eliminating individual privacy within a few short years; certainly much sooner than law enforcement can eliminate crime within our society. If we, therefore, justify massive electronic surveillance by our fear of rising crime, we may well deliver the lives of unborn generations into the vise of technological enslavement. Our children may live in a world of radio and laser beams, parabolic scopes, and government-induced mind control.

And for what rich benefits in present-day investigative shortcuts have we bartered away our children's freedom? The prevention of crime? The arrest and conviction of criminals?

Hardly. The fact is that electronic surveillance has been spectacularly unproductive over the years in the United States. It is slow, costly, and ineffective. It is seldom used in the investigation of crimes in any of the major categories. Very few murders are solved by the expediency of a wiretap. The bugging of motel rooms may uncover occasional marital infidelity but rarely, if ever, leads to the apprehension of a bad check artist.

It is in the field of vice and organized crime investigations that such techniques are most commonly used. The FBI engaged in the practice extensively in the late fifties and early sixties. Few, if any, convictions resulted from such electronic surveillances. More information and more convictions resulted from the use of informants and other proven methods of professional police work than from all of the supersensitive bugs used during those years.

The hard truth is that untold man-hours have been needlessly used and paid for so that investigators can monitor the bedroom activities of a variety of subjects throughout the nation while serious crime runs rampant in the streets. The shocking disclosures concerning the FBI's extensive illegal electronic surveillance in the 1960s of the late Martin Luther King, Jr. is a case well in point.

If electronic surveillance has any role to play in a democratic society—and the answer is not yet settled in America, ethically or legally—surely it must be regulated by strict court supervision, administered by adherence to the constitutional standards of probable cause such as those that apply to warrants of search and arrest.

Recording the Surveillance

A written record of surveillance operations should be maintained. The log should be maintained in chronological form. It should be clear and concise and not overburdened with the use of obscure symbols and abbreviations. It should record in detail the activities of the subject and the surveillants.

Among other things, the surveillance log may prove invaluable to officers relieving on-duty surveillants, as a foundation for further investigations in companion cases, and as evidence in a court of law. It may also be used as an objective evaluation of the surveillance operation itself and as a training aid for police investigators.

UNDERCOVER INVESTIGATIONS

Undercover activity is simply another form of surveillance. It is surveillance from the "inside," so to speak. Much of the same preparation required of a normal surveillance operation is also required prior to mounting an undercover investigation. An investigator must be so well prepared for his projected "role" that he is capable of gaining the confidence of a criminal suspect or of infiltrating a group suspected of engaging in criminal activities.

Often an undercover operation is the only means by which the desired information may be obtained. And the value of such information is considerably enhanced by the fact that it is eventually presented in court by an agent of the government rather than by an informant with an unsavory background and reputation. In addition, the police officer is better trained in such work than a confidential informant and generally is more aware of the kind of creditable evidence that must be developed either for prosecution or intelligence purposes.

Undercover operations are most commonly used in the investigation of vice crimes, particularly narcotics violations, and in cases involving organized crime associations, domestic militant groups, and national security cases.

As previously stated, it has been estimated that in the late fifties and early sixties, approximately two-thirds of the membership of the National Executive Committee of the Communist Party USA was comprised of FBI undercover operatives. Whether an exaggeration or not, certainly the use of such undercover personnel has been and is a major investigative technique of the FBI that has paid considerable dividends over the years.

An undercover assignment is the most sensitive type of investigative work. It can also be an extremely dangerous undertaking. The careful selection of the undercover agent for a particular assignment, then, is of utmost importance.

There are no general qualifications that fit an individual for undercover work. There are specific qualifications that fit a particular investigator for a designated case. Often the case itself will determine the sort of individual that will be used. A white officer would not, except under very peculiar circumstances, be chosen to infiltrate a black vice ring in a predominantly black ghetto area. In addition to race, matters of age, ethnic background, personality, intelligence, cultural factors, and so on must be considered.

The better the undercover agent fits into a social environment that he is to infiltrate, the more likely are his chances of running a successful operation.

Above all, however, the undercover agent must have the temperament, the self-confidence, and the resourcefulness to withstand the stress and strain of such an assignment. If an officer, otherwise thoroughly qualified, is assigned to an undercover narcotics investigation and becomes so upset and disoriented by the nihilistic milieu in which he finds himself that he is unable to function without the physical and psychological support of a variety of drugs with which he is in daily contact, his usefulness as a police investigator is rather obviously impaired.

Finally, he should be an officer who has demonstrated sound judgment under pressure in his past assignments. Undercover work is an unstructured, uncertain activity at best. The ability to remain calm, to think, and to make sound decisions in the face of sudden changes of circumstances is indispensable. Criminal suspects and their cohorts simply will not play their own roles according to a preconceived script. The undercover officer must be able to improvise. His life and the lives of others may well depend upon it.

In actual practice, unfortunately, many police officers are ill-chosen and underprepared for such assignments. It is not uncommon for police agencies to assign newly graduated recruits from the police academy to undercover jobs. Aside from the obvious fact that they are previously unknown in the vicinity as police officers, there are few other advantages in choosing such personnel. Young trainees generally do not have the professional experience or the proven abilities normally required for such work. In a particular case, such an assignment might be well-justified. As a general practice, however, it is not to be recommended.

Role Preparation

An undercover operation should never be undertaken without a thorough understanding of the purpose of the investigation and of what is expected of the investigator. He should familiarize himself with the information already possessed and with the law applicable to the type of case under investigation.

Certainly the undercover agent must have a thorough knowledge of the subject of the operation, whether it be an individual or a group target.

If an individual is the subject, his entire personal history should be absorbed by the investigator. Such background information would include the subject's full name, as well as any aliases or nicknames used in the past or suspected to have been used; a complete and accurate physical description; addresses, past and present, business and private; occupational specialty; educational level; and emotional and psychological characteristics, including prejudices, habits, and vices commonly indulged in.

The subject's family background should also be carefully

examined and assimilated, as well as the identity and nature of his associations. Failure to determine that a target subject is a borderline psychotic married to a blatant nymphomaniac is tantamount to using two heaping spoonfuls of strychnine in one's after-dinner coffee.

If the subject target is a group or an organizational structure, the personnel, purpose, and operating procedures of the subject must be thoroughly digested prior to initiating the undercover operation. Although the FBI has successfully infiltrated such groups as the CPUSA and the KKK, not every group target is so readily susceptible to penetration. A major factor in the FBI's inability to apprehend Patty Hearst for eighteen agonizing months was the impossibility of infiltrating the SLA. This particular radical group was too small and cohesive to achieve penetration. Thus, the Bureau was cut off from a major source of information.

Likewise, only one FBI informant has been known to have infiltrated the Weather Underground. Certainly such penetrations cannot succeed without a thorough understanding of the aims, principles, and group psychology of the subject target.

In addition, the undercover agent must have a thorough understanding of the topographical location in which he is to operate. A police officer born and raised in a middle-class environment is not necessarily suited for undercover work in a poverty-riddled ghetto. The agent must know how to operate in the assigned neighborhood. Utilizing such everyday services as restaurants, grocery stores, public transportation facilities, and the like can be a bewildering task to one unfamiliar with the system of the location. The undercover agent cannot afford such confusion.

Cover Story

Another important element in the preparation for an undercover assignment is the development of a cover story for the agent. It is nothing short of a complete fictitious background compatible with the role to be played by the agent. It should include an assumed name (and possibly a host of aliases), a familial history, a chronological listing of residences, an educational and employment profile, a criminal record, and so on.

Depending upon the nature of the case, the cover story should be complete to the smallest detail. If the undercover agent is portraying a character with a criminal background, then precautions should be taken to document that background in case it is checked upon by a suspicious target subject. It is not at all unusual for members of foreign espionage rings or organized crime cartels to make such background checks on a would-be new associate.

Though the cover story must be thorough, it must be plausible. It is foolish to claim levels of skill for the agent which are beyond his capacity to demonstrate. An agent who is smuggled into an underground militant group for the purpose of rendering medical assistance to a seriously wounded member is up the proverbial creek without a scalpel if he possesses no medical expertise whatsoever.

The cover should be deep but not so complex as to confuse the agent if he is challenged upon some of the details. Though necessarily comprised of lies, the cover should be based upon realities within the agent's own knowledge. If the script has him growing up in, say, Denver, Colorado, then he must possess a familiarity with Denver and the surrounding territory, including a knowledge of the people, customs, terrain, and climate.

Of course, the undercover agent must be instructed as to how far to carry his pose if confronted. An alternate cover may be prepared in case the subject discovers the agent's deceit. Or the agent may be instructed to terminate the operation. What if the agent is arrested by another police agency that is unaware of his official status? The circumstances of the case, along with previous instructions, are controlling.

The author once served with an undercover team posing as railroad employees, assigned the task of identifying an unknown individual who had been destroying railroad property by setting a series of homemade bombs. The author and two fellow agents were surveilling a suspect neighborhood one night from a detached freight car with the use of infrared binoculars, having used the same vantage point for three nights past. Although we had developed a rather informed estimation of the moral and ethical standards of that particular neighborhood, we had not obtained the slightest evidence concerning any railroad property abuse. About three in the morning, when the last shade had been finally drawn and the last round of musical beds performed, a squad of local police officers and a brace of irate husbands suddenly swooped down on the freight car with guns drawn and demanded that we come out with our hands up or be blasted out. It took a lot of fast talking to convince them that we were federal agents in search of a "mad bomber" and not a trio of perverted peeping Toms. Under the circumstances, however, it was either blow our cover or be blown to kingdom come.

Once an undercover operation begins, the agent must live the role without deviation until the operation is either concluded or terminated. He must at all times dress the part, talk the part, act the part; he may even come to think the part before his assignment is over. He must sever all possible connections with his police employees and family that might in any way cause him to be linked to them by the subject target. Badge, credentials, police weapons, jewelry, sentimental objects relating to his "real" life—all must be left behind.

Such necessities make for a lonely, alienated life indeed.

Official Communications

Communications between the undercover agent and headquarters should be kept to an absolute minimum. All such communications should be accomplished by the use of secret methods and in a manner that will in no way arouse suspicion.

Telephone contacts should generally be made by the use of dial phones in a public telephone booth. Switchboard calls should be avoided if at all possible. Routine should also be avoided. To avoid tapping or countersurveillance, a different phone booth and hour should be used for each communication.

Obviously the investigator should not place a call to the

public number of the police agency involved. Unlisted numbers should be used and these numbers should be memorized, never written down. In addition, the party on the receiving end of the call should be fully aware of the circumstances of the under-cover operation so that the message will be received and properly interpreted.

A code system should be devised in the event that an emergency call must be made under difficult circumstances. The code must be clear and simple in order to avoid all possibility of misunderstanding.

For example, in the Watergate case, Bob Woodward arranged a spur-of-the-moment confirm-or-hang-up telephone code with a confidential source in the Justice Department. If there was any reason why the reporters should hold back on a proposed story that Bob Haldeman had been named before a grand jury as one of the persons in control of a secret trust fund (illegal) to be used for President Nixon's re-election, then the Justice Department lawyer should simply hang up the phone before Woodward counted to ten. If he did not hang up, it would mean the story was valid. Such instructions were much too complicated. The lawyer misunderstood the instructions and remained on the line after the count of ten, intending to warn Woodward *off* the story. Woodward thought the man had approved the story and ran it in the *Washington Post*. It set the investigation of the Watergate conspiracy back a number of weeks when the story was clearly shown to be incorrect.

Notes and written reports should not be used unless absolutely necessary. The circumstances of the case, however, are always controlling. It may be that in a particular operation, the placing of phone calls is extremely risky, or in another case, the information to be relayed is unusually complex. In such cases, written reports may be necessary.

If written reports must be used, it must be done with utmost care. The reports must be written under absolutely secure circumstances and mailed at once. Reports, notes, exposed film and the like should never be kept on the agent's person or in his possession. The danger of discovery is simply too great.

Either a prearranged mail drop should be used, a "dummy"

address, or a designated post office box. Information should never be mailed to police headquarters. Return addresses should likewise be avoided. And the mail pickup should be accomplished with as much attention to security as the writing and posting of the communication.

It must be remembered at all times that either groups or individuals engaged in or contemplating criminal activity are highly paranoid and, therefore, extremely suspicious of any activity that seems even slightly unusual.

As far as actual meetings between an undercover operator and his contact are concerned, they should be avoided if possible and carefully prearranged if absolutely required. The likelihood of surveillance cannot be taken lightly, nor can the possibility of accidental discovery.

If a rendezvous has been arranged and the agent feels that he is being tailed, or even suspects that he is, it is the better course of action to simply abandon the contact rather than attempt to lose the tail, unless it can be accomplished with indisputable naturalness.

Of course, provision must always be made in advance for emergency situations. A system of audiovisual signals may be used. If a contact has been arranged, the signal to disregard may be the wearing of a certain item of clothing, the raising or lowering of the windows on one's auto, the peculiar manner of blowing one's car horn, the ordering of a certain drink or selection of food, and the like.

Such audiovisual signals are to be used when needed, not only by the undercover agent but also by his headquarters' contacts. If, for example, headquarters had developed certain information unknown to the undercover agent that indicates a strong likelihood of his imminent discovery, there should be some means by which a warning may be communicated. Again, code words in telephone contacts, visual signals such as the parking of a red vehicle bearing some identifiable marking in front of the agent's undercover residence, or the receipt of an apparently innocuous but coded piece of junk mail are just a few examples of how such a warning might be flashed.

It goes without saying, however, that not every eventuality can be foreseen. No amount of preplanning will eliminate the necessity of a high degree of judgmental skill on the part of the undercover agent. The decision to pass or punt is still made on Sunday afternoon, not on the practice field or at the Monday morning breakfast table. Careful preparation can help, but it cannot dictate all the decisions to be taken in advance.

Terminating the Operation

If, for whatever reason, it becomes desirable to terminate the operation, whether a success or not, the undercover agent must devise an appropriate withdrawal scheme. By all means, he must not just abruptly disappear.

Ideally, his withdrawal should be preplanned at the time of planning the original operation. He should be furnished with a number of alternative methods. Above all, his withdrawal must be accomplished so as not to incur the suspicion of the subject person or group, and it should be done in such a manner as to allow for a resumption of the operation if it should become desirable, either by the same undercover agent or another.

For example, a college girl working as a narcotics undercover agent, if warned by her control officer that it is time to suspend the operation, might purposely fail a big examination and use such failure as an excuse to withdraw from school. Or a prearranged withdrawal plan might be activated by sending her a letter from "home" announcing the serious illness of her "mother."

The Undercover Agent
and Criminal Conduct

Can an undercover agent initiate, incite, or participate in criminal activity? The issue is clearly and simply stated; the answer is fraught with shadow and confusion. Factors of ethics and law are involved, and there are no clear guidelines by courts or police administrators to assist the police investigator in the performance of his duties.

Does the end ever justify the means? In the case of *Lewis* v. *United States,* 385 U.S. 206, the U.S. Supreme Court stated that there are circumstances when the use of deceit is the only practicable law enforcement technique available, that it is only when the government's deception *implants* the criminal design in the mind of the defendant that the defense of entrapment arises.

The problem seems to be in deciding how much deceit, when employed, and under what circumstances. Can the undercover agent carry deceitfulness to the point of participation in the crime? What rule of law exempts the agent from being charged as party to the crime?

Perhaps it is the type of crime involved that is the controlling factor. An officer may be permitted to participate in a relatively minor crime in order to obtain information concerning a more serious offense. But who is authorized to make such a decision?—the undercover agent, his supervisor, the head of the police agency involved, judicial authority?

In other words, an undercover man might be allowed to participate in the crime of procurring an act of prostitution, but not in the plotting and execution of an act of murder for hire. Let us examine the facts of one of the most recent Supreme Court decisions on the subject and consider its ruling.

In the 1973 case of the *United States* v. *Russell,* 411 U.S. 423, previously mentioned, the defendant had been convicted in the trial court for having unlawfully manufactured and processed methamphetamine ("speed") and of having unlawfully sold and delivered that drug. His only defense to the charge was one of police entrapment. An appellate court had reversed the conviction solely on the grounds that an undercover agent had supplied an essential chemical for manufacturing the drug. The appellate court concluded that as a matter of law, an intolerable degree of governmental participation in the criminal activity charged would constitute a valid defense. The Supreme Court reversed that ruling and reinstated the conviction of the trial court.

There was never any dispute of the fact that the undercover man, an agent of the Federal Bureau of Narcotics and Dangerous Drugs, actually provided the essential ingredient in the manufacture of the drug produced and sold by the defendant. There was also testimony that the chemical supplied by the government agent was generally difficult to obtain. In the trial court, the judge had given the jury the standard entrapment instruction, to wit: "Where a person has the willingness and the readiness to break the law, the mere fact that the government agent provides what appears to be a favorable opportunity is not entrapment."

The judge further instructed the jury, however, to acquit the accused if the jury had "a reasonable doubt whether the defendant had the previous intent or purpose to commit the offense . . . and did so only because he was induced or persuaded by some officer or agent of the government."

From its earliest rulings on entrapment, the high court's rationale has always focused on the predisposition of the accused to commit the crime. A line has always been drawn between setting a trap for the unwary innocent and the unwary criminal. In *Sorrells* v. *United States*, 287 U.S. 435, the Supreme Court held in a 1932 case that the entrapment defense prohibits law enforcement officers from instigating criminal acts by persons "otherwise innocent in order to lure them to its commission and to punish them."

Another line of cases, however, has developed the nonentrapment rationale that a conviction cannot stand where the participation of a government investigator is so enmeshed in the criminal activity that the prosecution of the defendants would be repugnant to the system of criminal justice in a democratic society. Following this rationale, it can be seen that the appellate court in the *Russell* case attempted to broaden the traditional notion of entrapment, which focuses on the predisposition of the defendant to commit the crime charged, to require an acquittal where there has been "an intolerable degree of governmental participation in the criminal enterprise."

The Supreme Court, however, upon review refused to accept the contention that the undercover agent's involvement in the case constituted such an "intolerable participation." The high court adopted the earlier view that acquittal is required only when the government implanted the criminal design in an otherwise innocent mind.

There was a dissenting opinion in the *Russell* case in which four justices concurred.

The Court is obviously still sharply divided as to the proper basis, scope, and focus of the defense of entrapment. Nor have such decisions adequately addressed the issue of criminal liability on the part of an undercover agent who instigates and *participates* to *any* degree in a criminal act.

It would seem, therefore, that the law as it now stands would absolve an undercover policeman from any liability in the death of a purchaser of a drug incorrectly manufactured by a criminally inclined individual who was encouraged to manufacture such drug by the agent, even though the agent provided an essential ingredient of the drug which the manufacturer did not possess and without which the drug could not have been made.

Should an undercover agent, then, ever initiate, incite, or participate in the commission of a criminal act? Ethically, perhaps he should not. Legally, perhaps he may do so and avoid criminal responsibility for his acts.

ORGANIZED CRIME INVESTIGATIONS

In what ways are investigations of organized crime activities different from all other criminal investigations? Are special methods and techniques required to investigate such criminal violations?

Consider for a moment the following recitation of factual situations from varying parts of the nation.

A young deputy sheriff in middle Georgia has been engaged in an intensive investigation of narcotics trafficking in his county and is on the verge of presenting evidence to the local district attorney. He and his wife are found murdered in their rural home, victims of shotgun blasts fired in both instances from point-blank range. Their killers and those who hired them are unknown.

In a large metropolitan city on the northeastern seaboard, a group of businessmen form a corporation, open a corporate bank account with a sizeable deposit, lease a store, and place a number of orders, on credit, for merchandise with a variety of companies. A large porportion of the orders are comprised of such items as jewelry and appliances, and like items that are easily converted into cash. The merchandise is sold and the cash is carefully milked from the company, along with the original bank deposit in the corporate account. The company is forced into bankruptcy by its creditors since, as planned, it has no money with which to pay its debts. A successful scam operation has been concluded, no one is charged with a crime, no one is punished.

In a midwestern city, a homeowner in his early sixties, dressed in bathrobe and slippers, steps onto his front porch to pick up the morning newspaper and a man rises out of the shrubbery beside the porch and fires three shots from a handgun with a silencer attached. It is nearly two hours before a postman discovers the victim lying in the flower bed. The hit man and his motive are unknown, the case is unsolved.

In yet another medium-sized city in the southwest, a series of thundering explosions destroys a multimillion dollar factory in the dead of night, instantly swelling the local unemployment rolls by some 800 out-of-work employees. Some weeks later, the company officials file an insurance claim, asking for $30 million for loss of business and $10 million for the destroyed building itself. There are no direct links between the officers and the fire-bombings.

In a sparsely populated rural area of the far west, an ongoing scheme of importing illegal aliens from across the

Mexican border for purposes of cheap labor is under intensive investigation. In less than a two-year period, a dozen men and women who have been cooperating with the investigation with law enforcement agencies, are systematically murdered. Some are discovered shot and bludgeoned to death, others drowned in a local river, one man is brutally beaten and then hanged in his own garage. The investigation is at a standstill, potential witnesses are not to be found, the murders are unsolved.

What, if anything, do all of these incidents have in common?

Provable or not, all five incidents bear the unmistakable earmarks of organized crime activities, although not necessarily the ethnic stereotype with which we have all become so familiar as a result of such popular fictional motion picture successes of recent times as *The Godfather I* and *II*. American folklore is crowded with legends of criminal societies such as the Black Hand, Murder, Inc., the Purple Gang, the Mafia, and of more recent vintage, La Cosa Nostra.

The legends seem to operate cyclically. The twenties can be designated as the Capone era; the thirties gave us Murder, Inc.; the forties were dominated by Lucky Luciano and Lepke Buchalter; and in the fifties, organized crime really went public, so to speak, with the televised Kefauver hearings and the famous meeting at Appalachian. The sixties gave us Valachi's testimony, and the seventies have been dominated by the Big Books and the Fabulous Films. (Figs. 9.2–9.8.)

Why do such stereotyped exploits of organized crime so capture the interest of the American public? Perhaps the media appeal is rooted in the social phenomena of modern man's loss of identity and need for escape, for community involvement, and for a goal-oriented society. Perhaps the member of organized crime is seen to possess all of these psychic needs of modern man.

FIG. 9.2 Following his 1931 conviction for tax evasion, Al Capone smiles on his way to the Atlanta Federal Penitentiary. (United Press International Photo)

But if this American legend is indeed a stereotyped vision of organized crime, what then, is the reality of this social phenomena that has come to be so much a part of our daily lives, and how is it of any special interest to the criminal investigator?

The Reality of Organized Crime

There are likely as many different definitions of organized crime as there are readers of this text. The same probably holds true for the citizenry of our country. But the problem can never be addressed either from a social studies or criminological viewpoint until a workable definition can be devised and accepted.

The President's Commission on Law Enforcement and Administration of Justice, Task Force Report: Organized Crime, 1967, has described organized crime as:

FIG. 9.3 Albert Anastasia, the reputed executioner for Murder, Inc. (Wide World Photos)

. . . a society that seeks to operate outside the control of the American people and their governments. It involves thousands of criminals, working within structures as complex as those of any large corporation, subject to laws more rigidly enforced than those of legitimate governments. Its actions are not impulsive but rather the result of intricate conspiracies, carried on over many years and aimed at gaining control over whole fields of activity in order to amass huge profits.

This description is accurate to some extent and inaccurate in other respects. It is too restricted in conception, too broad in operation, and far too easily applicable to other institutions currently at work in today's society (not excluding the CIA and most of our major business corporations!).

What quality of an organization's activities is it that brings such behavior within an acceptable definition of organized

FIG. 9.4   Meyer Lansky, the supervisor of the Syndicate's gambling
interests in the Caribbean   (Wide World Photos)

crime? If it is not the act itself—murder (assassination), extortion, bribery, and the like—then what is it? Is it the goal of the organization—to acquire power or great sums of money? Are such goals in and of themselves antisocial in nature?

Organized crime, then, would seem to defy any simple definition. Is it possible that there is no one conclusive definition, simple or otherwise, and that the scope of the definition depends entirely upon who is making it and for what purpose?

It has already been suggested elsewhere in this text that *any* crime, organized or not, is that activity that the powerful among us say is criminal and that anyone who commits such an act is therefore deemed to be a criminal. But we know beyond dispute that many such criminal acts are committed by people in our society who are *not* considered to be criminals and are not punished for their acts.

Might it not be best, then, to avoid attempting a definition of organized crime that is so rigid and confining in its terms as

FIG. 9.5 "Lucky" Luciano, former New York vice overlord (Associated Press Wirephoto)

to exclude a considerable amount of activity from discussion and analysis in light of the overall crime problem in our culture?

For how can we determine who the members of organized crime are, according to such a restricted definition? Are these people card-carrying members of a totalitarian association of lawbreakers numbering in the millions? Do they wear uniforms or bear identification numbers on their backs? How does the ordinary citizen who occasionally behaves himself in a similar manner fit into the scheme of things?

Perhaps the President's commission settled upon such a limited definition in order to dramatize the problem so as to mobilize public interest and concern. It is much easier to explain a single exotic group like La Cosa Nostra to the American people than attempt to explain the infinitely more complex existence of organized crime in its broadest context. It is much easier to focus attention, interest, hatred, and fear upon one

FIG. 9.6   Louis "Lepke" Buchalter leaving court after the first day of his trial. He was charged with operating a dope ring that used attractive young women to smuggle narcotics.   (United Press International Photo)

man, one group, one idea, than some less identifiable and far more complex target.

In terms of relevance to contemporary law enforcement, however, such an attitude would seem to be self-defeating regarding the matter of crime prevention and control. It would be much more helpful to construct a working definition of organized crime that can accommodate all activity that can be seen to have a bearing upon the larger concept of organized antisocial conduct.

A Working Definition

It might be said to begin with, that organized crime consists of a set of human interactions that occur over a continuous period

FIG. 9.7 Joseph Valachi, convicted murderer, telling the Senate Permanent Investigations Committee how he was initiated into La Cosa Nostra by having to burn a crumpled ball of paper in his hands while taking the oath to "live by the gun and the knife and to die by the gun and the knife" and to be burned to ashes if he ever informed against his associates (Associated Press Wirephoto)

of time. Such activity may be performed by individuals who belong to a more or less permanent group or organization, or who merely engage in certain recurring patterns of behavior. These group activities, then, may be referred to as the work of criminal societies or of loosely connected networks of crime.

Societies are hierarchically structured and usually are engaged in a wide variety of criminal activities, while a network of groups or loosely connected individuals usually evolve around one or two economic activities that bind them together

Fig. 9.8 Racketeer Johnny Dio, called to testify before the Senate Rackets Committee, stares at photographers. Seconds later, he struck a United Press photographer on the ear. (Wide World Photos)

in a common interest. La Cosa Nostra is clearly an example of the former. (Fig. 9.9.)

La Cosa Nostra, the present-day mutation of the old Mafia, is comprised structurally of twenty-four known "families" located in various cities throughout the country. Each family is more or less autonomous and is made up of a ruling boss, one or more underbosses, a consigliere (legal advisor), a number of lieutenants or captains, and a varying number of shock troops known as soldiers or button men who actually perform the on-going work of the family on the operational level.

Although these families are linked historically to the old Sicilian Mafia, La Cosa Nostra is not the same organization merely transplanted to America. Indeed, it is Italian dominated, not Sicilian. The gang wars of the twenties and thirties between

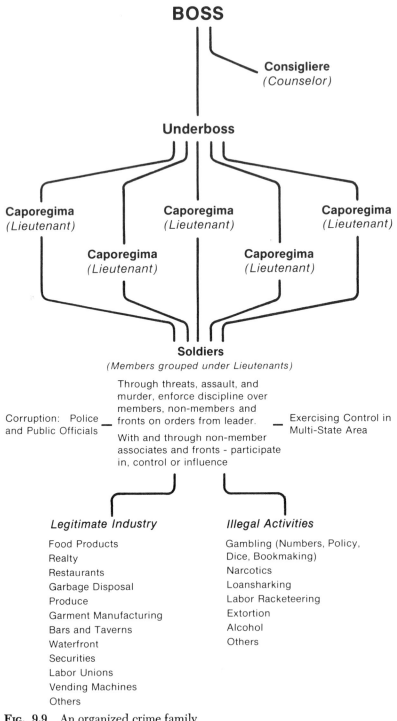

BOSS

Consigliere
(Counselor)

Underboss

Caporegima
(Lieutenant)

Caporegima
(Lieutenant)

Caporegima
(Lieutenant)

Caporegima
(Lieutenant)

Caporegima
(Lieutenant)

Soldiers
(Members grouped under Lieutenants)

Corruption: Police and Public Officials

Through threats, assault, and murder, enforce discipline over members, non-members and fronts on orders from leader.

With and through non-member associates and fronts - participate in, control or influence

Exercising Control in Multi-State Area

Legitimate Industry

Food Products
Realty
Restaurants
Garbage Disposal
Produce
Garment Manufacturing
Bars and Taverns
Waterfront
Securities
Labor Unions
Vending Machines
Others

Illegal Activities

Gambling (Numbers, Policy, Dice, Bookmaking)
Narcotics
Loansharking
Labor Racketeering
Extortion
Alcohol
Others

Fɪɢ. 9.9   An organized crime family

the Sicilian groups and the Italian groups in America finally ended in a loose merging of the two, and that is what exists today. Consequently, neither the term Mafia nor La Cosa Nostra is, in fact, a proper identification, but the name by which the society is called is less important than the reality of the society's existence.

The "family" is the most significant level of operation, and families range in size from 20 to 1,000 members. Some cities have more than one family. New York, for example, has five. The entire membership of La Cosa Nostra is estimated by most experts to be something less than 6,000.

There is a National Crime Syndicate that coordinates the activities of these twenty-four families in relationship to the operations of each other and as regards the activities of other nonfamily criminal groups involved in organized crime.

The Syndicate is governed by a commission that consists of from nine to twelve members, each of whom is the head of one of the twenty-four families. Only the most powerful families are represented on the commission. The personal makeup of the commission is obviously subject to change for a variety of reasons.

Below the commission is a council, made up of members of families in a given geographical area. Council members are not necessarily members of the ruling commission. Every family has a representative on the council in its territory.

Below the Council is the family, the most significant unit in the organizational hierarchy. Ultimate power is distributed among the families, and no individual member enjoys any significant personal power unless he is the head of a powerful family. There is no Boss-of-Bosses in the National Crime Syndicate, and just as soon as any one individual relinquishes his control over his family in order to exercise total domination over the Syndicate as a whole, it will be only a matter of time before he is removed from power entirely, by one means or another, fair or foul. Once he has given up his power base, he is no longer a significant factor to be reckoned with.

An example of the second type of organized crime activity, the network of group participation, might be the pattern of international cooperation in criminal commerce that finds the Turkish farmer growing the poppy, the Corsican chemist processing it into heroin, the Italian entrepreneur exporting it to the U.S., and the enterprising black hoodlum selling it in his ghetto neighborhood.

The important factor for law enforcement in such an extended, all-inclusive view of organized criminal behavior is the realization that even if all the established criminal societies now recognized by the experts were to evaporate overnight, there would be very little, if any, diminution of organized criminal activity.

This expanded definition of organized crime includes, then, the nationally known crime families of La Cosa Nostra, but it would be a grave mistake to conclude that organized crime is monopolized by any one particular ethnic group. In fact, the greatest threat to American society and the dominant challenge to law enforcement is posed by the semiautonomous, local and regional criminal groups or associations who operate more or less independently, yet assist one another when economically desirable.

Organized crime is an interjurisdictional operation—industry, if you will—that is engaged in the business of supplying goods and services to a large number of people upon demand. It feeds a public need. These acts are said to be criminal. The primary difference between these and other crimes, however, is that these are for the most past consensual crimes. The goods and services provided, the criminal acts themselves, are desired by the consuming public. There is no victim in the traditional sense.

Of course traditional crimes *are* committed. It is a violent business. (Fig. 9.10.) But for the most part, the murders, the beatings, the intimidation, are secondary in nature, used primarily as "sales gimmicks" in promoting the principal product —such as gambling, narcotics, prostitution, pornography, loansharking and the like.

Without the public demand, therefore, there could not be organized crime as we know it. There would be no reason to organize, for there would be no product to market. It is axio-

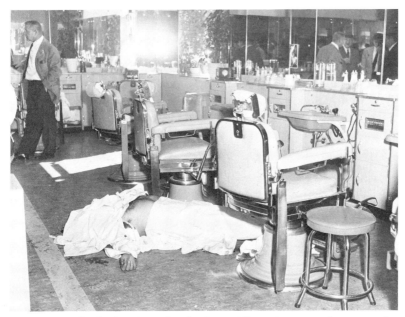

FIG. 9.10   The body of Mafia chieftain Albert Anastasia lying on the
floor of the barbershop in the Park Sheraton Hotel in New
York. Two masked men, who were never caught, blasted him
while he was having a shave.   (Associated Press Wirephoto)

matic that the public does not wish to "buy" bank robberies,
rapes, muggings, or homicides. It *does* wish to purchase narcotics, illegal liquor, prostitutes, gambling chances, etc.

Problems of Police Control

In a free democratic society, law enforcement has no chance of
preventing such desires being satisfied once the great majority
(or even an active insistent minority) of people begin to express such desires. In thinking that the police can control or
eliminate the supply of these goods and services, we have set
for them an impossible task. For it is a task that it is beyond
their capability to perform.

In the final analysis, we have brought organized crime upon ourselves. With our mania for legislating morals, we have given the organized criminal a "product" already packaged and promoted, and all he has to do is to distribute it.

We have apparently learned little or nothing from our experience with Prohibition in the 1920s. At that time, there was no such thing as a national organization of criminals. Wherever ethnic groups existed—Italian, Irish, Polish, Jewish, and "native American"—criminal societies and networks of similar ethnic flavor also existed to prey upon the helplessness of their own kind. But this version of organized crime was local, or neighborhood in kind, and ethnically oriented. The Volstead Act changed all of that.

Borne on the illegal waves of Prohibition suds, organized crime went national. The local scope and extent of their activities shifted from the ethnic neighborhood concept to one of city-wide, statewide, territorial, and eventually national proportions.

Suddenly a large segment of the public wanted and demanded an illegal product. Criminals, therefore, provided a quality service, and the public respected them for their "professionalism." Law enforcement had to contend not only with the criminals but with the public's complicity as well. In particular, the sale of illegal liquor had the overwhelming support of the middle and upper classes.

Was the seller any more criminal than the purchaser?

In time, the criminals became the popular heroes, the cops the "bad guys."

Obviously, criminal societies and networks were active in other forms of illegal activity simultaneously, but all the attention was centered upon bootlegging. It was just such official and public myopia that aided in the growth of organized crime as we know it today.

Cooperation between groups in different localities was soon necessary in order to distribute the product according to the national need and demand. Enormously high profits, low risk, and public and official sanction made competition inevitable, and such criminal alliances began to proliferate throughout the country. (This explosive growth also explains the violence of the period.) It was a period of rampant competition with no legitimate regulations.

Advances in transportation and communications also assisted the "nationalization" process, not to mention an Americanization of many ethnic groups that facilitated a merger—at least in business activities—that had never existed previously.

By the time we came to our national senses and insisted upon the repeal of Prohibition, it was too late. The enormous profits had been reaped and invested in diversified criminal activities, and the benefits of national organization and cooperation were too impressive to turn away from. There would be no looking back to the days of neighborhood, ethnic control. Crime had indeed organized. It had become diversified and multijurisdictional, and so it would remain.

But we as a society learned little from the experience. We have continued to pass laws against such human desires, knowing that the laws cannot be adequately enforced, and then we have completely turned our backs on the people who are supposed to enforce the laws. Police departments in general are totally unprepared to handle the assignment. They are undertrained, undereducated, undersupported, and grossly underpaid. Most departments don't even have organized crime units, and many departments that do have such units are completely controlled by organized crime elements in the community.

Local criminal justice jurisdictions, then, serviced by their traditional structure of law enforcement, simply cannot meet the current challenge of organized crime. Although the foundations of organized crime societies and networks are based upon such traditional activity as gambling, narcotics, prostitution, loansharking and the like, they are also deeply involved in the infiltration of legitimate businesses and labor unions, and the corruption of government officials. Methods such as extortion, terrorism, arson, monopolization, and tax evasion are commonplace.

Unless law enforcement and the criminal justice system in its entirety adopt new strategies to combat this insidious menace, unless society revises and restates a good many of its traditional values so long and foolishly held, organized crime will become even more pervasive in its power and influence in America. The perpetuity of the democratic process compels us to develop these strategies for survival.

Strategies for Survival

The greatest harm to society from organized crime is the insidious corruption that it spawns in its wake. It infects every institution and every individual that it touches. We must, therefore, accept the one hard fact of life where organized crime is concerned: it cannot exist on a large scale without official protection and social indifference.

We have simply been unable as a people to swallow this bitter pill. We want to look to some vast, foreign-dominated, evil organization that is responsible for the major ills of our society rather than face our own guilt. It is a magic mirror into which we gaze; we look at the reflection of our own image and see something else entirely.

Once we called it the Mafia. Now we call it La Cosa Nostra. We refuse to call it what it is: ourselves.

What, then, can be done short of a massive dose of social reform to remove the great citizen demand for illegal goods and services?

On the law enforcement level, an effective coordinated attack must be waged. Law enforcement must become at least as efficient and imaginative as organized crime. In short, law enforcement, too, must organize.

The first line of attack must be on the state level, for it is the primary responsibility of the state to control crime, whether of the traditional variety or of the organized crime type of violation. But how should the state proceed?

1. The office of state prosecutor should be created by legislation or by administrative action under existing statutes pertaining to the powers of the governor and attorney general of the state.

Such a prosecutive officer would be empowered to investigate and prosecute organized crime cases that extend beyond the limits of city and county jurisdictions. In addition, this officer would have the authority to conduct investigative hearings throughout the state, to subpoena witnesses and evidence to such hearings, and to request witness immunity.

In addition to prosecution and investigative functions, such a state prosecutor would also be empowered to collect and analyze intelligence data concerning the operations of individuals and groups engaged in organized crime.

A state prosecutor would serve to supplement the present system of local district attorneys, not to replace them. Yet it would be an effective means of removing an otherwise ineffective district attorney, whether for reasons of corruption or incompetence. At the present time, less than thirty states have anything like such a special prosecutive officer on a statewide basis.

2. Special investigative grand juries with statewide jurisdiction should be legislatively created in all states. The investigative grand jury, state and federal, has recently evolved into the single most effective discovery procedure in organized crime cases.

The statewide investigative grand jury can respond to the realization that organized crime is a statewide, multijurisdictional activity beyond the powers of local grand juries to investigate. At this time, less than a half dozen states have such statewide grand juries.

3. A general witness immunity statute should be legislatively established on a statewide basis. Laws are not self-operating. Crimes can only be established in a court of law upon a solid construct of witness testimony. Organized crime cases are hindered by a wall of silence in much larger numbers than ordinary criminal cases, and for obvious reasons.

Once a witness is granted immunity from prosecution based upon his testimony, however, a reluctant or evasive witness would then be judicially compelled to testify or be imprisoned for contempt. A majority of the states have already enacted general witness immunity statutes.

4. Where organized crime is involved, state law enforce-

ment agencies must be legislatively granted broad arrest and investigative powers.

The obvious limitations of local law enforcement agencies in combatting organized crime activities of a multijurisdictional nature, makes it imperative that a state agency be empowered to function without jurisdictional disadvantage in this area.

In addition to such state efforts to combat organized crime, the federal government must step up its own efforts in this regard. Although it can never play the major role in this respect, it does have a crucial contribution to make. If organized crime exists in significant proportions in a given city, county, or state, then it is axiomatic that local and state government have been corrupted to a proportionate degree. Federal action in such instances can serve to throw off the yoke of corruption and turn the reins of government back into the hands of honest officials.

Since 1967, the federal approach in this regard has been largely by way of the federal strike force. A team of prosecutors and investigators from all law enforcement agencies operating in the area of the particular target location, collects and analyzes all available intelligence, investigates all allegations of criminal conduct, follows all leads, and gathers all available evidence bearing on the subject of the investigation. Then, under the supervision of a special U.S. attorney, a special investigative grand jury is convened to hear evidence presented by the prosecution.

Strike forces obviously vary in size and agency involvement, depending on the particulars of the matter under investigation. Federal strike forces investigating organized crime in a wide variety of jurisdictions throughout the nation have been remarkably effective in relation to any other approach taken regarding this problem.

Organization, cooperation of law enforcement agencies— local, state, and federal—a careful exchange of intelligence, and a vigorous multijurisdictional prosecutorial approach, and organized crime can be dealt a series of continuously crippling blows. It cannot be put out of business, certainly not by law enforcement tactics alone, however innovative they might be. But its concentrations of power can be broken up, its leaders systematically imprisoned, its profits curtailed, and, above all, its corrupting influence upon local government reduced significantly.

Contributions of the Individual
Police Officer

Crime—organized or not—is a revolt against society's way of doing things, a refusal to conform to the will and dictate of others for the public good. Organized crime, then, is just a little more revolt, better coordinated, and much more difficult to understand and control.

Local law enforcement must educate and train its officers from the lowliest recruit up through the highest administrators in each agency. In addition, a special group of officers and investigators should be given intensive training on a broader scale than the average recruit, and these officers should then constitute a special cadre of organized crime specialists with no other police duties to perform. Every police agency of moderate size and above should maintain a specially educated and trained intelligence unit to deal with the problem of organized crime.

This is not, however, intended to minimize the role of the policeman/investigator in the field. These individuals rather than the specialists are in the first line of attack, and their role is a crucial one.

It is the field officer's task to collect the facts and relay them to the special intelligence unit for compilation, analysis, and the development of enforcement policy. There can never be enough specialists to collect such detailed minute information as names, business and residential addresses, vehicle make and licenses, and social friends and business associates of suspected members of organized crime activities. Only the officer on the street can accomplish such tasks.

Street contacts of the patrol officer, for example, may develop leads concerning a numbers operation in a particular neighborhood that an intelligence officer would personally be unable to develop.

An investigator who is engaged in running down leads on a suspected case of arson should keep in mind the possibility that even if arson is established, the motive may not have been a one-shot attempt of the perpetrator to collect illegal insurance proceeds. The incident might be part of an organized crime arson ring operating over an extended territorial and time period. In a recent period, for example, a middle-Georgia gang of arsonists burned more than a dozen homes and business establishments over a two-year span, accumulating over a half million dollars in insurance benefits. And the same group netted over $50,000 in insurance claims fraudulently filed as a result of a series of staged automobile accidents. The astute criminal investigator must be aware of such potential implications of every case he investigates.

A recent LEAA (Law Enforcement Assistance Administration) *Police Guide on Organized Crime* published by the U.S. Department of Justice, indicates a number of ways in which the officer/investigator who is trained and educated in the modus operandi of organized criminals, may render direct assistance to the specialized investigatory unit in his or her agency. Though not an all-inclusive list, the following illustrations from the guide are helpful in apprising the nonspecialist of certain signs or symptoms of organized crime that may come to his attention in the course of his regular duties.

1. A candy store, grocery store, drug store, or other retail establishment seems to be doing a brisk business—many customers coming and going. But the customers do not remain in the store very long and do not leave with packages or other evidence that purchases were made. The store may have a meager selection of merchandise, which raises the question of how it can attract so many customers day after day. This could indicate the presence of a policy operation at the writer level or the place of business of a bookmaker's commission man.

2. At about the same time each day, a package is delivered to a newsstand, bar, or other location. Later the package is picked up by another individual. The newsstand or whatever could be a policy drop—the place to which a policy writer sends his slips and/or day's receipts.

3. A number is chalked on a street lamp pole. The same number is observed in other locations. It might be the winning number for the day's policy play.

4. You are called to investigate a beating in a bar or at a location near a factory or other place of employment. The incident may occur on a payday or within a couple of days thereafter. The beating may have resulted from the impatience of a loan shark who has not been paid on schedule.

5. A parked car—often double parked—is observed daily at the same location and at the same time. The driver remains in the vehicle while a number of "friends" come up to say hello. Such a situation may indicate bet-taking activity.

6. A well-dressed individual is often seen driving an expensive late model car in the area. No one seems to know what his occupation is. One patrolman pursued observations similar to this and found out that the individual was a policy operator—and had been for twenty-one years—without so much as an arrest. On the basis of this information and further investigation, a special squad of detectives made a case against the operator and his employers.

7. A shopkeeper complains about poor business and notes that as a result he had to borrow money recently. With a few comments to the patrolman about the high interest rates, the shopkeeper might disclose the imposition of an interest rate above the legal maximum. If so, the shopkeeper may have been dealing with a loan shark. If the shopkeeper advises that he cannot keep up with the payments, the officer might find an opportune time to ask for the identity of the shark. Depending on the desperation and temperament of the victim, the suggestion to cooperate may bring positive results.

8. After arriving at the scene of an assault, a patrolman learns that the victim is a union official. This information should be noted because if there have been other similar assaults in the city, the overall total, when analyzed by an organized crime intelligence unit, may strongly indicate an attempt by racketeers to gain control over a union local.

9. Merchants complain about another price rise by the cartage company that removes their garbage or trash. They also mention that there is either no competitor to deal with or if there is one, it will not accept their business.

Not infrequently, this is an indication that an organized crime group is trying to monopolize the cartage business or to limit competition through territorial agreements.

10. During a routine check of a restaurant, a patrolman recognizes several organized crime figures at a table, or many double-parked cars are spotted in front of a bar that is either known or suspected as a meeting place for racketeers. The patrolman should jot down the license plate numbers and phone in his observations immediately, so that investigators can be dispatched to the scene. Such signs indicate that underworld figures are meeting for one reason or another. However, they also may be indicia of hidden ownership of the bar or restaurant by organized crime. In some instances, bars can be closed down if they are frequented by criminals.

11. A new set of vendors begins to service a business—a restaurant, for example. The linen supplier is new, as are the meat provisioner, fuel oil company, and cartage firm. Perhaps new vending machines or jukeboxes are observed being installed. Some of these suppliers are recognized as enterprises run by organized crime. These are fairly solid indicators that organized crime figures have purchased, or have otherwise secured a degree of control in the business being serviced.

12. A rash of vandalism strikes a number of establishments engaged in the same type of business—such as dry cleaning. Racketeers may be trying to coerce reluctant owners into joining an association or into doing business with mob-controlled vendors.

13. Appliances are seen being loaded into the storeroom of a sporting goods store. Scams or bankruptcy frauds frequently involve the ordering of goods (on credit, of course) unrelated to the customary line of the business.

14. Determining who the bettors are in your area can be as important as knowing who the bookmakers are—indeed, many times the identification of a bettor leads to the identification of a bookie. Patrolmen have identified bettors through conversations with those on their posts—sometimes even by observing who buys racing forms. In some instances, you may even get close enough to a bettor to observe the number dialed when a bet is placed. Observations such as these could trigger an investigation leading to the prosecution of the upper echelon of organized crime's gambling hierarchy.

15. Just as identification of the bettor is important, so also is the identification of addicts and loan shark customers. In two separate incidents, an arrested burglar revealed, under questioning by a patrolman, that he was stealing to finance his heroin purchases; while another arrested thief said he had to raise money to keep up with his loan shark payments. This information led to the arrest of a pusher in one case and the loan shark in the other.

16. Make a habit of checking out new businesses that set up shop in the area. If the enterprise is one that requires a license—such as a bar—ask to see it if for no other reason than to observe who the owners are, ascertain the identity of the company that distributes or services the jukeboxes, et cetera. If, for example, the distributor of the jukeboxes or vending machines is a company controlled by the organized underworld, so also might be the bar in which they are located.

17. You note pickets outside one or two stores in the same line of business. The picketing may be a perfectly legitimate tactic, or it may represent an attempt by organized crime to coerce employers into doing business with an underworld firm, to extort payments in return for labor peace, to convince employers to join an "association" and pay substantial dues, or to demonstrate the advisability of hiring a "labor consultant" who is able to resolve such troublesome activities as picketing.

18. A cheap hotel appears to be doing a reasonably brisk business. Its patrons travel light—many do not carry luggage. A bar has a reputation for being a clip joint; charges of watered-down liquor are frequent. These signs indicate a possible call-girl operation at the hotel and B-girl activity at the bar.

19. A truck is loaded at a location other than a depot or shipping dock. Goods are transferred from a truck of a well-known company to an unmarked truck or vehicle. A warehouse that is almost always empty is now full. Unusual activity at an unusual time occurs in a warehouse area. Merchandise is transferred from a truck to the garage of a residence. Any of these activities could point to a hijacking. License numbers, locations, times, and other facts should be noted.

20. A group begins to congregate at a certain street location at certain times during each day. The group could be composed of addicts waiting for a pusher to make his rounds.

21. A business establishment suspected of being mob-controlled burns to the ground. One possibility is that arson was committed to collect the insurance.

22. Certain individuals always seem to frequent a certain bar although none of them lives in the neighborhood. Perhaps they use the bar as a bet-taking center.

23. A club shuts down at irregular times—sometimes early in the afternoon, other times at mid-evening. Do these times coincide with the completion of racing or when the results of other sporting events become available? If so, the club may be a base for gambling operations.

24. A known racketeer frequently meets with certain unidentified individuals. If possible, note the license plate numbers of the vehicles of these individuals as well as the time and location of the conversations. Racketeers, like most everyone else, are victims of habit and associate with each other.

25. Many cars pull up and park in front of the suburban home of a suspected racketeer, who is ostensibly throwing a party for friends. Jot down license plate numbers and call in the information promptly. The party may be bona fide, or the real purpose of the gathering may be to conduct underworld business, as was the case at the famed Appalachian meeting, where an alert officer noted unusual activity at a country estate and blew the whistle on what turned out to be a nationwide assembly of high-ranking members of the organized underworld. Knowledge of who associates with whom is highly important—whether the occasion is a bona fide social activity or otherwise.

If organized crime is to be impeded to any degree of effectiveness, then the law enforcement attack must come from both the street level and the specialized intelligence units. Although law enforcement cannot do the entire job of controlling organized crime, neither will a social restructuring alone materially affect the problem.

Meanwhile, law enforcement must begin the battle. It must not wait until society decides its own course of action. Indeed, law enforcement must attempt to awaken society to the danger it faces from organized crime, to educate society as to the true nature of this sinister evil among us, and to suggest a policy designed toward its control and eventual eradication.

• DISCUSSION QUESTIONS

1. *There are said to be two types of surveillances, stationary and moving. The character of such surveillances, however, may vary in at least four ways. What are these four techniques of surveillances?*

2. *What is the crux of the Federal Communication Act of 1934? What is the current status of the act?*

3. *How do congressional statutes affect the President's power to eavesdrop electronically in national security cases? With a warrant? Without a warrant?*

4. *How useful has electronic surveillance been to law enforcement over the years? In what kind of cases is this technique most effective? Least effective?*

5. *Should an undercover agent initiate, incite, or participate in criminal activity? Does the end ever justify the means? How does the U.S. Supreme Court stand on this issue?*

6. *What is the administrative structure of an organized crime "family"?*

7. *What is the administrative structure of the National Crime Syndicate?*

8. *What was the dominant factor enabling organized crime to expand from an ethnic neighborhood concept to one of national proportions? Explain.*

9. *Is there a significant difference between the terms "Mafia" and "La Cosa Nostra"?*

10

- *Interviews and Interrogations*

A criminal investigation is a search for truth. Truth is determined by gathering all of the facts concerning a given incident by way of a systematic, planned operation designed to resolve all pertinent issues.

Truth, however, is a relative quantity as to time and place and personal viewpoint. The investigator must separate fact from fantasy, observation from opinion. He must distinguish between fact and inference. He must eliminate the influence of bias, his own as well as that of witnesses, suspects, informants, and victims.

Truth is obtained for the most part through the verbal techniques of communication. Interviewing, however, is not an informal conversational process. It is, rather, a planned attempt to obtain purposeful information. The process of interviewing is an art, not a science. It cannot be taught, but it can be learned. It can, in fact, be developed to a highly creative level of achievement.

How can it be so developed? Thomas Edison said that genius is one percent inspiration and ninety-nine percent perspiration, and so it is with the art of successful interviewing. One learns only by constant striving and by practice. And although it can't be learned entirely in a classroom, there are, of course, certain fundamentals to be made aware of, certain techniques to master prior to adoption of the realistic trial-and-error approach.

Can one imagine that a "showboat" like Broadway Joe Namath is such a genius on the football field by working out with Hollywood starlets during the week and by reporting on Sunday afternoons to toss four or five touchdown passes among ten or twenty brilliant completions before hitting the old celebrity trail again?

Of course he doesn't. At the heart of such expertise lies hours and hours, days and months, and even years of intensive training and attention to detail. If the incomparable Muhammed Ali did not have the legs, the hands, the mental agility, and the heart to go with the rapid-fire mouth and tongue, he would long ago have been reduced to some lesser calling in American life, such as politics, perhaps, or used-car huckstering.

The timing of a Namath or an Ali is not unlike that of a hard-hitting prosecutor or a crafty defense attorney who can nail a waffling witness to the dock with a series of cogent, penetrating questions. The best athletes, the best courtroom lawyers, the best surgeons, carpenters, and seamstresses are those who have mastered the fundamentals of their profession, craft, or art. And so it is with the police investigator.

In many respects, the investigator has the most demanding task of all. He must, at times, be all things to all men. Cop, yes, but also psychiatrist, sociologist, legal scholar, actor, con man, public relations expert, athlete, and, all too often, scapegoat.

Reference is made to a *good* investigator, a pro, not just a slug who pulls his shift and draws his pay and commutes like every other nine-to-fiver on the Mediocre Express. The good investigator *works* at his art, just like a painter struggles with his pictures, and a musician runs his scales.

Of course a mule *works* behind a plow. Something more than physical effort is required. But an investigator doesn't have to be a genius and is probably better qualified if he isn't. There is an old saying about law students: "A" students make the best professors, "B" students make good judges, and "C" students are so mediocre they can't do anything but make money.

Then what is the primary asset that a successful investigator must have? An ability to handle people—all else is secondary.

For the most part, police investigators "handle" people by the interview process. Interviewing is one of the most common investigative techniques, constituting in most cases the major source of information. Even physical evidence is often discovered as a result of persistent and knowledgeable interviewing. It cannot be overstressed that the effectiveness of an investigator rests to a considerable extent upon his ability to conduct such interviews.

INTERVIEWS

Definition

What is an interview? It is the planned, purposeful, verbal communication between the police officer and another person. It is designed to ascertain the truth of a situation by obtaining and testing answers to pertinent questions concerning an alleged or suspected violation of the law, or other matters of interest to the law enforcement agency involved.

Although there are occasions when an interview must be conducted more or less spontaneously, it is fair to say that generally speaking, an interview will probably not be successful unless it has been planned and organized in advance with a definite purpose in mind.

The objective is always to obtain as much information as possible, while giving as little as possible. A combination of disparate factors will determine how successful an investigator is in this respect. And although there is no $2 + 2 = 4$ combination that can be learned and thereafter relied upon, there are certain traits and qualifications that have proven common to the personal makeup of most successful interviewers.

Qualifications of the Interviewer

The most important of these seems to be an ability to convey a sincere concern for humanity, and, in particular, for the interviewee from whom the desired information is being sought.

Will Rogers, the late humorist, once said that he'd never met a person he didn't like. And Rogers did not lead a sheltered life. Whether or not he was given to lying or at least hyperbole is immaterial. The criminal investigator does not have to like every individual with whom he has contact. It does help, however, if he likes mankind in the abstract. If even this is asking too much, it is absolutely necessary that the qualities of pity and compassion for the unfortunates among us have not been blunted by the sordidness he has seen, the injustice of life, and the inhumanity of man. It is only in this way that the investigator can make "contact" with the interviewee.

And the rapport that exists between the interviewer and the interviewee will in all likelihood determine the outcome of the interview. How such rapport is established, however, is one of those imponderable dilemmas that so frustrates the unsuccessful interviewer who must look on while an accomplished associate deftly opens a veritable floodgate of repressed information.

The establishment of rapport is the natural result of a combination of personality traits that are either genuine or so convincingly evinced that genuineness is accepted by the interviewee. Actual rather than feigned sincerity is to be desired. A "performance" on the part of the investigator is usually apprehended by the interviewee, and even though he may have no personal motive for withholding information, his attitude, consciously or unconsciously, will then be less than cooperative.

In addition to such obvious qualities as intelligence and an easy skill with words, a successful interviewer should possess an insatiable curiosity about life and all its vagaries. Only by this trait can he develop a sufficient body of knowledge and breadth of interests as to relate successfully to the diverse worlds of the interviewees with whom he will be confronted.

On the other hand, naiveté is a trait to be avoided. The investigator should be skeptical by vocation if not by nature. He must understand the infinite complexities of human nature and never become smug or self-satisfied by his own deductive powers. He should always be suspicious without showing it. And he should be persistent. He should endeavor to obtain answers to all critical and crucial questions. If at all possible, he should obtain all desired information in the first interview. But he should not hesitate to conduct reinterviews whenever indicated.

In this regard, it should be pointed out that all information obtained by way of interviewing must be tested prior to acceptance. This is done by checking the interviewee's statements against statements of others, by verifying certain claimed facts through resort to formal records and other written documents, by requestioning the interviewee with a variation of approach, and the like. There are obviously many reasons why a witness might give false or inaccurate information. He might have something to hide in his own life, whether it pertains to the investigation at hand or not. He might be afraid to tell the truth. He might not know the truth in spite of the fact that he supposes he does. He may simply have made a mistake in relating the information. The investigator must make certain that questionable words and phrases are understood. He must determine what the interviewee means by the use of such words and phrases.

In order to conduct such an interview and obtain and retain the good will of the interviewee, an investigator should exhibit a manner that is courteous, cordial, and, if the occasion dictates, friendly. Such a manner will soften the edge of the investigator's persistence.

An investigator should be flexible in his technique and analytical with regard to the information as it is received. As his analysis of the information and of the interviewee's attitude, personality, and truthfulness indicate a shift in technique, he must be willing and flexible enough to alter his approach in the continuing interview. Such shifts and alterations may very well take place numerous times in the course of a single interview.

Patience, then, is a prime virtue of the successful criminal investigator. He must be willing to spend whatever length of time is required to obtain the desired information. It may take the bulk of the time allotted to the entire interview merely to gain the interviewee's confidence and prepare the atmosphere for meaningful questioning. Obtaining information about a robbery suspect may only be fruitful after a thirty-minute session of Monday morning quarterbacking concerning the previous day's Super Bowl encounter. Likewise, a woman interviewee may not relate to a male investigator until she has satisfied herself as to the extent of chauvenistic tendencies that he possesses.

After each interview, the investigator—especially the inexperienced investigator—should spend a period of self-examination as to the manner in which he conducted the interview and the relative success or failure of the encounter in light of the predetermined objectives. It is also a useful practice to subject oneself to the constructive criticism of an associate who witnessed the interview.

Conducting the Interview

An interview pursuant to a criminal investigation is not a happening. It should be carefully planned in advance and staged with such care and consideration as will afford every psychological advantage to the investigator.

This is not to say, however, that no consideration is to be given to the convenience of the subject of the interview. On the contrary, in many cases, the time and place of the interview can be selected entirely with the subject's comfort in mind. The rule of thumb should be to make the decision based upon the need for privacy and sufficient time to enable the interview to be as thorough and far-ranging as the needs of the case dictate.

In major criminal cases, of course, most interviews should be conducted in the investigator's own office. Under such circumstances, the investigator should control the interview at all times. It should be conducted in a simple, sparsely furnished room. The atmosphere should be businesslike but not frightening. Lighting should be adequate so that facial expressions and body nuances are clearly discernable, but the use of the third-degree naked light bulb tactics must be scrupulously avoided.

Upon initiating an interview, the investigator should introduce himself and produce his credentials and, unless the nature of the case determines otherwise, disclose or confirm the purpose of the interview.

The investigator might be well-advised at this point to expect any one of an infinite variety of reactions to such introductions. Respected community businessmen have been known to experience instant cardiac arrest upon glimpsing an IRS agent's credentials. Nor is a sigh of relief and a blurted confession of embezzlement of company funds uncommon to an FBI agent's experience. As likely as not, the original purposes of such inquiries may very well have been routine background investigations of a third-party applicant for a government job. The investigator, however, must be prepared for any eventuality.

After the introductions have been made, the investigator should normally delay any immediate inquiries into the case at hand while endeavoring to establish the necessary rapport between himself and the subject of the interview.

Interviewees come in all sizes, shapes, and colors. This is where the investigator's general knowledge and experience of life become so important. Though individuals should not be stereotyped, there are certain traits and characteristics more or less common to most members of any particular subgroup within our society. An investigator must be aware of such group distinctions and must use to the best advantage his knowledge of man's likes and dislikes, his hopes and aspirations, his fears and prejudices. Without the necessity of being judgmental, an understanding of human nature—its strengths as well as its weaknesses—is the raw material in the process of establishing rapport with another human being. For example, the investigator may try discussing the weather with a farmer, the economy with a housewife, and the latest rock band sensation with a high school student. As soon as he feels the atmosphere is such that the witness will be responsive to his questioning, he may then direct the interview accordingly.

In planning the interview beforehand, the investigator has reviewed the facts and the evidence presently accumulated, has analyzed the theory(s) of the case, and has familiarized himself as much as possible with the background of the witness. He has therefore fashioned for himself a general scenario of what he desires to cover in the interview. And prior to actually beginning the interview, he has written down in his notebook the date, time, and place of the interview, the file number of the case, the name and address of the interviewee, and perhaps a checklist of issues and questions to be pursued in the body of the interview.

The investigator should initially allow the witness to relate his statements in his own words, uninterrupted by questions or observations. Although mental notations should be made of erroneous or contradictory statements, no written notes should be taken at this stage of the interview. It is not uncommon that an otherwise cooperative witness will become intimidated by the premature attempt to record his observations, either by notetaking, the use of a stenographer, or any of the variety of recording devices presently available to the criminal investigator.

After the witness has related whatever information he "thinks" he possesses, and the investigator has had an opportunity to assess his potential for truthfulness and reliability, he may then be ready to proceed to the more direct question-and-answer stage.

The investigator knows generally the kind of information he is seeking. If he is investigating a suspected criminal offense, he hopes to establish the actual commission of the crime. If a crime has in fact been established, then he knows he must obtain evidence that will establish the elements of the offense. Since most witnesses have a tendency to ramble and digress to the point of irrelevancy, it is the responsibility of the investigator to control the interview so that it conforms to the predetermined needs of the inquiry.

That is not to say, however, that the interviewee is given no leeway in his responses. It is impossible for an investigator to know everything he will need in advance of an interview. Witnesses often possess valuable information that neither they nor the investigator are aware of. The investigator must be alert to the possibility of obtaining additional information as well as to the information he seeks. Controlling the interview, therefore, does not mean turning a deaf ear to all that the investigator has not planned to hear.

In fact, it bears restating at this point that the most crucial mistake a criminal investigator can make—be it in regard to the testimony of a victim of a crime, a witness or suspect, in regard to physical evidence of whatever nature, or to an overall theory of the case at hand—is to become blindly committed to a point of view already developed, no matter how sound and well-reasoned it might appear.

It is this very tendency, perhaps, that historically has mitigated against raising the specialty of criminal investigation to a science in the full sense of the term. Even scientists all too often fall into error precisely because of this disastrous tendency. To become absorbed in a hypothesis is more often than not a one-way ticket to disaster. The true scientific merit in believing passionately in a hypothesis is that we should then be stimulated to an even deeper inquiry into its validity, that we should devise even more stringent tests of its reliability. All too often, scientists—and criminal investigators—become so committed to a hypothesis, a theory of the case, that rather than testing it in any way and risking repudiation of the belief as held, they skirt all around the issue or follow leads of such remote lines of cognate investigation that their premise is in no way endangered. The modern, professional criminal investigator—as well as generally the scientist—must come to terms with this tendency first by recognizing and acknowledging its existence and its power for harm, and then by guarding vigilantly against it in his performance of duty.

For example, refer for a moment to our hypothetical rural murder case previously discussed. How beneficial to the investigation it would have been had the sheriff been willing to put to the test his rather hasty and not very well-founded theory that the deceased man's wife had killed her husband and daughter because of an obscure rumor of some sort of incestuous relationship.

So, the investigator must approach his interviewee with an open mind. And it is during the direct questioning phase of the interview that the investigator should first begin testing the information as it is received. Discrepancies and misunderstandings should be patiently cleared away. And if the investigator is adroit enough, this may often be done without the witness's awareness of the confusion in the first place. Such confusion may be the result of lies or honest mistakes. The investigator must be able to distinguish between the two and vary his questioning technique accordingly.

His technique, whatever variation used, should be kept as simple as possible. His questions should be short, clear, and directly on point. The witness should be allowed to answer one question before another question is put to him. Nor does control of the interview require that the investigator restrict the witness to yes or no responses. Qualification of answers should always be permitted and elicited whenever necessary. Precise questioning will prevent the witness from wandering too far afield in pursuit of irrelevant matters.

A special word of caution. The investigator should consciously guard against suggesting the answers to his questions whether by word, expression, or gesture. He wants to learn what the witness knows and not what the investigator hopes he knows.

Of course, not every witness is as amenable to the control of the investigator as might be desired. Each witness is unique, and the investigator's technique must be adapted accordingly. Witnesses may obviously be distinguished as to age and sex, and perhaps only slightly less obviously as to race and national origin. However, every nuance of personality and social distinction must be recognized and evaluated by the successful criminal investigator.

The crucial task for the criminal investigator in this connection is to determine the category in which a given witness falls as soon as possible, so as to shape his questioning accordingly. Fitting one's method of interviewing to the personality variables of each witness can only be perfected through accumulated experience. There are certain guidelines, however, that may prove helpful, especially to the novice investigator.

Classification of Witnesses

One should make the external classifications at once, such as matters pertaining to age, sex, race, and national origin. An investigator, for example, must be instantly on guard against the danger of accepting as literal truth the description of an event as seen by an imaginative, impressionistic child of tender years. On the other hand, an older child quite often makes a better witness than an adult because his powers of observation are heightened by childish curiosity long since blunted in the vision of his care-worn self-centered elders.

Teenagers, however, are notoriously poor witnesses, apparently due to their preoccupation with themselves and their peers. Unless unusually stimulated—generally by an issue that affects them personally, such as the war in Vietnam—such youths are generally uninterested in their external surroundings. The operations of government and most all social institutions are not only uninteresting to this age group, they are also often viewed by them to be unnecessary and untrustworthy. Great tact and flexibility are required on the part of an investigator who must interview such a witness. Certainly such anti-authoritarian witnesses cannot usually be bullied or cajoled into cooperation.

Information derived from elderly witnesses must also be received with caution. Physical and mental infirmities may affect the accuracy of information in spite of the best intentions of the witness. And unfortunately—and a sad commentary it is upon our times—all too often the elderly citizen has developed a lonely bitterness against society that renders his observations cynical and self-serving.

Middle-aged persons, however, are generally supposed to make good witnesses. This interpretation is a generous one. It seems more accurate to state candidly that there are few, if any, "good" witnesses in any category. Some are simply less bad than others. This is about the best claim that can be substantiated, even though the middle-aged witness is commonly reputed to be a person of experienced observation and mature judgment.

The reality is that the average citizen is neither trained nor motivated to observe and understand facts beneficial to police investigation. Even well-intentioned witnesses to a crime generally provide something less than accurate information of what they saw, heard, or felt. A knowledge of human nature and potential is absolutely necessary on the part of the criminal investigator in evaluating information obtained from a witness, regardless of his or her category.

A witness may have something to hide or simply may be a congenital liar. Another may be an honest witness with nothing significant to offer. Still another may be terrified by even so slight a contact with a police officer that he is incapable of assisting in the investigation unless handled with extreme sensitivity. Witnesses may be ignorant, unobservant, cunning, suspicious, antiestablishment oriented, timid, fearful, egotistic. In every instance, the investigator must make an assessment as to the reliability of the information.

The assessment can best be made by obtaining as much knowledge about the witness as is possible under the circumstances. It would obviously be of considerable benefit to the investigator to know that the complaining witness in an alleged rape case has been "raped" seven times previously in the past two months. Or if a witness tells you that he has received most of his information by way of supersonic intergalactic isotopes, it would be quite useful to be aware of the fact that the unfortunate fellow has a history of mental disorder. If he has become unduly agitated as a result of having related his story, you might want to consider playing along with him by offering to "insulate" him. One recommended technique of accomplishing this is by suggesting that the recipient of such "messages" should extend a lengthy chain of paper clips from his belt loop, down the inside of his pants leg, and into the instep of his shoe. Similar "grounding" techniques have been used with uncommon success by FBI agents over the years.

Certainly the questioning of the victim of a crime must be conducted with care and sensitivity, the more so depending upon the type of offense involved. The victim may be in a highly emotional state, extending even to the point of temporary paranoia. A wrong word or gesture can produce explosive results under such circumstances. The list of such victims is long and varied, such as child victims of sex crimes, a woman who has been assaulted and/or raped, or the victim of a humiliating domestic dispute, to mention only a few.

Imagine the following brief series of questions being put

to a rape victim in the emergency room by a male criminal investigator.

"So you're tellin' us you went out an' got yourself raped?"

"What were you doin' by yourself on the street after dark in the first place?"

"Were you wearing a coat, or was that flimsy little skirt an' blouse all you had on?"

"If you didn't know this guy, how come you stopped an' had conversation with him?"

"When he dragged you into the bushes did you scream, did you try to resist; did you hit him, bite him, try to kick him in the balls?"

"Did he use a weapon, other than the obvious one?"

"Are you sure you weren't out there lookin' for exactly what you got?"

"Are you tryin' to tell us that way down deep, when all's said and done, you didn't enjoy it even a little bit?"

Gross. Utterly insensitive. Exaggeration beyond the point of usefulness? Over fifty thousand rapes are reported in the United States every year; ask the women who have been interviewed by police how many of those questions they have heard.

Psychological Implications

It has been said that a police officer should be a person of many talents with a broad sphere of knowledge. He must at times be conversant with the law of the land in more than superficial detail; he must have a basic understanding of emergency medical procedures; he must function as part sociologist, part family counselor, and part economic advisor. It is a staggering responsibility. No other professional in American life is faced with such varied demands. And no other professional is so ill-equipped to discharge such responsibilities. Underpaid, under-educated, and undertrained, most police officers find the task is beyond their capacities. Still, the effort must be made.

It is therefore imperative that the criminal investigator who aspires to a level of professional competence in the performance of his duties must do all within his power to achieve such distinction by self-education, self-awareness, self-knowledge, and a wide-ranging understanding of human nature in general.

Why does so-called civilized man continue to murder, rape, steal, and connive, as if the accumulated history of man meant nothing? Why does man lie and cheat and debase his species like none other extant? The criminal investigator simply must make such inquiries his own. He must study man, the product, the raw material with which he must deal.

In order to rely upon information furnished by a witness, including victims and suspects, an investigator must know enough about that witness to enable him to evaluate the quality of the information in question. How was such information obtained? How was it perceived by the witness? Is it the whole truth, a composite, a fantasy?

Psychologists have written at length concerning the ways in which we perceive events. It is commonly believed that man has a tendency to view things as a whole rather than in their individual parts. The principle of *pragnanz*, the law of "good figures," was recognized by the gestalt method of psychology that contended that simple symmetrical figures were more easily perceived than were irregular figures. The law of *pragnanz*, then, deals with the principles of psychological organization.

Another gestalt principle important to law enforcement is known as the *law of closure*. This simply recognizes the inclination or tendency of man to complete his fleeting impressions by making good figures out of those shapes that are irregular or incomplete. The mind has a tendency, for example, to complete the picture of an unclosed circle, to extend the line, to fill in the gap.

The concept of "gestalt," then, implies organization. The

word "gestalt" implies an entity of concreteness and individuality, of something detached and having a shape or form as one of its attributes. A "gestalt" can therefore be said to be a product of organization, and organization is that process that leads to a gestalt.

Furthermore, the human mind abhors a vacuum. There is a tendency, therefore, to interpret and complete a thing perceived. One places an interpretation on things perceived by filling in the details by reason of one's experience and total knowledge. Obviously, due to the incompleteness of one's experience and knowledge, one is often mistaken in this completion process.

Such rules would seem to apply to social conditions as well. One who has knowledge and experience in a certain field, who is familiar with a particular subject, is more likely to make a good witness concerning matters related to that specific field or subject. Whereas a person who observes something but does not understand that which he sees will in all likelihood not make a good witness. For example, if a house painter had occasion to observe a delicate brain operation, the description of what he saw in the operating arena is not likely to coincide with the surgeon's own description of what the operation actually entailed.

Another general tendency that must be considered by the investigator is that of man's inclination to judge empty space as being larger than it actually is, and to judge the same space as smaller if it is filled with objects.

And the necessity of judging distances gives witnesses considerable difficulty. An investigator must always make certain that distances are accurately measured, never estimated. However, when a number of persons do estimate a distance, the average of such estimations is quite likely to be very close to the actuality.

Observation and Description

The same generalization applies to descriptions of persons. Extract the common factors from all the descriptions, and a rather close likeness will generally result. It must always be borne in mind, however, that witness information will be governed by subjective perception rather than objective reality. The way one person perceives a thing will usually be at great variance with the perception of another. In Laingian terms, the question can even be asked as to whether one person can *ever* perceive the reality of another person.

For example: If I perceive you and you perceive me, I do not perceive the *real* you but only my perception of you, and you do not perceive the *real* me but only your perception of me.

A person's perception is always governed by certain pre-existing perception-sets. You see a thing the way you are conditioned to see it, and you are conditioned to see things according to the way in which you are oriented by your total experience, environment, and knowledge. In short, you are the sum of your experiences, and you interpret life accordingly. Even your behavior, therefore, is governed by subjective perception, the way you see the world and the way you fit into the scheme of things (or believe that you do).

Try to imagine, for instance, the variety of interpretations that resulted in the collective mind of the voting public some years ago in a hotly contested Deep South senatorial campaign, when one of the antagonists referred to the other (the loser) thusly: "Are you (the voters) aware that ——— is known all over town as a shameless extrovert? Not only that, but this man is reliably reported to practice nepotism with his sister-in-law, and he has a sister who was once a thespian in New York City. He matriculated with coeds at the University, and worst of all, it is an established fact that before his marriage he habitually practiced celibacy."

Of course, the conscious mind cannot remember all of life's experiences. What is left in our minds after we have forgotten the thing itself is called the *apperceptive mass*. It is the residue of life's experience that will serve as a background with which to relate current stimuli. The more one learns, the greater one's experience of life, the larger the apperceptive mass, and the easier one can learn more. Psychologist William James advocated that one should experience as much as possible in order to grow.

The criminal investigator, then, must concern himself with the diverse factors affecting human perception if he is to evaluate witness information with any hope of accuracy. In addition to the perceptive-sets affecting the way a person views things, certain physical factors must also be considered as having a bearing upon the reliability of witness information.

Opportunity of observation must be considered. What was the distance from which the witness claims to have observed an event? What position, what angle? What was the illumination?

The physical condition and capacity of the witness is of great importance. Matters such as eyesight, hearing, and physical dexterity, may very well be controlling as to whether or not the witness could possibly have observed an event in a particular fashion.

The effect of environmental conditions such as fog, dust, rain, snow, and the like might render the details of a given witness statement suspect.

Witness description, then, is based primarily upon the sense of sight and secondarily upon the senses of hearing, smell, touch, and taste. We have seen how unreliable these sense perceptions may be. Each one of the senses is subject to mistaken apprehensions in the trained investigator as well as in the untrained layman.

Consider for a moment an example taken from Richard Powell's novel *The Philadelphian*. The incident involved the courtroom testimony of a witness in a murder trial. The deceased's butler was testifying to the effect that on the night his employee was murdered, the butler heard a shot in the drawing room and rushed downstairs to investigate; that upon his arrival in the study, he discovered the body of his employer and two empty whiskey glasses nearby. A window to the garden was open and the assailant was gone.

In the course of the defense attorney's cross-examination of the witness he (the butler) testified that he had sniffed each of the whiskey glasses and was able to ascertain the kind of whiskey that each man had been drinking by their distinctive bouquets. His employer drank only expensive Scotch and Napoleon brandy. The defendant always drank a very raw, cheap rye. He therefore deduced that the last person with his employer that night prior to his death was indeed the defendant.

The defense attorney asked the butler to demonstrate his highly developed sense of smell. On the defense table sat three glasses of whiskey labeled A, B, and C and a pitcher of water. The defense attorney poured himself a glass of water using a fourth unlabeled glass, then offered glass A to the witness to test. The butler sniffed the glass of whiskey a few times and then identified it as a cheap rye with a very short aging period.

The defense attorney handed him the second glass marked B. The witness spent some moments sniffing the aroma and finally announced rather triumphantly that it was Royal Tartan Scotch, unmistakably heavy and rich of bouquet, with a definite aroma of peat smoke.

The defense attorney then fumbled around on the table and handed the witness a third glass for testing. The butler lowered his head to sniff the contents, expecting Napoleon brandy of course, and then arrogantly accused the attorney of having given him the lawyer's own glass of water.

The attorney assured him that he'd not made such a mistake, that it was indeed the correct glass. The witness patronizingly assured him it was water, that he could even smell the city chlorine in it, and to prove it, he unexpectedly took a sip from the glass.

He choked, gasped, and erupted into a fit of coughing.

With much embarrassment and humiliation, he finally identified the contents of the glass as pure gin.

A humorous scene indeed, effectively done. And whether Mr. Powell based his scene upon an actual event or not, the appropriateness to our purpose is evident. What had happened, of course, was that the defense attorney had tricked the pompous witness into mislabeling the third glass. He had so filled his nose with fumes that his sense of smell was altered by the time he got to the third glass, so altered that he couldn't even distinguish gin from water. Obviously, the little experiment was anything but wasted upon the attentive jurors and the witness's previous testimony was weighed accordingly.

Such mistaken identifications—either of persons, physical objects, or events, etc.—can be catastrophic. It should be remembered that mistaken identity is still perhaps the major factor in the conviction of innocent defendants. Yet subject identifications do and must play an important role in criminal investigations. Traditionally, subjects are identified by a witness's verbal description, by an examination of photographic records, by fingerprints and palmar impressions, by footprints and voiceprints, and on occasion by the assistance of artists' renderings. (Fig. 10.1.) The evidentiary value of such identifications will be discussed in a subsequent chapter.

Modus Operandi Files

In conjunction with the photographic files, *modus operandi* files are often most useful in effecting subject identifications. Most medium-sized-and-above police agencies today maintain such files. A *modus operandi* file, or MO file, is simply a repository

FIG. 10.1   At right is a drawing made by a Chicago police department artist of the slayer of eight student nurses as described by the one survivor. At left is a police photograph of Richard Speck. (Wide World Photos)

of information that affords an investigator an opportunity to ascertain common patterns of behavior as being applicable to a particular suspect.

A suspect's MO is a combination of his habits, techniques, and eccentricities that, when examined as a unit, often serves to reveal his identity as if it were a fingerprint impression of his character and personality.

Custodial Identifications

One-on-one visual identification by a witness is to be avoided in all but those instances of absolute necessity. Generally from six to ten persons, in addition to the suspect, should be included in a police lineup for identification purposes. Although the suspect has no right to refuse to participate in a lineup, he is entitled to certain procedural safeguards.

Among other rights in this regard, he is entitled, after indictment, to the assistance of counsel; he should be allowed to choose the position in which he desires to stand during the lineup; and he should never be exhibited in such a way as to cause him to stand out from the others in the lineup.

The right to counsel after charges are made was enunciated in the 1970 case of *Kirby* v. *Illinois*, 406 U.S. 682. The court held in a five to four decision that although the right to counsel did not apply to a police-arranged lineup before any formal charges had been brought, that such a right must be extended to an accused once he has become the subject of a criminal prosecution.

In addition to participation in the lineup itself, a suspect may also be required to perform certain tasks, such as walking, talking, putting on clothing, removing clothing, gesturing in a particular manner, etc. Of course, the other members in the lineup must be made to perform the identical tasks. In addition, samples of such things as the suspect's blood, hair, voice, and handwriting may be taken, along with his fingerprints, footprints, and palmar surfaces, without violating his constitutional rights, which are said to apply only to testimonial evidence.

The use of fingerprints for identification purposes has long been held admissible in evidence, as has more recently the use of photographs. But the increasing utilization of such scientific evidence raises many issues yet to be determined, constitutional and otherwise. The U.S. Supreme Court has generally approved the use of such techniques, so long as their use is narrowly circumscribed. As late as 1972, the Supreme Court held that the compelled production of voice exemplars for spectrographic analysis did not violate the defendant's constitutional protections, thus clearing the way for the use of voiceprints in evidence. Each state is free to determine its own rules of evidence and many states have already accepted the use of voiceprints in court.

Investigators should insure that where more than one witness is required to view a lineup, that each witness views the lineup separately and any identifications that are forthcoming should be made separately so as to avoid comparisons of details by the witnesses. Of course it goes without saying that a written description of the suspect should be obtained from each witness prior to viewing the lineup.

Self-awareness

It must always be uppermost in the investigator's mind that everything said above concerns not only the way a witness perceives an event or thing, but also affects the perception of the investigator. He too is subject to perception-sets, to social and cultural taboos, and to contemporary environmental factors. He too is subject to physical ailments and impaired faculties. He too is a creature of deep-rooted prejudices.

The police officer all too often is conditioned to see life exclusively in terms of black and white, right and wrong, good and bad, innocence and guilt. A youth with long hair is probably a drug user; a black is a social militant; a lawyer is a crook. Reformists are bleeding-heart liberals; exponents of rehabilitation are coddlers; police unions are pawns of left-wing subversives whose activities are directed from a foreign shore.

Investigators must guard against such mind-sets. They

must strive to recognize and to accept their own human weaknesses, and to pursue objectivity and detachment in the performance of their duties.

Consider the following incident that occurred in one of the author's classrooms: The author was lecturing to a class of some fifty students, at least thirty of whom were law enforcement officers, when the door suddenly burst open and a particularly irate young man exploded into the room at precisely 8:15 P.M.

The dialogue that followed went something like this:

"What class is this, mister?" the intruder demanded.

"Fundamentals of Criminal Investigation. May I help you?"

"If your name's Greg Metter then you're the one who's gonna need the help."

"Are you threatening me, young man?"

"If you're the crud that gave me that stinking W-F, I damn sure am. This is my last quarter and now those twerps over at the registrar's office say I can't graduate."

"Well I'm sorry about that, but it certainly isn't my fault—"

"The hell you say! Now don't you go tryin' to weasel out of it with those oily words of yours. I know what a cunning linguist you are. In my opinion you're nothing but a lousy pedagogue—"

"Listen, son, I'll talk to you about this after class—"

"Don't call me son, you pernicious perigrinator! Or I'll take you outside and fix your dastardly clock!"

At this point in the young man's outburst, which had lasted no more than sixty seconds, Officer Barbarella invited the intruder to leave by saying: "Get the hell out of here, you turd."

"Yes, please leave now," said the instructor politely. "We are trying to complete our class on the fundamentals of criminal investigation with an emphasis on observation and identification."

"I don't give a good damn what you're tryin' to do, you demented, asinine—"

"I told you to get outa here, turd."

The intruder paid no heed to the growling officer, but rather continued to berate the defenseless instructor with a string of odd crudities that appeared to wound the instructor with their pertinency.

Officer Barbarella, however, could brook no further public exercise of the constitutional freedom of speech. He rose to his feet, badge gleaming on his broad chest, hefting a crippling weight of "heat" on his right hip, and exited from the classroom —preceded, as it were, by the hapless intruder who was flapping precariously on the business end of a deftly executed wrist-lock.

By the time the instructor could get outside and come to his frantic colleague's assistance, Officer Barbarella had the young psychology instructor toe dancing like a cat burglar up the side of the building wall.

Of course the incident had been staged and rehearsed well in advance. The only oversight was that it was a two-man script; no allowance had been made for Officer Barbarella's impromptu audition.

As soon as the instructor re-established control over the class, it was immediately assigned the task of preparing a complete, detailed, eyewitness incident report of the entire transaction. It might prove informative as well as interesting to compare some of their observations.

Actual Description of Intruder	Composite Description of Class
White male	Boy
6'5"	6'1"
190 pounds	130–245 pounds
Age 26	Age 18–20
Dark brown hair, bushy, collar length	Brown shoulder-length Afro

Actual Description of Intruder	Composite Description of Class
Small, close-set brown eyes	(Apparently no eyes)
Fair complexion	(No race, color, or creed)
Tan suede coat	Brown corduroy coat
Open, white flowered print sport shirt	White shirt and tie
Blue flared dacron slacks	Levi's
Brown zippered boots	(Apparently bare-footed)
Pronounced southern accent	Lower middle-class to poor white trash

Actual crimes committed	Class indictments
None	Trespass
	Illegal entry
	Indecent assault
	Libel and slander
	Criminal conversa-tion

Definitions according to modern dictionary usage:

crud   disparaging vernacular epithet
twerp   disparaging vernacular epithet
turd   disparaging vernacular epithet
cunning linguist   a person who uses language with crafted eloquence
pedagogue   teacher or schoolmaster
perigrinator   incessant traveler
demigod   a mythological being with more power than a man but less than a god.

Composite class narrative of incident:

Subject entered classroom anywhere from 8:10 to 8:45 and began to browbeat the cowering instructor with abusive language. Said if instructor's name was Grog Meddle he was going to need his cock fixed later outside. Called instructor a crud, a turd, a bastard, a preverted [sic] cunnilinguist and a goddamned demigod, among other flagrant irregularities. Subject was ejaculated from the class by Officer Barberossa.

It should be noted that only one student came to the defenseless instructor's assistance. The others withheld action apparently in hopes that the subject intruder would punch the cunning instructor in his cruddy mouth.

The entire class flunked the exercise.

(The instructor lost a friend in the psychology department.)

A humorous incident, yes. Staged, yes. Unrealistic in observation response? No. It is precisely such misapprehension of observed phenomena as this that the criminal investigator (if not the college student) must guard against. He must be aware of his own tendencies toward misapprehension, as well as those of others.

It is sufficiently difficult to accurately describe a person one has seen casually, or even intimately, over a long period of time. It is immeasurably more difficult to describe a person one has observed for only a matter of minutes or even seconds.

For example, consider this instance of a bank robbery that occurred some years ago in a southern metropolitan city. A lone bandit passed a holdup note to a teller and in less than sixty seconds had joined his accomplice who was waiting outside in the getaway car. They had robbed the bank of more than four thousand dollars.

The subsequent investigation led the police to the perpetrators, and both men were arrested within thirty-six hours with more than thirty-seven hundred dollars still in their possession, including two hundred dollars in marked bait money handed out by the alert teller. Prosecution and conviction should have been simple.

The perpetrators were eventually convicted, but it was not simple nor without embarrassment. From photographs of the suspects the bank teller positively identified the man who had remained outside in the getaway car as the one who had passed her the note!

Generally, descriptions will vary in direct proportion to the number of witnesses involved. The investigator must know how to help witnesses remember what they have seen. The key factor in identifications is association. The witness must be encouraged to compare physical characteristics with a standard of measurement. Who did the suspect look like; was he as tall as so-and-so; were his eyes as blue as Paul Newman's?

There are six important basic elements of physical description: age, height, weight, peculiarities, clothing, and facial features. See Fig. 10.2 for a sampling of facial characteristics that the criminal investigator must use and understand in perfecting his own descriptive powers and in assisting witnesses.

In addition to such facial characteristics as shown in Fig. 10.2, such items as hairstyle; forehead width and slope; eyebrow shape and eye size; nose line, width and base; ear size, shape, and relation to the head; lip width and thickness; mouth size; and chin shape, length, and slope must all be considered. Any visible scars and marks should of course be noted.

It is the unique combination of all such individual facial and body characteristics that makes one person look different from all others, or similar to someone else. By carefully questioning witnesses as to such aspects of a suspect's appearance, the investigator will have a better likelihood of deriving a working description of the suspect in question. A true likeness, mind you, occurs only in rare instances. But at least it is a starting place. The important thing is for the investigator to remember that that is *all* it is: a starting place.

HEAD SHAPE

ROUND   BULGING BACK   FLAT BACK

FLAT TOP   EGG SHAPED   POINTED

FACE SHAPE

ROUND   RECTANGULAR   OVAL   BROAD

LONG   FULL   TRIANGULAR   TRIANGULAR   SQUARE

Fig. 10.2 Facial characteristics

INTERROGATIONS

An interrogation is the questioning of a suspect or a reluctant witness, the nature of which is more adversarial than that used in a nonadversarial witness interview. Information is more difficult to obtain from a suspect, therefore the investigator's skill must be of a higher order. Many of the same techniques, principles, and human implications, however, are as applicable to interrogations as to interviews.

Since the interrogation process is of an adversarial nature, the legal restrictions are greater than in the procedure relating to interviews—and for good reasons.

Historically, in America and elsewhere, police have imaginatively employed force and terror tactics as a routine adjunct to their interrogation techniques. Experience has shown that such "third degree" tactics are not merely the creative discoveries of novelists and filmmakers, but rather the warp and woof of everyday police reality. Only in recent years has a body of legal decision been forthcoming that is designed to halt such sordid infringements on the collective constitutional rights of our citizenry. Perhaps no other aspect of the criminal justice system, save the issue of capital punishment, is more likely to engender heated emotional debate than is a discussion of the U.S. Supreme Court's rulings in this vital area of law enforcement.

The leading case of *Miranda* v. *Arizona*, and others, will be discussed at length in the following chapter dealing with confessions, admissions, and written statements. It is only necessary to make here a clear enunciation of what the law presently requires of a criminal investigator who is called upon to question a person suspected of having committed a crime.

Pursuant to the *Miranda* decision, prior to interrogating a suspect or any person who is significantly deprived of his freedom, an investigator must:

1. identify himself and inform the suspect of the general nature of the offense

2. advise the suspect that he does not have to answer questions, but that any answers he does give may be used against him

3. inform him that he has the right to legal counsel of his own choosing and is entitled to have such counsel present prior to and during periods of questioning

4. tell him that if he desires such counsel yet cannot afford to retain a lawyer, the state will appoint counsel at no expense to him.

It is crucial to understand that the *Miranda* ruling only prevents the *interrogation* of suspects; it has no bearing at all upon statements *voluntarily* furnished by suspects in custody. Suspects are not prevented from talking, if they so desire; police, however, are prevented from interrogating unless the above warning has been given, acknowledged by the suspect, and his right to remain silent is waived accordingly.

What constitutes a waiver of a suspect's rights? The burden of proving such a waiver is always on the state. It must be shown in clear, unequivocal terms that the suspect was advised of his rights, that he understood them, and that such **rights** were knowledgeably and voluntarily waived. Any evidence indicating the use of tricks, threats, or coercion of any kind will invalidate any confession, admission, or statement subsequently given by the suspect. Ideally, the suspect's waiver should be written, dated, signed, and witnessed.

The primary object of interrogation is not, as is often supposed, to obtain a confession from a suspect. It is rather to obtain information. Information gained by the exercise of the technique of interrogation may be classified as a confession, or admission, or as a statement. Each of these classifications will be independently discussed in the following chapter. Suffice it to say at this point that a confession is an acknowledgment of guilt, whereas an admission is an incriminating statement that indicates but falls short of acknowledging guilt, and a statement is simply a declaration of facts concerning the case under investigation or even concerning extraneous matter.

Such information may very well establish innocence as

well as guilt. It may be decisive in preventing the filing of charges in a given case or indeed in the avoidance of an unwarranted arrest action. It may be used primarily to develop leads, to locate physical evidence, to aid in the investigation of other crimes, and for many other like purposes unrelated directly to the proof of guilt of any particular suspect.

Procedure

How should an interrogation of a suspect be conducted in a modern democratic society? It is not a simple question to answer. Police manuals and texts on the art and science of criminal investigation have traditionally counseled an array of tactics that, according to such sources, have proven effective in the past. And perhaps there is no reason to suppose that such tactics would not prove successful today and in the future. What are some of these recommended tactics?

Initially, the investigator should thoroughly acquaint himself with all background information available on the subject prior to interrogation. Such information is developed from police records and all other sources of information available to the investigator. Statistics clearly indicate that many criminals are repeat offenders. They not only have extensive records, but also are well-known personally to large numbers of police officers. An investigator on a current case should confer with officers who have had previous contact with the suspect, regarding his character and personality, including his weaknesses and strengths, *modus operandi*, and any significant details that might be advantageous to the investigator during the interrogation.

The factor of absolute control over the interrogation, psychologically as well as physically, is uniformly urged. Privacy is suggested as the best means of obtaining such dominance over the suspect to be interrogated. The investigator's office is commonly regarded as the best location to afford such privacy. The room should be simply furnished and softly lighted. Ideally, there should be a two-way mirror to enable investigators to observe the suspect outside the room without his knowledge, and the room should be wired so that the suspect may be surreptitiously recorded and overheard. Under such circumstances, the suspect should be adequately deprived of every psychological advantage. He is without family, friends, or counsel to lend moral and legal support. Every advantage is on the side of the interrogator, and the atmosphere is overwhelmingly authoritarian.

The investigator is further exorted to exude confidence, positiveness, and perseverance. He must use every strategy short of physical force to persuade the suspect to cooperate by giving the desired responses. He is counseled to use such stratagems as kindness, compassion, and sympathy. Where these are unsuccessful, however, he must be equally adept in the use of deception and appeals to the emotions. In the tougher cases, he must be relentlessly persistent, without, however, resorting to duress or coercion.

It should be of no great surprise that such tactics have met in the past with a certain degree of *pro forma* success. The Court of Star Chamber, as we have seen, was also not without its successes. And there are similar "success stories" of a more recent vintage in our own country and in others.

These, then, are some, a few, of the techniques and stratagems to be used by the police interrogator—*if* the desired goal of an interrogation of a suspect is solely a confession of guilt at any cost save physical violence. The matter of confessions will be discussed at length in the following chapter.

1. *What is the distinction between an interview and an interrogation?*

2. *What is the primary objective of an interview/interrogation?*

3. *What is the most important qualification of an interviewer?*

4. *Why should a criminal investigator possess a broad liberal education background in addition to whatever specialized knowledge he possesses?*

5. *What role does psychology play in the interview/interrogation process?*

6. *What general factors should the investigator consider prior to conducting an interrogation?*

11

• Confessions, Admissions, and Written Statements

The interview and interrogation process is not an end in itself. In this regard, the medium is not the message. The goal is, or, as we have suggested, should be, the desire to obtain information. And not just *any* information, but information that will stand as admissible evidence in a court of law.

The information that is obtained by the interview-interrogation technique will be supplied by persons who fall into a variety of categories such as: a victim of a crime; a witness to a crime; a perpetrator of a crime; a suspect; or a witness with general background knowledge helpful to the investigation. The character of the individual supplying such information, then, will determine the category of the information itself.

A confession is an acknowledgment of guilt. "Yes, I killed her. I am the murderer."

An admission is an incriminating statement that indicates guilt but that falls short of a confession. "Yes, I was in her apartment last night. We had some drinks and there was an argument."

A statement is a declaration of facts or opinion, which may or may not be applicable to the case under investigation, made by a person who may or may not have any personal connection with the case. "She was a fine girl. I used to hear them arguing and would wonder why she would put up with such an unpleasant man."

Formal Written Statements

Confessions, admissions, and statements should be reduced to writing whenever possible. Such formal written statements should be obtained under the same procedural limitations as those that apply to the conduct of interrogations. Such statements must be freely and voluntarily given, of course, and a written and witnessed waiver to this effect is always to be desired.

The content of such statements to a considerable extent is dependent upon the questions put to the examinee by the investigator in the interview or the interrogation. It is by his direction that much irrelevant and immaterial information may be excluded. Witnesses, victims, and suspects alike have a tendency to ramble; the investigator must deftly control such tendencies.

The methods of reducing the statement to writing will vary according to the prevailing circumstances. Many factors may be taken into consideration, such as the attitude of the person giving the statement, his intelligence, temperament, cooperativeness; the nature and quantity of the information to be recorded; the physical accommodations of the place in which the statement is being developed; the capabilities of the investigator in such matters as typing skill, linguistics, and the like; and the availability of stenographic assistance and/or mechanical recording devices.

The day is quite likely not too far distant when all criminal investigators will carry pocket-sized electronic recording devices with which to reduce instantaneously all oral statements, confessions, and admissions to a record. Such a capability will obviously be an advance in operational efficiency, but whether or not it will serve to advance the cause of justice remains to be seen.

Will Rogers, the late American humorist, once observed that anyone who believes that civilization has advanced is an egotist. It might not be too much of an exaggeration to suggest that law enforcement cannot claim to have advanced significantly so long as the expediency of solving crime by confession continues to play a major role in the criminal investigation process.

Not that the use of the confession is without historical precedent. The Caesars, the kings and queens of antiquity, the Popes, and the Inquisitors have all relied eagerly upon the confession as a means of controlling socially aberrant behavior. And in this respect, history has taught us moderns well. Today, millions of helpless people the world over are being crushed and brutalized by the use of confessions extorted by torture, deceitfulness, and trickery. Technology has shrunk the highways of the world so that the likes of Brazilia, Lisbon, Belfast, Athens, Moscow, Saigon, Peking, and Havana are little more than commuter suburbs of Washington, D.C. We can no longer turn our backs on the atrocities committed throughout the world, and at home, in the name of justice.

We may grant that most modern American police agencies seek confessions out of a sincere desire to solve crime and do not engage in the overt use of violence and torture. But the question remains—should confessions, however obtained, serve primarily as the basis for a charge or a conviction in a criminal case? And further, given the nature and atmosphere of the criminal interrogation process, is it possible to obtain *any* confession freely and voluntarily without the use of duress or coercion? Isn't it possible that the interrogation of any suspect under police control in an authoritarian atmosphere constitutes duress?

We have seen that, according to the instructions of the police manuals by which such interrogations are to be conducted, every opportunity is to be taken, planned in advance, that is calculated to make the suspect as physically uncomfortable as possible and as psychologically disadvantaged as the investigator's experience and ability will allow. Under such circumstances, is there anything free and voluntary about *any* information provided by the suspect?

The value of confessions, historically, may have been vastly overrated. Just solutions to crime are rarely dependent upon confessions. A modern professional police agency relies little, if at all, upon the expediency of the confession. Professional law enforcement relies upon evidence that is subject to proof in court. A confession is not hard evidence per se; it does not *prove* the matters to which it refers. Confessions are usually conclusive only in cases in which the police already possess overwhelming evidence of the suspect's guilt.

It has been suggested that police can more wisely spend

their time and effort investigating rather than interrogating. The pursuit of objective evidence by using the latest scientific methods of criminal investigation is a far superior technique of solving crime than is the intensive interrogation of custodial suspects.

A case in point occurred in New York City in 1964. Two young female roommates were murdered, and a nineteen-year-old suspect confessed to the crime. In fact, the suspect confessed before news cameras in a police-arranged interview wherein a sixty-page signed confession was exhibited to the media. Along with the confession was a photograph that the police *said* was a picture of one of the dead girls and that was found on the suspect at the time of his arrest. Although the suspect subsequently repudiated his confession, it was not until a year had elapsed that a new suspect was inadvertently arrested for the same murders. Closer investigation then established the fact that the original suspect possessed an IQ of sixty, that he was interrogated extensively without the benefit of an attorney's advice and would have "confessed" to virtually any crime that had been forced upon him, and that the damning photograph in his possession at the time of his arrest was *not* a picture of the murdered girl after all.

The first suspect was released by New York authorities, and the second suspect was then tried and convicted, one must *suppose* upon valid credible evidence gathered by the criminal investigators handling the case.

Such mishandling of criminal investigations have wide-ranging repercussions that lead not only to citizen suspicion of police operations in general, but also to legislative and judicial restrictions upon investigative procedures. And there can be little doubt that such cases have been a major factor in the disfavor of capital punishment in recent years.

Of course it is now widely argued, especially in police circles, that recent decisions of the U.S. Supreme Court have so restricted the police investigator in his dealings with the criminal suspect, that the question of the use of confessions is a moot point in any event. The police have been so hamstrung by the courts, according to this argument, that every advantage is now with the criminal violator. It should be of considerable value for the criminal investigator and the student to obtain a thorough understanding of the body of law applicable to this controversial and utterly crucial aspect of the criminal investigative process.

In 1972 the U.S. Supreme Court finally brought the letter of the law into line with the spirit of the law. In the case of *Argersinger* v. *Hamlin*, 407 U.S. 25, the Court held that the Sixth Amendment to the U.S. Constitution, by reason of the Fourteenth Amendment, was applicable to the states. Therefore, the assistance of legal counsel was assured to every citizen charged with a crime in which a jail sentence of *any* length of time might be imposed upon conviction. Historically, such was not always the case.

In fact, the courts required the passage of many years in which to broaden the application of the Sixth and Fourteenth Amendments by way of a series of carefully limited decisions. In 1932, in a famous (or infamous) Alabama rape case, popularly known as the *Scottsboro Boys Case*, 287 U.S. 45, the Supreme Court ultimately guaranteed a lawyer in cases in which life was at stake. In a 1963 case, *Gideon* v. *Wainwright*, 372 U.S. 335, the Court extended the rule to include all felony cases. And it was not until the 1972 case of *Argersinger* v. *Hamlin* that the Court went further still to include *any* case involving a *potential* jail sentence of *any* length of time.

But exactly at what point in the proceeding is the accused entitled to the benefit of legal counsel? In the 1959 case of *Spano* v. *New York*, 360 U.S. 315, the Court ruled inadmissible a confession extracted from the defendant after a prolonged and persistent interrogation without the presence of his attorney. Then in a landmark case, *Escobedo* v. *Illinois*, 378 U.S. 478 (1964), the Court extended the defendant's right to counsel to include the interrogation room as well as the courtroom. A thorough examination of the landmark case of *Miranda* v. *Arizona* (1966) will follow subsequently.

What we have seen thus far is the development of the law concerning the right of all persons, irrespective of financial status, to have the assistance of legal counsel from the very

moment of arrest, during the interrogation process, and throughout the trial procedure. Such rulings have placed clear restrictions on the police in the areas of interrogation, admissions, and
confessions. These restrictions are designed not to hamper police work, but rather to safeguard the rights and liberties of all
citizens.

Of course, the injustices of the *Scottsboro* cases were not
the first of their kind, nor will the lack of due process in the
initial *Escobedo* trial be the last of such abuses. There really
isn't much new or unusual about any of these cases. Consider,
if you will, this extrapolated report of an earlier criminal proceeding of considerable historical and judicial importance.

The incident occurred some years ago in a large capital city
well-known throughout the world. The government charged the
defendant with having conspired with others to violate the law
of the land. It was clearly a political charge in nature, but effective as to the purposes of the government involved. The defendant was a peaceful, nonviolent man—a pacifist, if you will.
He refused to countenance war, cruelty, or injustice. An unprejudiced man, he believed that all men, irrespective of race,
color, or creed should enjoy the equal application and protection of the law.

Admittedly, he was an agitator, a social activist, and an
orator who could command the minds and emotions of the
masses. He was generally an unpleasant, antiestablishment figure, with his long hair and beard and simple mode of dress. And
he made no secret of his association with known criminals and
members of the counterculture. The government was angered
and intimidated by the continued success of his speeches. In
time, the defendant's message began to have a disrupting effect
on the government's conduct of its domestic and foreign policies.

The final conflict occurred between them during the height
of a great march on the capital city. Hundreds of thousands of

citizens had assembled to present their grievances once and for all to the ruling powers. Now the defendant was not exactly their leader; he was, however, their major spokesman. So the government decided, for reasons of security, that it was too dangerous to allow him to speak freely under such volatile circumstances. They determined on the expedient of "preventive arrest."

But they didn't know exactly where the defendant was at the moment; he was named and identified, but his precise location was as yet unknown to the authorities. Finally, after much investigation through normal sources of information, a paid informant advised the authorities where the defendant was staying. That same night, without a warrant, arguably without probable cause, a uniformed contingent of officers arrested him.

Of course there was a great protest. His people didn't want to let him go; they far outnumbered the arresting officers, and a potential riot was in the making. But the defendant, true to his pacific tendencies, cautioned his followers not to resort to violence. He voluntarily submitted to arrest.

He was immediately taken before the court. He was not arraigned, he was not asked to plead one way or the other, nor was he allowed witnesses in his favor. The administration of justice was swift, sure, and final. He was charged with treason and sedition, tried summarily, convicted, and sentenced to death.

The sentence was appealed and upheld.

The legal implications involved in the case were these:

1. The defendant, when accused of a crime, offered no defense and did not take the stand in his own behalf.

2. An informant testified against the defendant, and his testimony was not contradicted by the accused. Instead, the latter chose to remain silent. (In many of our jurisdictions today, silence under such circumstances still may be used as evidence of guilt.)

3. Although the defendant had not been advised of his rights, had not been arraigned, and had no access to the advice of counsel, he was nevertheless interrogated in open court. When asked by the judge if he was guilty as charged, his only reply was: "Thou sayest it."

The death sentence was carried out with dispatch, and the defendant was executed by crucifixion.

The Founding Fathers certainly had sufficient precedent upon which to base their inclusion of the Bill of Rights when framing the U.S. Constitution, by which all citizens were granted the equal protection of the laws. Has a defendant more innocent of the charges against him ever been railroaded at the bar of justice than the subject of the foregoing case? It has been suggested, though not that unanimously approved, that in a democracy it is better to let countless guilty persons go free rather than to risk the unjust conviction of a single citizen.

In this connection, let us now make a rather extended historical jump from the case of one Jesus of Nazareth to that of Ernest Miranda versus the State of Arizona.

MIRANDA v. *ARIZONA,*
384 U.S. 436 (1966)

Issues raised in this case penetrate to the very roots of the American concepts of criminal jurisprudence. Broadly stated, the Court was concerned with the restraints that society must observe pursuant to the U.S. Constitution in prosecuting an individual for the commission of a crime. Specifically, the Court dealt with the admissibility of statements obtained by interrogation from a suspect under police custody and the necessity for adhering to certain minimum procedures that insure that the individual is accorded his rights under the Fifth Amendment to the Constitution not to be compelled to incriminate himself.

Ernest Miranda and three young companions were arrested and charged with the crime of rape. All of the defendants were interrogated for varying lengths of time, separately, under controlled authoritarian circumstances. Miranda eventually signed a confession, and the other three defendants signed inculpatory statements. Miranda, an indigent Mexican-American, was found to be a seriously disturbed individual with pronounced sexual fantasies and another defendant was an indigent black who had dropped out of school in the sixth grade. All four defendants were tried and found guilty by a jury.

The case was appealed, and the U.S. Supreme Court ultimately reversed the convictions. The Court held that any person accused of a crime must be clearly advised that he does not have to answer questions asked by police while in their custody, and that anything he does say can be used against him in a court of law. The Court further held that such a person is entitled to have a lawyer and that if he cannot afford one, counsel will be provided at government expense. The Court found the facts to be uncontroverted that none of the defendants had been so warned of his constitutional rights and accordingly reversed the convictions.

The rationale of the Court's decision was as follows: The specific wording of the U.S. Constitution requires nothing less than what the Court has ordered. "No person shall be compelled in any criminal case to be a witness against himself," and "the accused shall have the Assistance of Counsel." In the words of Chief Justice John Marshall, these precious rights were fixed in our Constitution "for ages to come" (*Cohens* v. *Virginia,* 6 Wheat, 264, 387 [1821]).

The Court's ruling in the *Miranda* case, in summary, was as follows:

> . . . the prosecution may not use statements, whether exculpatory or inculpatory, stemming from custodial interrogation of the defendant unless it demonstrates the use of procedural safeguards effective to secure the privilege against self-incrimination. By custodial interrogation, we mean questioning initiated by law enforcement officers after a person has been taken into custody or otherwise deprived of his freedom of action in any significant way. As for the procedural safeguards to be employed, unless other fully effective means are devised to inform

accused persons of their right of silence and to assure a continuous opportunity to exercise it, the following measures are required. Prior to any questioning, the person must be warned that he has a right to remain silent, that any statement he does make may be used as evidence against him, and that he has a right to the presence of an attorney, either retained or appointed. The defendant may waive effectuation of these rights, provided the waiver is made voluntarily, knowingly, and intelligently. If, however, he indicates in any manner and at any stage of the process that he wishes to consult with an attorney before speaking, there can be no questioning. Likewise, if the individual is alone and indicates in any manner that he does not wish to be interrogated, the police may not question him. The mere fact that he may have answered some questions or volunteered some statements on his own does not deprive him of the right to refrain from answering any further inquiries until he has consulted with an attorney and thereafter consents to be questioned.

The Court went on to discuss its findings in depth. The facts of the case established that all four of the defendants were interrogated in an incommunicado, police-dominated atmosphere and subsequently produced self-incriminating statements without having been given full warnings of their constitutional rights. The Court felt that the nature and setting of such custodial interrogation was the controlling aspect of its ruling. It reviewed a series of cases in which incommunicado police interrogations produced so-called confessions by resorting to physical brutality in the form of beatings, hangings, whippings, and the like. Although such cases dated as far back in American history as the 1930s, as late as 1961, the Commission on Civil Rights reported that a considerable body of evidence indicated that "some policemen still resort to physical force to obtain confessions."

The Court agreed that such cases were now the exception rather than the rule but felt strongly that unless proper limitations were affixed to custodial interrogations, there could be no assurance that such practices would not flourish again in the future. It was unacceptable, the Court said, to do justice by obtaining a proper result by irregular or improper means. The ends do not justify the means, particularly in the field of law enforcement.

Of particular interest to the student of criminal investigation is the Court's emphasis upon the psychological rather than the purely physical aspects of custodial interrogation. The Court clearly recognized that coercion can be mental as well as physical.

Police interrogation is calculatedly a private matter. Privacy results in secrecy that in turn results in minimal public or judicial knowledge as to what occurs in the interrogation room. The Court, however, reviewed at length and in great detail a variety of police manuals and textbooks that served as a rich source of information concerning past and recommended police practices in this regard. The Court felt that by considering such data, since it was used by law enforcement agencies themselves as guides to the most enlightened and effective police techniques, it was possible to obtain an understanding of current procedures in use throughout the country.

Initially, the Court remarked upon the emphasis in such texts and manuals of the element of privacy. It cited from one text as follows:

> If at all practicable, the interrogation should take place in the investigator's office or at least in a room of his own choice. The subject should be deprived of every psychological advantage. In his own home he may be confident, indignant, or recalcitrant. He is more keenly aware of his rights and more reluctant to tell of his indiscretions or criminal behavior within the walls of his home. Moreover, his family and other friends are nearby, their presence lending moral support. In his own office, the investigator possesses all the advantages. The atmosphere suggests the invincibility of the forces of the law.*

* Charles E. O'Hara, *Fundamentals of Criminal Investigation* (Springfield, Ill.: Charles C Thomas, 1956).

Such tactics, the Court said, were designed to put the subject in a psychological condition in which his statement is nothing more than a confirmation of what his interrogators already know—that he is guilty of the offense under investigation. Any explanation that might indicate innocence is actually discouraged at this point.

The Court further noted the stress placed upon the patience and perseverance of the interrogator by quoting from the same text as follows:

> In the preceding paragraphs emphasis has been placed on kindness and stratagems. The investigator will, however, encounter many situations where the sheer weight of his personality will be the deciding factor. Where emotional appeals and tricks are employed to no avail, he must rely on an oppressive atmosphere of dogged persistence. He must interrogate steadily and without relent, leaving the subject no prospect of surcease. He must dominate his subject and overwhelm him with his inexorable will to obtain the truth. He should interrogate for a spell of several hours, pausing only for the subject's necessities in acknowledgment of the need to avoid a charge of duress that can be "technically" substantiated. In a serious case, the interrogation may continue for days, with the required intervals for food and sleep, but with no respite from the atmosphere of domination. It is possible in this way to induce the subject to talk without resorting to duress or coercion. This method should be used only when the guilt of the subject appears highly probable.

The Court also found that such texts and manuals recommended that the suspect be offered legal excuses, or at the least, mitigating circumstances, for his actions in order to obtain an admission of guilt. The investigator might say something like "I know you didn't plan to kill her in advance, Snookie. But when you caught her in bed with Joe Stud and she began to taunt you, and Joe laughed in your face, why, you just couldn't help yourself. And it was under those circumstances that you shot and killed the two of 'em, right Snookie?"

When such techniques prove unsuccessful, the Court found that the investigator was then urged to alternate this more-or-less buddy-buddy approach with a show of some hostility. The "Mutt and Jeff" act requires that one investigator, "Mutt," contends that he knows the suspect is guilty and will waste no time with any pussy-footing questions. He wants a confession and that's all there is to it. There will be no deals, no cooperation, no leniency. The suspect will either talk or they will "throw the book at him."

"Jeff," on the other hand, is a kindly soul. He understands human nature; everyone is weak, everyone is susceptible to a mistake. He wouldn't want to see a member of his own family mistreated by a "hot head" like his partner "Mutt." If the suspect will cooperate, "Jeff" will intercede for him in every way possible, but he can't control "Mutt" much longer, and the suspect must make up his mind without undue delay. It should be noted that "Jeff" is always present during "Mutt's" aggressive tirade and is visibly upset by his partner's tactics. "Mutt" is never present, however, when "Jeff" delivers his compassionate appeal for the suspect's cooperation.

The Court further found that many police manuals and texts often encourage the use of trickery and other deceptive stratagems, such as false legal advice and promises of assistance that are beyond the investigator's authority to make and his power to deliver.

The Court held that even without the use of brutality or any of the above techniques, the very fact of custodial interrogation exacts a heavy toll on individual liberty and trades on the weakness of individuals. Nor is it uncommon for interrogation procedures to succeed in fostering false confessions. Since the interrogation environment is created for no purpose other than to subjugate the individual to the will of his examiner, unless adequate protective devices are employed, the Court felt that no statement obtained from a suspect under such conditions can truly be the product of his free will. The compelling atmosphere of the interrogation procedure, not an independent decision on the suspect's part, caused him to speak.

The Court announced loudly and clearly, then, that it is

well settled that the Fifth Amendment privilege is available outside of criminal court proceedings and serves to protect persons in all settings in which their freedom of action is significantly curtailed from being compelled to incriminate themselves. And the burden of proof rests upon the government to show uncontrovertedly that the suspect was aware of such rights.

It is not sufficient for the government to contend that the suspect did not request a lawyer prior to police interrogation. Failure to ask for a lawyer in no way constitutes a waiver of a suspect's constitutional rights. It must be shown that he was clearly advised of such rights. The accused who does not know his rights, said the Court, may be the person who most needs counsel. That the accused knowingly and intelligently waived his privilege against self-incrimination and his right to counsel, is the burden imposed by the Court upon the prosecution.

Most importantly for the criminal justice student or police officer, the Court made it clear that its decision was in no way intended to hamper or tie the hands of police in the investigation of crime. On the contrary, it was intended to assist the police in a more professional execution of their duties. That the ruling has done exactly this is more or less evident by a careful reading of the entire, rather tutorial decision of the Court. One is forced to wonder, however, how many police officers have troubled themselves to read the decision. From the tenor of executive and administrative pronouncements from the police hierarchy—state, federal, and local—in the years following the ruling, it seems unlikely that many high police officials have a very clear understanding of the philosophical and practical purport of the decision.

Just how has the *Miranda* ruling affected the art of interrogation and the status of custodial response? Apparently, very little. To a large extent it has been pretty much ignored as a practical matter, both by police and citizen alike. The most significant effect has been vocal condemnation and dire warnings of disaster unless police hands are "untied." As far as the "street" is concerned, it has had little or no impact. If police have but slight evidence against a suspect, he keeps his mouth shut. If police have an abundance of solid evidence to back a charge, the suspect often confesses—with or without the benefit of legal counsel.

Studies have indicated that when the so-called *Miranda* warning is actually given by police—and it often is—it is done in such an off-hand or abusive manner that it has no meaning one way or another. Police officers have memorized the half dozen or so salient requirements of the ruling, and they spout it off while handcuffing a suspect or otherwise pursuing their normal police duties. Often they carry small 2-by-4-inch cards with the warning printed on the face and distribute these as if they were calling cards to citizens suspected of crime.

Likewise, there seem to have been as many confessions obtained by police after the *Miranda* ruling as before. Is there, perhaps, something about the condition of police arrest that all but guarantees some degree of suspect response in a considerable percentage of cases? It seems likely that there is indeed.

Rather than serving as a detriment to police investigation, there is ample reason to believe that the ruling, if implemented according to the spirit of the decision, would in fact assist police in becoming more professional in their investigations and therefore more successful. Many countries have completely abandoned the use of confessions many years ago. In such countries, interrogation of suspects, if used at all, is designed to elicit information, not confessions of guilt. That this distinction is not readily apparent to many American police officers is at the very heart of the problem.

Even the success of such U.S. police agencies that long ago voluntarily adopted operational guidelines similar to the requirements of the *Miranda* ruling has not served to inspire confidence in the majority of agencies that still refuse to modernize their approach. Nearly two decades prior to *Miranda*, the FBI conducted its investigations pursuant to similar standards, excepting only the guarantee of an attorney, which it did not have the authority to offer. In view of such voluntary warnings, the FBI then had to establish its cases by the development of solid, incontrovertible evidence. In order to gather such evidence, the Bureau had to remain abreast of every modern development in the art and science of criminal investigation. If it was unable, in spite of its highly professional methods, to obtain substantial evidence of guilt in a given case, it simply did not make an arrest.

More often than not, the Bureau makes an arrest only after an indictment by a federal grand jury. It should be noted that guilty pleas are entered in over 85 percent of all FBI cases, and over 95 percent of the cases that actually go on to trial result in a conviction. Clearly, cases that depend upon confessions obtained by intensive police interrogation cannot compare favorably with those based upon the collection of objective evidence.

Police spokesmen who continue to decry the "evils" of the *Miranda* decision should consider one additional fact of the matter. *Miranda* was never intended by the Court to apply to juvenile crime, nor have later rulings to date expanded such coverage. Therefore, the ruling cannot be said to have contributed to the drastic increase in juvenile crime in the years since the decision, and since the vast increase of *all* crimes during these years has unquestionably been attributed to juvenile offenders, then the *Miranda* case can in no way be held responsible for our present-day plight. It has not tied the police officer's hands in his war against crime. It has not opened the prison gates and released a tidal wave of criminals upon an unprotected society. It has merely instructed the police to conduct themselves according to the rules laid down long ago in the U.S. Constitution.

How many police officers realize that neither Ernest Miranda nor any of his codefendants walked free as a result of the Supreme Court's decision? All the Court said was that the confessions could not be used, that the interrogation procedures were unconstitutional. In fact, Miranda and the other defendants were retried on the same charges and all were either convicted or plead guilty. The police had gathered ample objective evidence—including the victim's positive identification—to substantiate the defendant's guilt without resort to the tainted confessions at all.

It is most important that the student and/or police officer should not be deluded by the import of the *Miranda* case. The significance of the ruling has been expanded—mostly by emotional rhetoric—far beyond its intrinsic value and general application. The decision merely restated rights of citizenship that we all possess by virtue of the Constitution. Its only real application, however, is to the segment of our society that is unaware of such rights, or cannot understand what they mean. The professional criminal understands his rights, as does the intelligent businessman, the politician, the famous, the wealthy, and the educated. None of these requires the warning of a police officer that he does not have to talk if he doesn't care to, that he is entitled to the services of an attorney. He *knows* all of this, and he will more often than not avail himself of all the rights to which he is entitled.

To whom does the *Miranda* rule then in fact apply? To the poor, the ignorant, the sick, and the retarded. They are simply reminded, or advised, perhaps for the first time, that the Constitution applies to them, too. And is this asking so much? Dare we ask anything less if democracy and justice are to exist in fact as well as in concept?

AFTER *MIRANDA*

Judicial erosion as well as practical disregard for the spirit of the *Miranda* decision set in almost immediately after it was handed down. First, the decision was held not to be retroactive to convictions in cases that were tried prior to June 13, 1966 (the date of the Court's *Miranda* ruling). Then, in the case of *Harris* v. *New York*, 401 U.S. 222 (1970), the Court by another 5–4 vote, held that in-custody statements, even though excluded by the *Miranda* rule from being used in court in the government's case in chief, could nevertheless be used by the prosecution to impeach the credibility of a defendant who has testified in his own behalf.

The majority held that such a ruling would not jeopardize the intention of the *Miranda* decision by encouraging impermissible conduct on the part of police officers. The novelty of this reasoning was delineated by the minority opinion that considered such use in court of otherwise incompetent evidence as a clear violation of the defendant's Fifth Amendment privilege against self-incrimination, as well as an invitation to police officers to abuse the procedural restrictions laid down in *Miranda*.

The *Miranda* ruling unhesitatingly (albeit by a 5–4 decision) proscribed the use, for *any* reason, of any incriminating statement without the full warning and effective waiver as set forth in the decision. The *Harris* ruling must have an undermining effect upon that objective. What it quite logically suggests to police is that they may interrogate an accused in violation of the *Miranda* ruling, knowing full well that the results cannot be used in the prosecution's case in chief, but hoping all the while that the defendant will exercise the constitutional effrontery of testifying in court in his own behalf, in which situation the results of such illegal interrogation may *then* be used to impeach his court testimony. The majority opinion in the *Harris* case might aptly be entitled: *Now You Have It* (constitutional protection) *And Now You Don't.*

In *Michigan* v. *Tucker*, 417 U.S. 433 (1973), the Court again modified *Miranda* by holding that testimony of a witness whose name was obtained by police by virtue of an improper interrogation of the defendant was properly admitted at trial. The Court thus drew a distinction between substantive violations of a defendant's Fifth Amendment rights and the mere failure of police to interrogate according to *Miranda* requirements. Such a ruling would appear to cast the *Miranda* requirements in the mold of mere guidelines rather than constitutional standards.

In yet another decision contracting the *Miranda* rule, the Court held in the 1975 robbery-murder case of *Michigan* v. *Mosley* that police may question suspects in some cases even after they have insisted upon their rights to remain silent.

In a 6–2 ruling, the murder conviction of the defendant Mosley was allowed to stand even though the defendant had undisputedly exercised his right to remain silent while being interrogated concerning the robbery under investigation. Some hours thereafter he was questioned by homicide officers concerning the murder and was tricked into confessing by using one of the oldest ploys in the book—he was told (falsely) by a detective that one of his friends had implicated him.

The defendant was convicted and sentenced to life imprisonment. A state court of appeals overturned the jury verdict, holding that the police had no right to question the defendant about the murder because he had elected to remain silent when initially questioned about the robberies.

In restoring the original conviction, the Supreme Court noted that the *Miranda* ruling did not specifically state under what circumstances, if any, a resumption of questioning is permissible after a defendant has once exercised his right to remain silent. The Court went so far as to suggest that *Miranda*, if extended to excessive lengths, might be taken literally to mean that such a defendant could never be questioned again by a police officer at any time and on any subject. This interpretation itself might be called "excessive," to say the least.

For more than three decades, the trend of the U.S. Supreme Court's decisions in the field of criminal law has been to interpret the U.S. Constitution in favor of citizen's rights as opposed to the ease of police investigations and government prosecution. This trend can be said to have culminated in the strict rules for custodial interrogation and the admission of confessions in court as announced in *Miranda* v. *Arizona*.

Can there be any question, however, that the pendulum of case law is now swinging the other way? How far it will extend is a matter of speculation. Practical considerations suggest themselves. Justice William O. Douglas is no longer a member of the Court. Justice Thurgood Marshall is ailing. In their dissenting opinion to the *Mosley* ruling, Justices William J. Brennan and Thurgood Marshall saw the decision as "yet another step toward the ultimate overruling of *Miranda*'s enforcement of the privilege against self-incrimination." Justice Byron R. White (one of the original anti-*Miranda* members of the Court) called for exactly that result in his concurring opinion.

Will *Miranda* stand?

Will individual rights prevail?

Will police pursue the path of professionalism or revert to the rule of expediency?

Whatever the courts do, police service is ultimately responsible for keeping its own house in order. It can voluntarily adhere to the rule of fairness and decency; it can place self-imposed limits of action upon itself; it can opt for professional objective-oriented investigations. Advantages in performance and public esteem would certainly outweigh any disadvantages attending the adoption of such standards.

• DISCUSSION QUESTIONS

1. *What role has the confession traditionally played in criminal investigation?*

2. *What is the status of the confession in modern criminal investigation? What role should it play?*

3. *What is the controlling case concerning the role of the confession in police investigations? What are its salient points? What effect has it had on modern police work?*

12

• *The Fourth Amendment: Arrest and Search and Seizure*

On the morning of September 9, 1956, a federal narcotics agent and a Denver police officer watched at the Denver Union Station as a young black male alighted from an incoming Chicago train and started walking rapidly out of the station. He was carrying a tan zipper bag in one hand, with the other thrust deeply into the pocket of his raincoat. The officers quickly overtook the man, stopped him, and placed him under arrest. Then they proceeded to search him. They found two envelopes containing an unknown quantity of heroin clutched in the hand inside his coat pocket and a hypodermic syringe in the tan zipper bag. The man was subsequently tried and convicted of knowingly concealing and transporting narcotic drugs. In part, his conviction was based upon the introduction in evidence of the two envelopes containing 865 grains of heroin and the syringe that had been taken from his person pursuant to his arrest. The Federal District Court found that the defendant was arrested without a warrant but with probable cause, and that the search and seizure were incident to a lawful arrest and therefore justified; the Court of Appeals affirmed the decision. On certiorari, the U.S. Supreme Court examined the facts upon which the case was made.

The arrest was determined to have been based primarily upon information supplied by a paid informer of past reliability. In early September, the informant had advised the federal narcotics agent that the defendant had recently "set up" in Denver and was "peddling narcotics to several addicts." A few days later, he advised the agent that the defendant had gone to

Chicago by train and would return with three ounces of heroin in his possession. He provided the agent with a detailed physical description of the defendant—"a young, light-brown Negro male, about 5′8″ and 160 pounds"—and of the clothing he would be wearing. He further advised that the defendant would be carrying a tan zipper bag and that he customarily "walked real fast." The Court found that the information provided by the informer had been reliable in the past and was accurate in this instance on all points. Was the arrest and subsequent search and seizure, therefore, legal?

The Court held in the affirmative. It found that the narcotics agent had every reason to believe that the information supplied by the informer would prove true in its entirety. After all, the agent had verified by sight everything the informer had told him concerning the incident, except whether or not the defendant actually had the heroin in his possession. It was reasonable under the circumstances to suppose that he did, and this was all that was required of the agent.

Under the law, said the Court, an agent is authorized to make an arrest without a warrant where the violation is committed in his presence or where he has reasonable grounds to believe that the person about to be arrested has committed or is committing such violation. The Court went on to point out that probable cause does not require certitude, that probable cause exists where the facts and circumstances within the arresting officer's knowledge are sufficient in themselves to warrant a person of reasonable caution to believe that an offense has been or is being committed.

It would seem, then, that the law of arrest and search and seizure is well settled in the U.S., and that law enforcement officers have merely to perform their duties according to the clarity of the law. Not so. Few areas of the law have been so exposed to the winds of shifting constitutional standards as that of search and seizure incidental to a lawful arrest.

Even though the arrest aspect of the problem has not been so troublesome as the subsequent search and seizure, the entire "transaction" is so closely intermeshed that it is expedient to consider the problem as a whole.

ARRESTS AND APPREHENSIONS

The authority of a law officer to make an arrest is governed by federal law and the state law in the jurisdiction where the arrest is contemplated. Generally, the police officer enjoys the same right to effect an arrest as does the private citizen. That is, he may make an arrest, with or without a warrant, for the commission of a felony or a breach of the peace committed in his presence, as well as for such an offense not committed in his presence but which has in fact been committed and for which he has reasonable cause to believe was committed by the person to be arrested. Neither citizen nor police officer has the authority to arrest for misdemeanors other than by a warrant.

Police arrest, then, is the act of taking an offender into official custody and imposing restraint upon him, coupled with the formal notification that he is under arrest. Physical restraint without notice of arrest may on occasion be employed. For example, police may detain a citizen for questioning, or hold one in protective custody. The British employ an interesting phrase for the act of all arrests: so-and-so, according to the public police announcements, is "helping with the investigation."

It is difficult to offer advice as to the manner in which an arrest should be executed. The circumstances of each case will determine the method to be used. Safety is the overriding concern of the arresting officer: the safety of innocent third parties, himself, and the person to be arrested. It bears restating that a successful arrest is one in which the suspect is taken into custody by the use of the minimum amount of force necessary, with as little personal injury and loss of life as is possible under the circumstances.

No arrest, therefore, should be a spur-of-the-moment operation if it can be avoided. Whenever possible, it should be planned in advance to include whatever assistance in personnel and material is necessary or helpful. The place and time of arrest should be determined by the officer in charge, not by circumstances. Alternative courses should be considered in light of the suspect's possible reaction to notification of arrest. Potential for violence and/or escape should always be minimized by the tactics of arrest.

Executing the Police Raid

Planning and preparation is the key element in all police raids. Such operations must be mounted with the forethought and attention to detail as one finds in a minor but important military operation. A police raid must be conducted with the utmost secrecy, speed, and superiority of manpower. The element of surprise is crucial more often than not.

What is the purpose of a police raid? Generally, it is to effect an apprehension of one or more individuals, and/or to obtain evidence of illegal activities, and/or to recover stolen property or contraband.

In order to be useful, a raid obviously must be conducted under color of legal authority, that is, upon the basis of a duly authorized search warrant, or a warrant of arrest, or both. The only other circumstance when a raid may be legally executed without the authority of a judicial warrant is when the operation is conducted by a team of officers acting in "hot pursuit" of a suspect reasonably believed to have perpetrated a felony that has in fact been committed.

Reflect for a moment upon the police raid on the motel room in the hypothetical multiple murder case previously discussed on page 69. The police had obtained a description of the perpetrators of the crime and of their automobile, as well as some digits of the license plate number. There was little or no question that the vehicle parked at the motel was the car that had been involved in the crime. The description of the room occupants given by the motel clerk matched the description of the men previously given by the woman survivor of the carnage in her family grocery store. There certainly was reasonable cause to believe that the killers were in the motel room. The sheriff, it will be remembered, argued for an immediate raid operation, in opposition to the state patrol's urging that the raid be delayed until a search warrant could be obtained. What, then, are the legal implications that should have been considered?

A felony had, in fact, been committed—not in the presence of the police officers, however. The controlling question is, was there reasonable cause to believe that the persons about to be arrested were the perpetrators of the felony?

In this situation, the answer is probably yes. But it was also a risk that was probably unnecessary and unwise to take. It does not require much delay in order to obtain a valid search warrant. Why jeopardize the entire case by taking such precipitous action?

Even in situations in which sufficient time is taken to obtain a valid warrant, opportunity for mistake abounds. Consider, for example, this recent case that occurred in a southern state. A couple was awakened in the dead of the night by a loud knock on their apartment door. The woman cracked the door on its chain lock, but before she could extract any identification, a police officer jammed his foot against the door and thrust a piece of paper at her which he claimed was a search warrant. Before the frightened woman's husband could reach the door, the officers kicked it in.

Six officers then burst into the apartment and began to manhandle the partially nude couple while shouting instructions at them. Then the officers proceeded to disassemble the astonished young couple's apartment. But after having almost totally demolished the apartment without finding any incriminating evidence of criminal activity, the officers realized the error of their ways, suspended the search, and departed as suddenly as they had appeared.

No explanation was forthcoming, no apologies, and no offer to pay damages since the raid was "legally" conducted in spite of the fact that the information upon which the warrant was issued was, in fact, erroneous.

If such miscalculations can occur even when at least procedural requirements are met, how much greater is the likelihood of error and injustice when police act without sufficient legal justification?

Raids, however, are a necessary function of criminal inves-

286 · CRIMINAL INVESTIGATION

tigations. It therefore bears repeating that the paramount concern in all such operations is the safety of the members of the team and of innocent third parties, including those persons who may be in the company of the suspect, yet are not believed to have any involvement with criminal activity. In this regard, the understatement often exhibited by our British counterparts in law enforcement should not pass unnoticed, especially in view of such an instance as the unfortunate midnight raid on the apartment of the young American couple.

On November 8, 1968, Scotland Yard investigators arrested the last suspect in connection with Britain's great train robbery of 1963 in which $7 million in bank notes was stolen. (Most of the money has yet to be recovered, see page 75.) Investigators rang the suspect's doorbell at 6:30 A.M., and when, in pajamas and bathrobe, he sleepily answered the call, they quietly informed him that he was under arrest. His wife was invited to join the group in the living room for several hours of "conversation" before the suspect was finally removed to police headquarters. News reports duly announced that the suspect was "helping police with the investigation."

In the U.S., however, relations between the police and the criminal element of our society are not governed by such genteel rules of etiquette. (Consider the televised "shoot-out" staged by the LAPD and the SLA revolutionists in May of 1974, witnessed electronically by most of the entire world.) Nevertheless, the police officer should attempt to execute an arrest with as much civility as the circumstances will allow.

Effecting the Arrest

He should identify himself at once by displaying his badge or credentials and then by notifying the suspect that he is under arrest. The arrest should be made in a firm, businesslike manner with no trace of equivocation. Once the decision has been made to arrest, there should be no doubt left in the suspect's mind as to the officer's intention or resolution. A preliminary search should then be accomplished, as thoroughly and as inconspicuously as the circumstances permit; a more complete search should be undertaken as soon as is practicable. At this point, the suspect should be advised of his constitutional rights and transported to an authorized place of detention.

It must be acknowledged that not every arrest can be executed as a matter of routine. The officer must be prepared for every eventuality, including defensive stratagems of deceit and trickery, physical and/or emotional collapse, and violence. Nor in reality can every arrest be carefully laid out in advance. After all, the police officer does have the authority, and the duty, to make arrests for felonies that occur in his presence or that he believes the suspect to have committed elsewhere. Still, he must make such arrests with the same concern for safety as is the case with more carefully planned and executed arrests; he simply has less lead time in deciding upon the best course of action.

Use of Force

Obviously, not every suspect is amenable to the idea of arrest. How much force, then, is permitted in making the arrest of a reluctant suspect? The answer is simply stated. Only that force that is necessary under the circumstances of the case. The answer, however, is not so simply resolved.

To a considerable extent, the issue of how much force is permissible in making a police arrest is controlled by the classification of the offense. In misdemeanor cases, the police officer is not permitted to use force that is likely to cause grave bodily harm in executing an arrest. Neither firearms or other weapons are justified in such cases, except in self-defense or in the defense of innocent third parties. It is difficult to counsel a police officer to tolerate resistance to a lawful arrest; however, it is more acceptable to allow a misdemeanant to escape than to inflict serious bodily harm. The suspect has simply made matters worse for himself—now he is chargeable for having resisted a lawful arrest, an offense that is in some states a felony in and of itself.

Of course in this event, the neat little situation arises that if resistance to a lawful arrest is a felony itself, then the police officer is at that point no longer seeking to arrest a misdemeanant but rather one who has committed a felony in the officer's presence. What degree of force is now permitted in effecting the arrest of a felon?

The general rule is that whatever amount of force is necessary to effect an arrest of a felon is permissible, including the use of deadly force. Such force may be used by the officer to prevent the felon's escape, to protect the safety of third parties, and in self-defense.

The control word here is *necessary*. The police officer may use such force as is necessary to accomplish the arrest. Merely because an officer is dealing with a felon does not of itself authorize the use of force in making the arrest. Every arrest should be made with the minimum amount of force necessary. Ideally, no force should be used if the apprehension is possible without it. Always, the use of force should be a last resort. This is one of the most important determinations a police officer has to make in a democratic society. It requires the exercise of mature judgment, often in moments of stress and of limited opportunity for reflection.

For example, should a police officer fire at a fleeing felon? Perhaps. But one must consider the circumstances. Suppose the felony having been committed was the crime of embezzlement or larceny of an item valued at fifty-one dollars. Or suppose the offense was the sale of an ounce and a half of marijuana. Or perhaps the suspect is wanted for armed robbery or for the shotgun slaying of his wife and her lover. In one instance, the fleeing felon is armed; in another, he is not. Are there not shades of culpability involved in such situations that would affect whether or not an officer would use force, and if so, to what degree in order to prevent the felon's escape?

Of course there are. And it is no simple matter to resolve, especially in the heat of the moment. Still, the police officer must make such decisions in the face of life and death implications. What he does will be determined by the quality of his training, education, and experience, and not in the least by his general philosophy of life.

As a general rule, no one tells the police officer when to strike with his club or when to fire his weapon. These are for the most part determinations he must make for himself. There is ample evidence to support the contention that police brutality and misconduct, verbal and physical, is generally directed toward members of the lower, less affluent classes of society, white and black alike.

Each police officer should examine his own character, therefore, in an effort to determine why this is so. He should also examine the performance of his fellow officers in this regard. There is no place in the profession of modern police work for the use of unnecessary force, no matter whom it is directed against. All too often, the hard-nosed police officer is heard to observe that we have become too soft, that we coddle lawbreakers, and that we have to teach them to fear and respect the law. Sadly, such attitudes do nothing but instill contempt and hatred for the law and all of its representatives.

Although the day is not yet come that violence has been conditioned out of our social fabric, the day has long since passed that police service should have taken the lead in diffusing the violent character of its own response to social conflict. The use of institutional violence as a tactic of social control is inexcusable. The failure of research and development aspects of police service to produce an array of nonlethal weapons and control devices to keep pace with the many advances in sophisticated weapons of destruction, is indicative of our collective social mind-set in this age of technological miracles. To advocate disarming American police along the lines of the British experience (even at a time when our friends across the Atlantic are seriously reconsidering their own position on this matter) would be the ultimate in speciousness. But to advocate a reassessment of the usefulness, as well as the ethics, of indiscriminate police force would seem to be the primary hope for an acceptable solution to the problem of violence in our society.

That violence is almost endemic in our body politic hardly needs explication. Contrary to popular belief, however, fostered primarily by official dictum and a gaggle of self-seeking political demagogues, the rate of police injury and death as a result of such lawlessness is *not* constantly rising. The rate has in fact changed little nationwide since 1963. The rate of civilians killed by police, however, *is* rising steadily. And still the hard-liners call for more forceful, aggressive police work. It is our national shame that the call is not for more professionalism.

SEARCHES AND SEIZURES

The moment of arrest is one of the most crucial points in the criminal justice process. The outcome of the entire case may well hinge upon how the police officer conducts himself at this juncture. The time of arrest often affords the opportunity to gather evidence that is absolutely vital to the development of the case. A search of the person arrested and of the area in which the arrest is made may very well produce conclusive evidence of the suspect's guilt or innocence. Such a search might produce evidence linking the prisoner with the crime under investigation (numbered currency taken in a bank robbery), the crime scene itself (paint smears in a case of hit-and-run driving), or with the victim (pubic hairs and vaginal stains in a rape case). In addition to the offense for which the prisoner has been arrested, evidence on his person or at the scene may connect him with other offenses, past or ongoing in nature. But what is the competency of such evidence in a subsequent court of law?

It depends upon how the evidence was obtained. It also depends to a large extent upon the philosophical makeup of the U.S. Supreme Court at the particular point in time. In a 1969 case, Justice Byron R. White wrote a dissenting opinion in which he stated that "Few areas of the law have been so subject to shifting constitutional standards over the last fifty years as that of the search 'incident to an arrest.'"

Generally, the search incidental to an arrest should be confined to the person of the individual apprehended and to the vicinity in which the arrest occurs. A search may be characterized as preliminary or thorough in nature.

Preliminary Search

The primary purpose of a preliminary search, customarily executed at the time of arrest, is the discovery of concealed weapons (for obvious reasons) and the location of incriminating evidence. There is no set procedure for conducting such a search; it must always be determined by the circumstances of the case. Haste, carelessness, and indifference, however, are to be guarded against at all times. The consequences of a botched preliminary search may include the escape of the prisoner, injury to an innocent bystander, and death for the offending police officer.

Although this kind of search is often referred to as a "frisk," it is in fact somewhat more thorough than this term would imply. In 1968 the Court approved the police procedure of stop-and-frisk in the case of *Terry* v. *Ohio*, 394 U.S. 1. It limited the "frisk" to something less than a full search allowing only a "protective search" for weapons. A preliminary search of a suspect in custody, however, is considerably broader in scope.

It must be systematic and complete within the limits of its design. A variety of techniques may be used. Perhaps the most common is the wall search. The prisoner is instructed to face the wall—or the police sedan, or a tree, etc.—and lean forward with his arms outstretched. In this off-balance position, he is extremely limited in mobility. The search may proceed with one officer, or two, or more, depending upon the situation.

The prisoner's clothing and limbs must be methodically searched. If restraining devices are required in order to conduct the search, the double-locking type of handcuff is the most reliable method. The prisoner's hands are cuffed behind his back and he now leans against the wall with his head, more off balance and disadvantaged than before. But a special warning is in order. The handcuff can be used as a lethal striking weapon as well as a restraining device. More than a few police officers have been severely injured by a prisoner wielding a metal handcuff fastened to one wrist. Extreme caution must be observed at all times, regardless of the slight stature or seemingly pliant personality of the prisoner. Such a readily improvised weapon is a devastating equalizer.

As a general rule, a prisoner's hands should never be hand-cuffed in front of his body. If for any reason it does become necessary to do so, a belt or necktie or short piece of rope should be used to further secure the hands. In transporting a prisoner by a vehicle, his hands might effectively be neutralized by hand-cuffing them under his knees.

It should also be noted that handcuffs are not failure-proof. Handcuffs may be "shimmied" by using a thin strip of flexible steel inserted between the cam groove and the claw shank. Experienced police officers will know the advisability of a thor-ough preliminary body search.

Custodial Search

Once the prisoner has been transported (by use of official police vehicle only) to the place of detention, he is then afforded a complete body and clothing search in conjunction with the booking process. Especially in the case of serious crimes, it is the better procedure to conduct a thorough search of the pris-oner at this time, regardless of the extent of the preliminary search at the time of arrest. A complete strip search is advisable. For the most part, this in-house custodial search is conducted by personnel other than the arresting officers. It goes without saying that female attendants must be provided for searches of women prisoners.

Place Search

After the prisoner has been searched and adequately secured at the place of arrest, the surrounding area should be searched for weapons and other physical evidence. The legal doctrine of "immediate control" is said to determine the area in which a search incidental to arrest may be effected.

Generally, if the arrest is made on the street, his person and the immediate vicinity may be searched; if the arrest is made in a vehicle, the vehicle may be searched; if the arrest is made indoors, the house, hotel room, apartment, or area generally under his control may be searched.

Seizure

The term seizure in the jargon of criminal investigation is not to be confused with an epileptic fit. It is nothing more than the term the law applies to the act of taking into custody any physical evidence belonging to, or connected with the prisoner, located as a result of a search of the prisoner's person or the immediate vicinity in which the arrest is made.

It should not be surprising to the criminal investigator that a suspect about to be arrested or questioned by a police officer would make every effort to conceal, destroy, or dispose of incriminating physical evidence of any offense with which he might be charged. Bookies have been known to swallow wagering evidence, addicts to hastily consume entire vials of illegal pills; murderers habitually discard their weapons in garbage cans, rivers, and wooded fields; burglars and street thieves routinely furnish their homes and apartments with the stolen lucre until it can be profitably disposed of. The investigator must be alert to the patterns of behavior common to perpetrators of a wide variety of specific criminal offenses.

Even so, the question remains—how far can the criminal investigator go in effecting a search for evidence under such circumstances?

Legal Implications

The Constitution and statutory law have generally been interpreted to prohibit unreasonable searches and seizures by law enforcement officers in the absence of a valid search warrant or sufficient evidence to arrest the suspect and thereby conduct a search incidental to arrest.

Every police officer should be intimately aware of the precise wording of the Fourth Amendment. "The right of the people to be secure in their persons, houses, papers, and effects, against unreasonable searches and seizures, shall not be violated, and no warrants shall issue, but upon probable cause, supported by oath or affirmation, and particularly describing the place to be searched, and the person or things to be seized." It would seem that the controlling aspect of the prohibition is the word *unreasonable*. The citizen is protected against *unreasonable* searches and seizures.

It is informative and interesting to note how the Supreme Court has interpreted the Fourth Amendment at varying times. From the time the Court first approved searches without warrants when incidental to a valid arrest, the pendulum has swung back and forth between restricted characterizations of such searches and a more expanded view. The law enforcement officer, however, will search in vain for any standards of uniformity or certainty as to the extent to which he may go in executing a warrantless search and seizure. The only aspect of this entire controversy upon which the Court has been able to voice unanimity is in its displeasure with the present state of the law on the subject.

No case has included a more thorough examination of the Supreme Court's historical interpretation of the Fourth Amendment than the 1971 case of *Coolidge* v. *New Hampshire*, 403 U.S. 433. The facts of the case involved a particularly brutal murder. A fourteen-year-old girl left her home one evening in response to an unidentified man's telephone solicitation of a baby-sitter. She went out in a heavy winter snowstorm and was not seen again until after a thaw some eight days later. Her body was discovered by the side of a major highway several miles from her home. She had been sexually abused and murdered.

Some days later, police went to the home of the man suspected to have committed the crime and questioned him in the presence of his wife. He denied the accusations of his involvement in the case. He admitted to the ownership of three guns: two shotguns and a rifle. He was generally cooperative and agreed to take a lie detector test. He was driven to the police station where the test was to be administered, and in his absence, two police investigators questioned his wife. She voluntarily turned over to them four guns and some clothes that she thought her husband might have been wearing on the night of the victim's disappearance.

In the days that followed, the police developed a quantity of evidence to support the theory that the suspect was guilty of the girl's murder. The state attorney general, who had personally taken charge of the police investigation, and who ultimately was to serve as the chief prosecutor at the trial, personally signed the arrest and search warrants, which he was permitted to do under state law. Police then arrested the suspect at his home.

At the time of the arrest, two automobiles owned by the suspect and his wife were parked in the driveway in plain sight, both from the street and from inside the house. Both cars were towed to the police station, where they were searched and vacuumed for evidence.

In the trial court, the four guns, along with vacuum sweepings of the suspect's automobile and clothing, were introduced to establish the suspect's guilt. The prosecution contended, in spite of conflicting ballistics testimony, that the bullets found in the victim's body had been fired by one of the guns. It further argued that microscopic analysis of the vacuum sweepings of the car showed that it was highly probable that the victim had been in the car, and that similar scientific examinations of the vacuum sweepings of the clothes indicated a high probability that the clothes had been in contact with the victim's body. A jury found the accused guilty of murder, and the judge sentenced him to life imprisonment. The state high court affirmed the judgment. The U.S. Supreme Court accepted the case in order to determine the constitutional issues it presented.

Initially the Court held that the state attorney general was not the neutral and detached magistrate required by the Constitution to issue warrants and that the search and seizure, therefore, had to be considered as if there had been no warrant at all. If it could be justified, it had to be done on some other theory.

The state advanced three separate theories, any or all of which would sustain the petitioner's conviction. First, the state claimed that the search was incidental to a valid arrest and therefore legal. Second, the state contended that a warrantless search and seizure is justified whenever police have probable cause to do so. And thirdly, the state argued that the car itself was an instrumentality of the crime and might be seized as such because it was in plain view of the police at the time of the suspect's arrest.

The Court dismissed the first theory out of hand as having no applicability to the case. It cited *Chimel* v. *California*, 395 U.S. 752 (1969), to the effect that the only time in which police may make a search and seizure incidental to a lawful arrest is when a weapon might be immediately available to the suspect, or if physical evidence within reach of the suspect might reasonably be exposed to destruction or contamination. Clearly, no such possibilities existed in the instant case.

As to the state's second contention, the Court held that such a theory, relying upon a previous ruling in the case of *Carroll* v. *United States*, 267 U.S. 132, was untenable unless the facts of the case clearly established the impracticality of obtaining a warrant prior to the search and subsequent seizure of physical evidence. The Court held that in the instant case there was absolutely no reason why the police could not have obtained a warrant in advance of the search and seizure. The facts showed that they had long suspected that the car had played a role in the murder; that the petitioner knew he was under suspicion but had been cooperative and made no effort to flee or destroy evidence in the car; and that the car itself could not be said to constitute a danger of any sort that required an instant seizure.

Finally, the Court gave its attention to the third contention of the state, namely, the "plain view" theory. It reiterated that it is well-established law that under certain circumstances the police may seize evidence that is in plain view without a warrant. The problem with this doctrine, said the Court, is to identify the circumstances in which it is applicable. It noted that *any* evidence seized by police will be in plain view at the moment of seizure at the very least.

An examination of the cases that are grounded upon the

"plain view" doctrine show that what they all have in common is that the police officer in each case had a prior justification for an intrusion in the course of which he inadvertently discovered an item of incriminating evidence against the accused. The Court stated emphatically that the "plain view" doctrine cannot be used to implement a general exploratory search from one object to another until *something* incriminating is at last discovered. It is the specific evil of the "general warrant" against which the Constitution is braced.

The controlling aspect of the doctrine, said the Court, is that plain view *alone* is never sufficient to justify the warrantless seizure of evidence, and that the discovery of such evidence must be inadvertent. The Court held that in the instant case, the facts simply did not bring it within the perimeters of such restrictions. The police knew precisely where the car was located, they knew that they expected it to provide physical evidence in support of the suspect's guilt, and they had ample time and opportunity for obtaining a valid search warrant.

The Court further stated that the requirement of warrants of arrest and of search and seizure have been a valued component of constitutional law for decades and was not an inconvenience to be weighed against the claims of police efficiency. The warrant should operate as a matter of course, said the Court, citing the 1967 case of *Katz* v. *United States*, 389 U.S. 347, to check the well-intentioned but mistakenly overzealous performance of law enforcement officers.

Since evidence obtained in the course of the search was used in the trial in violation of the rule previously announced in the 1961 case of *Mapp* v. *Ohio*, 367 U.S. 643, to the effect that evidence obtained by a search and seizure in violation of the Fourth Amendment is inadmissible in state and federal courts, the Court therefore reversed the conviction in the instant case and it was remanded to the state court for further proceedings consistent with the decision.

The *Coolidge* case has not, of course, eliminated the confusion and controversy of the Fourth Amendment and its application to the rule of law. Each case must still be decided upon its merits and regardless of the Supreme Court's stated rationale in the decision of a particular case, the factor of reasonableness would seem always to be of major importance, whether explicitly or implicitly so.

In view of the historical complexity of the Court's decisions, a police investigator would be well advised to adhere to the following rather simple guidelines: Police must obtain a warrant when it is their intention to seize evidence outside the scope of a valid search incidental to arrest. The Supreme Court has announced the view that such a requirement is easily understood and may be applied with consistency by courts and law enforcement officers alike. Such a principle protects the citizen in the spirit of the Fourth Amendment without overburdening the police and, in fact, leads in the long run to police professionalism through improved efficiency.

Obtaining the Search Warrant

Whenever a police investigator determines that a search without a warrant may not be conducted pursuant to any of the above discussed exceptions to the Fourth Amendment requirement, it is his responsibility to obtain a warrant from an authorized impartial magistrate.

A search warrant by definition is a written order, signed by the magistrate as an authorized representative of the state, directed to a peace officer and commanding him to search for certain clearly enumerated items of property and bring it before the magistrate.

A search warrant may issue only upon probable cause and must be supported by an affidavit naming or describing the person and/or property and/or place to be searched. Investigators should insure that such affidavits in support of an application for a warrant communicate to the magistrate informative facts rather than conclusions.

By way of example, the information upon which the application is grounded may have been obtained by police observation, examination of records, or the use of informants. The exact wording of the application depends upon the particular case, but it is an exacting requirement and more than one case has been lost as a result of deficiencies in this regard. The police investigator *must* therefore be intimately conversant with the case of *Aguilar* v. *Texas*, 378 U.S. 108 (1964) and the line of cases that have developed therefrom in the ensuing years.

In *Aguilar*, a search warrant had issued upon an affidavit of police officers who swore only that they had "received reliable information from a credible person and do believe" that narcotics were being illegally stored on the described premises. Although the U.S. Supreme Court reaffirmed the principle that the constitutional requirement of probable cause can be satisfied by hearsay information, it held the affidavit for the search warrant inadequate for the following two reasons.

One, the affidavit failed to specify any of the underlying circumstances necessary to enable the magistrate to form an independent judgment as to the validity of the informant's conclusion that the narcotics were in fact stored where he claimed they were.

Two, the affidavit offered no supporting evidence that the informant was credible and reliable other than the simple recitation of the claim by the police officers making the affidavit.

In the case of *Spinelli* v. *United States*, 393 U.S. 410 (1969), the Court found it desirable to further explicate the principles of the *Aguilar* decision in a case in which the supporting affidavit went further than the *Aguilar* affidavit. Here the petitioner was convicted in the trial court of traveling from Illinois to Missouri with the intention of conducting gambling activities in violation of Missouri law. The FBI affidavit in support of an application for a search warrant included not only a report from an anonymous informant, but also a report of an independent FBI investigation purporting to corroborate the informant's allegations.

The Court, however, held that the affidavit fell short of the standard announced in *Aguilar*. The affiant swore that the informant was "reliable," but he offered the magistrate no facts in support of such a conclusion. Nor was there sufficient information as to the underlying circumstances from which the informer made the determination that the petitioner was conducting a bookmaking operation. In the absence of such information, the Court held that the affidavit must then describe the accused's criminal activity in such detail as would allow the magistrate to know that he was relying on something substantial and not on mere rumor or mistake or malice.

The Court further held that the FBI's independent investigation was insufficient in that it corroborated nothing more than a very small detail of the informant's information, namely that the accused was in fact using two specified telephones and was "known" to the FBI and others to be a gambler. Such simple assertions, said the Court, are not sufficient basis for a magistrate's finding of probable cause.

But in the next few years, while perhaps making it more difficult for law enforcement officials to justify searches and seizures without warrants, the Court also made it easier to obtain warrants. The requirements of cases such as *Spinelli* and *Aguilar* were eased somewhat in another 5–4 decision in 1971.

In *United States* v. *Harris,* 403 U.S. 573, the Court found adequate an affidavit based largely on the hearsay evidence of an informer who was described only as "a prudent person" who had recent "personal knowledge" of the accused's whisky sales and who further admitted that he himself had made several purchases of moonshine whisky from the accused.

The Court again reiterated that a bare statement by a police officer that he believed the informant to be truthful would not, in itself, provide a factual basis for crediting the allegations of an unnamed informant. The Court went on, however, to find that in the present case, the facts were such as to warrant the conclusion that the affidavit contained sufficient basis for believing the informant, and that when coupled with the police officer's own stated knowledge of the accused's background, the magistrate had sufficient information upon which to make an independent determination of probable cause.

Particular stress was placed by the Court upon the informer's declaration against interest in the affidavit. The Court concluded that such admissions carry their own indicia of credibility—in spite of the likelihood that the informer was paid for his information, either in legal tender or by favor.

Furthermore, the Court executed a complete about-face from the *Spinelli* decision, in which case it had held that a police officer's "knowledge" of a gambler's reputation was insufficient ground upon which a magistrate might determine probable cause, by holding that such knowledge of a moonshiner's reputation was sufficient to justify a search warrant. A judgment of conviction was thus reinstated.

Such, then, are the tangled paths through which the judicial mind must labor in order to erect the temple of case law by which the police officer, as well as the individual citizen, must govern his or her conduct. That the temple is constructed upon shifting sand is patently clear. That the police officer plies his way through a quagmire of twists and turns and stops and starts is equally certain.

CIVIL AND CRIMINAL LIABILITY OF THE POLICE OFFICER

No discussion of the intricacies of the law concerning arrest and search and seizure should be concluded without commenting upon the legal problems of a personal nature that the police investigator may face as a result of the performance of his duties.

Anyone can be sued, including police officers. In this day of increasing litigious citizen response to official abuses, fancied and real, it behooves the police officer to give careful consideration to the unpleasant but ever-present possibility of a lawsuit.

Succinctly stated, the officer is responsible for forseeing the consequences of his acts. Like any other citizen, to be held liable for his harmful acts, he must have acted negligently; and the negligence must have been the proximate cause of the injury. An officer, therefore, is required to guard against only those things that an "ordinarily prudent man" would guard against under the existing circumstances.

What is a tort? *Black's Law Dictionary* defines a tort as a private or civil wrong. There are three elements of every tort action: 1) the existence of a legal duty from a defendant to plaintiff, 2) a breach of that duty, 3) injury as a proximate result of said breach.

The law enforcement officer should be aware that the law

of torts is concerned with civil wrongs against another person or his property, as distinguished from the criminal law, which is concerned with public offenses against the whole of society. Criminal law punishes the wrongdoer in the name of the state by the imposition of fine, imprisonment, or both. Civil law—tort law—compensates the individual victim for the injury done him by the imposition of money damages.

The practical operation of a tort judgment is this: The officer's salary may be subject to garnishment; his property, both real and personal, may be amenable to attachment; and there will, of course, be significant legal fees and court costs expended pursuant to the proceedings. Few police agencies furnish legal counsel for their employees in civil suits, and few police officers have the financial wherewithal to view such an event as anything but catastrophic.

In the main, the individual police officer is responsible for his own conduct. If he is incautious, injudicious, or inhumane, he may pay a considerable price for such unprofessional conduct. On the other hand, the very nature of his duties places even the most ethical, dedicated, and well-trained officer in a precarious position indeed. What, then, are some of the more common areas of tort exposure facing the modern police officer?

Excessive Force

A police officer is entitled to use only that force that is necessary to make a lawful arrest. Refer back to page 283 for a discussion on the use of force.

Malicious Prosecution

The fact that suits for malicious prosecution are uncommon should not deter the police officer from an understanding of his liability for such excesses of duty. If an officer acts willfully or maliciously out of spite or out of a desire for personal revenge in prosecuting the accused (the plaintiff of the civil action), then the accused (plaintiff) may ask for punitive damages in the civil suit for malicious prosecution, as well as for compensatory damages. Compensatory damages compensate the victim for the injury done him; punitive damages punish the wrong-doer for his malicious or willful behavior. It is not unusual for such damages to be awarded in six-figure increments.

False Arrest and False Imprisonment

A false arrest or false imprisonment is generally defined as an intentional, unlawful, and unprivileged restraint of a person's liberty, either in prison or elsewhere, resulting in harm to the person so confined. If an officer acts, therefore, without proper legal authority, he may be held liable for damages, even if the person arrested is eventually found guilty. It is the penalty an officer must pay if he acts outside his authority.

Consider the following example. In the case of *Spicy* v. *City of Miami*, 280 So. 2d 419 (1973), two police officers found a subject in the front seat of a taxi in a dazed incoherent condition. They later testified that they smelled no alcohol on his breath. An intern who examined the subject said he believed the man had been drinking but offered no opinion as to whether or not he was drunk. The subject was nevertheless booked on a drunk charge and assigned to a cell. His condition progressively worsened and he was again taken to hospital, this time being diagnosed as suffering from a fractured skull. He died without regaining consciousness.

The estate of the deceased filed suit for false arrest and imprisonment and won a substantial jury verdict against the city and the arresting officers. The Florida Supreme Court, in sustaining the award for damages entered in the trial court, ruled that the two police officers could not make a bad arrest good by relying upon the doctor's findings, which were in fact made after the event. The arresting officer must exercise his judgment at the time of the arrest, said the court, not later upon the exercise of hindsight. The court supported the trial court's finding that there had been no reasonable cause for either the arrest or the imprisonment of the deceased.

Deprivation of Civil Rights

The law enforcement officer should be especially aware of the
fact that he or she may not only be liable civilly for violations
of a citizen's civil rights, but may also be subject to criminal
liability, at both the federal and state levels.

Title 42, United States Code, Section 1983, states:

> Every person who, under color of any statute, ordinance,
> regulation, custom, or usage, or any State or Territory,
> subjects, or causes to be subjected, any citizen of the
> United States or other person within the jurisdiction
> thereof to the deprivation of any rights, privileges, or
> immunities secured by the Constitution and laws, shall be
> liable to the party injured in an action at law, suit in
> equity, or other proceeding for redress.

A suit under this section may be filed in the United States
District Court and may also be tried in state courts.

Federal criminal prosecutions in cases of police abuse are
tried in District Court under sections 241 and 242 of the U.S.
Criminal Code. Section 242 makes the willful deprivation of a
citizen's federal rights by police officers acting under color of
state law a criminal offense. Such offenses may be punishable
by a maximum of a one-thousand-dollar fine, a one-year imprisonment, or both. The language of Section 242 closely ap-
proximates that of Section 1983 of the civil rights damage
statute.

Section 241 is a conspiracy statute that makes it a crime
for two or more persons to intimidate or deprive a citizen of
the free exercise or enjoyment of any right or privilege secured
to him by the Constitution or the laws of the United States.
The penalty prescribed by the act is a maximum fine of five
thousand dollars, ten years imprisonment, or both.

In the case of *United States* v. *Price,* 383 U.S. 787 (1966),
the U.S. Supreme Court by its ruling fashioned the civil rights
laws into a fine cutting sword that struck fear and respect,
however grudging, into the hearts of all government officials

who were predisposed to consider one particular group of citizen rights and privileges to be of less importance than other groups.

The ruling was handed down in a case that involved the brutal slaying of three civil rights workers near Philadelphia, Mississippi. (Fig. 12.1.) The three youthful victims, one black and two white, were working on a black voter registration project when they disappeared. They had been arrested by the Neshoba County Sheriff's Department for speeding, paid a fine, and were released. They were not seen again. Their automobile was found abandoned and partly burned a short distance from where they were last seen. Months later, acting upon information furnished by an informant, the FBI discovered the bodies of the three young men buried under a newly constructed earthen dam on a nearby farm. All three had been shot, and the black man had been brutally beaten and mutilated.

Eighteen persons were eventually indicted under the federal civil rights statutes, but the District Court dismissed the indictment on the ground that Section 241 did not embrace conspiracies in violation of the due process clause of the Fourteenth Amendment. On appeal, the U.S. Supreme Court ruled otherwise. It held that Section 241 did, in fact, embrace conspiracies to interfere with Fourteenth Amendment rights and privileges where state officials participated in such conspiracies.

What is action, then, that is considered to be "under color of state law?" It is the abuse of power that is possessed by sanction of the state. And, having clothed its agent with such "color of authority," neither the state, nor its agent, can claim that the actions of the agent are not in the line of duty.

How, then, do this and other such rulings affect today's law enforcement officer? The plain fact of the matter is that lawsuits based upon allegations of police brutality and violations of civil rights are being filed in ever-growing numbers. Convictions involving criminal penalties and civil damages in substantial amounts have been more or less common, rather than exceptional, in the last few years. Such considerations have involved not only the individual police officer, but his employing agency and even the governmental entity of which they are a part.

MISSING CALL FBI

THE FBI IS SEEKING INFORMATION CONCERNING THE DISAPPEARANCE AT PHILADELPHIA, MISSISSIPPI, OF THESE THREE INDIVIDUALS ON JUNE 21, 1964. EXTENSIVE INVESTIGATION IS BEING CONDUCTED TO LOCATE GOODMAN, CHANEY, AND SCHWERNER, WHO ARE DESCRIBED AS FOLLOWS:

ANDREW GOODMAN	JAMES EARL CHANEY	MICHAEL HENRY SCHWERNER

RACE:	White	Negro	White
SEX:	Male	Male	Male
DOB:	November 23, 1943	May 30, 1943	November 6, 1939
POB:	New York City	Meridian, Mississippi	New York City
AGE:	20 years	21 years	24 years
HEIGHT:	5'10"	5'7"	5'9" to 5'10"
WEIGHT:	150 pounds	135 to 140 pounds	170 to 180 pounds
HAIR:	Dark brown; wavy	Black	Brown
EYES:	Brown	Brown	Light blue
TEETH:		Good: none missing	
SCARS AND MARKS:		1 inch cut scar 2 inches above left ear.	Pock mark center of forehead, slight scar on bridge of nose, appendectomy scar, broken leg scar.

SHOULD YOU HAVE OR IN THE FUTURE RECEIVE ANY INFORMATION CONCERNING THE WHEREABOUTS OF THESE INDIVIDUALS, YOU ARE REQUESTED TO NOTIFY ME OR THE NEAREST OFFICE OF THE FBI. TELEPHONE NUMBER IS LISTED BELOW.

DIRECTOR
FEDERAL BUREAU OF INVESTIGATION
UNITED STATES DEPARTMENT OF JUSTICE
WASHINGTON, D. C. 20535
TELEPHONE, NATIONAL 8-7117

June 29, 1964

The three who were slain, Andrew Goodman, James Chaney, and Michael Schwerner, pictured on an FBI circular (United Press International Photo)

FIG. 12.1 Murder of Mississippi civil rights workers

Neshoba County Sheriff Lawrence Rainey (right) and his
deputy, Cecil Price relaxing during their arraignment along
with 17 others on federal charges in connection with the
deaths of three civil rights workers. Charges were later
dismissed.   (United Press International Photo)

Patrols combing rural Mississippi
searching for the bodies of the
murdered civil rights workers
(Shel Hershorn/Black Star)

It stands to reason, therefore, that any intelligent police officer will make it one of his major priorities to acquaint himself in considerable detail with the statutes and case law bearing upon such matters. When the chips are down, it will more often than not be the individual officer who suffers most for the privilege of serving his fellow man in an absolutely vital but routinely unappreciated job.

- **DISCUSSION QUESTIONS**

1. By what authority is the police officer's power of arrest governed?

2. What are the boundaries of the police officer's right to make arrests?

3. What force may a police officer use in effecting a valid arrest?

4. What is meant by the phrase "search incident to an arrest"?

5. Distinguish between a preliminary search and a stop-and-frisk search.

6. Define a search warrant and state the basis for the issuance of such a warrant.

7. What is a a tort and how does it affect the police officer in the performance of his duties?

13

- ***Rules of Evidence and the Criminal Investigator In Court***

"Officer Smith, please tell the court whether the victim was dead or alive when you first arrived on the scene."

"Dead, sir. I would estimate that she had been dead for at least . . ."

"Objection! Officer Smith's opinion as to the time of death is beyond his level of expertise."

"Objection sustained."

"Were you able to ascertain the cause of death, Officer Smith?"

"Yes, sir. The victim had been . . ."

"Objection. Counsel's question calls for a medical conclusion."

"Sustained."

"Officer Smith, did you observe that the victim had been shot?"

"Yes, sir. There was a gunshot wound in her chest. The murder weapon was . . ."

"Objection!"

"Sustained."

"Was a weapon found at the scene of the crime?"

"Yes, sir. A gun was lying beside the body."

"Were you able to determine the owner of the gun?"

"Yes, sir. It belonged to the defendant."

"How did you make this determination?"

"The victim's husband told me that a friend of the defendant told him . . ."

"Objection, Your Honor! Such testimony is obviously based upon hearsay."

"Objection sustained."

And so it goes.

The success or failure of a criminal prosecution depends largely upon the amount and quality of the evidence accumulated during the investigation and how much of that evidence is ultimately admitted before the trial court. Evidence is that information, tangible and intangible, that is placed before the triers of fact (the jury) to assist them in determining the truth or falsity of the allegations against the accused. To be admissible, all evidence must satisfy the standards of relevancy, materiality, and competency.

To assist the triers of fact, rules of evidence have been developed that are designed to exclude from the unskilled juror's consideration that evidence that experience and reason have proven to be wanting in validity and reliability. It is important for the police officer to note, however, that there are no uniform rules of evidence pertaining to all jurisdictions alike. Each state and the federal government are empowered to determine its own rules concerning the admissibility of evidence.

Categories of Evidence

There are two major categories of evidence: direct and circumstantial.

Direct evidence is that evidence that establishes the particular point at issue without the reliance upon inference or presumption. If such evidence is true, then it conclusively establishes the fact it seeks to prove. For example, if A testifies that he saw B surreptitiously remove a ten-dollar bill from C's wallet, such testimony, if true, is direct evidence of the criminal offense.

Circumstantial evidence on the other hand, is that evidence that establishes one fact, or series of facts, other than the point at issue, and that tends thereby to establish by inference the main fact at issue. For example, if A observes B surreptitiously adding a powdered substance to C's food, and C thereafter dies of food poisoning, A's testimony would be circumstantial evidence giving rise to a reasonable inference that B poisoned C.

Types of Evidence

There are numerous types of evidence that may be said to be direct or circumstantial, depending upon the particular case. Evidence may be corroborative in nature; that is, it serves to strengthen, confirm, or explain other evidence already before the court. *Prima facie* evidence is evidence that is sufficient upon its face to establish the fact that it seeks to prove. Some facts need not be proved by formal presentation of evidence at all. These facts are matters of such widespread common knowledge that proof is unnecessary. For example, $2 \times 2 = 4$, the city of Chicago is located in the state of Illinois, the Pope is a Catholic. A court is empowered to accept evidence of this type on its own authority and no proof will be required. Recognition of such evidence is known as judicial notice.

Evidence can be received in court in many forms—written, spoken, or visual—and all may tend to directly prove a fact at issue or to prove said fact by inference by way of proving another closely related fact. All such evidence, however, must be material, relevant, and competent.

Materiality

To be material, the evidence must tend to prove a fact or facts the proof of which has a direct bearing upon a significant issue of the case. If the evidence is important to the case, it is material. That the defendant stole a particular automobile would, of course, be material to the charge of auto theft. But testimony to the effect that the automobile, once identified, bore white sidewall tires would be immaterial to the issue.

Relevancy

Evidence is generally said to be relevant if it tends to prove or disprove any disputed fact that has a direct bearing on the point at issue in the trial. For example, if A has been charged in the hit-and-run death of B, it is relevant evidence that seeks to prove that A does not know how to drive an automobile. Such evidence might be taken as proof that A struck B because A could not safely manage the vehicle, or it might influence the trier of fact to feel that it was unlikely that A would in fact have been behind the wheel of the vehicle in question.

Competency

The term applies to legal fitness. To be competent, evidence must be legally sufficient. It must have been obtained and handled in a lawful manner, and a knowledge of the type of police action that will invalidate the use of evidence is an absolute necessity to the law enforcement officer. He must become intimately acquainted with the case law and controlling decisions concerning such investigative techniques as arrests, searches and seizures, interrogation, and eavesdropping and wiretapping operations. Evidence that is tainted by any procedural irregularities in any of these areas is inadmissible in a court of law.

Proof and the Trier of Fact

Proof is the legal significance of admissible evidence. Its legal significance is determined by the *trier of fact*. It must be noted that evidence is not fact. Evidence is always subjective material, open to many opposing interpretations. Evidence is not necessarily true. It is subject to mistake or misstatement. A witness may lie on the stand, exaggerate, or simply misconstrue an event to which he was witness. Nevertheless, it is all evidence. The trier of fact must interpret the evidence and seek the truthfulness of the issue.

In the American system, the trier of fact may be a judge (in preliminary proceedings and nonjury trials), but more commonly it is the jury sitting in a trial court or as a grand jury. In deciding the issue of guilt or innocence in a criminal case, the jurors apply the rules of law (as given to them in the judge's instructions at the conclusion of the case) to the facts as they determine them from the evidence submitted during the trial. The outcome of the case depends solely upon the opinion of the jurors as to what the evidence meant.

As to the matter of proof, the primary instruction that the jury will receive from the judge concerns the *amount* of proof that the prosecution must produce in order for the defendant to be found guilty.

Presumption of Innocence and Burden of Proof

The bedrock of American criminal jurisprudence is the presumption that *every* defendant is innocent until proven guilty beyond any reasonable doubt.

Historically, *reasonable doubt* has been interpreted to mean that state of mind that falls short of an abiding conviction, to a moral certainty, of the truth of the charge against the defendant. It does not require proof beyond any *possibility* of doubt since no such certainty can ever exist concerning the affairs of man.

This presumption of innocence, then, places the burden of proof in all criminal cases squarely on the prosecution. It must prove the defendant's guilt beyond and to the exclusion of any reasonable doubt. The defendant is never required to prove his innocence. In fact, the defendant is not required to prove anything. Since a jury verdict of guilty must be unanimous, all the defendant must do is to create a reasonable doubt in the mind of at least one juror concerning the allegations against him. It is primarily for this reason that the police investigator must scrupulously adhere to the guidelines for handling evidence as laid down by the controlling case law. And since these guidelines exhibit such chameleon-like characteristics, it is absolutely essential that the modern, professionally oriented police investigator develop some of the mole-like tenacity of the legal scholar.

Exclusionary Rules

Obviously, if there is a set of rules governing the conditions under which evidence will be admitted in a court of law, there must likewise have developed a set of rules setting forth the circumstances under which evidence will not be admitted. These latter rules are called *rules of exclusion.*

The purpose of such rules is to assist the layman juror who is generally inexperienced in technical legal matters by limiting the kind of evidence that is presented to the jury for its consideration. Fearing that the layman would not properly discriminate between fact and rumor and allegation and truth, the law therefore developed a set of rules limiting the evidence that a witness may offer specifically to those things and events about which he has a direct sensory knowledge. Therefore, A may testify that he saw B strike C with a blunt instrument; A may *not* testify that D told A that B struck C with a blunt instrument. The latter testimony, if offered to prove the truth of the allegation that B struck C with a blunt instrument would be hearsay and therefore subject to exclusion.

It might well be noted at this point, however, that there are exceptions even to the rules of exclusion. For example, had the above testimony of A to the effect that D told A that B struck C with a blunt instrument been offered in evidence merely to prove that D made such a statement, and *not* to establish the truth of the allegation that B struck C, then A's testimony would be admissible.

Bearing in mind then, that there are exceptions to all of the following types of evidence that are generally inadmissible, we will discuss a few of the more commonly excluded areas.

Opinion evidence is generally inadmissible. A witness must testify only as to facts within his knowledge and not as to any opinions or conclusions that he might have drawn from such facts. It is the function of the jury to draw opinions and conclusions from the evidence.

There are exceptions to the opinion rule. A layman, for example, may express an opinion on matters of common observation. Such opinions are permitted only concerning subjects within the average person's experience and knowledge. On the other hand, opinion and conclusions are admitted when offered by a qualified expert in the area of his expertise. An expert, for the purposes of this rule, is an individual skilled in some art, trade, profession, or science whose knowledge of the subject area extends beyond the common knowledge of the layman. A medical doctor, for example, may offer an opinion concerning surgical procedure but not an opinion on traffic engineering.

Evidence concerning a person's character and reputation is also generally excluded under the rules. Primarily, such evidence cannot be introduced for the purpose of raising an inference of guilt in regard to the accusation being tried. The mere fact that a defendant stole an automobile when he was seventeen, was convicted of possessing marijuana when he was eighteen, and has a reputation for spending considerably more money than he earns as a schoolteacher can have no bearing upon whether or not he is guilty of the crime of rape for which he is presently being tried.

Evidence of previous crimes or acts may be introduced, however, if they tend to show that the defendant did in fact commit the particular crime for which he is being tried. For example, evidence that the defendant has committed similar crimes using similar techniques as were used in the case at bar, would be admissible to prove the defendant's method of operation, or *modus operandi*. Or evidence might tend to establish that the defendant has a reputation as a receiver of stolen goods, which tends to show that the defendant had guilty knowledge or intent when he accepted the offer of a slightly used new Cadillac for the bargain price of a thousand dollars. Or a defendant may be interposing a defense of accidental death to a charge of wife-murder, in which case, testimony is introduced by the prosecution to the effect that two previous wives of the defendant had died by "acidental" means.

Such evidence, though admissible, is not conclusive of guilt. The fact that two of the defendant's previous wives died deaths of accidental violence may give rise to a justifiable inference of the defendant's complicity and may shift the burden of proving otherwise to the defendant. Yet the presumption of guilt is subject to contrary proof; it is rebuttable.

A conclusive presumption, on the other hand, is not susceptible to being rebutted by contradictory evidence. Such presumptions are considered final. Everyone is presumed to know the law, for example. A man cannot be the victim of the crime of rape. Children under certain statutory age are presumed incapable of committing a crime. These are conclusions that are required, in effect, as a matter of law.

Hearsay evidence—secondhand evidence, information derived from third parties rather than a personal knowledge of the witness—is generally inadmissible. However, due to the importance that such evidence often has in developing the truth as to allegations under criminal investigation, courts have over the years come to allow a considerable number of exceptions to this rule. Due to expediency, information having to do with statements and acts of the defendant, victim, or codefendants, written records, and the admission of prior testimony when witnesses are not available, are regularly admissible in criminal trials.

Spontaneous exclamations are admissible on the rationale that a person is likely to speak the truth if he speaks under the stress of excitement in the event. The utterance must concern the event itself and must be made without the opportunity for deliberation. Such statements are admissible when related by anyone who heard the statements uttered. Generally, only a person who committed the act, or participated in it, or who witnessed it may be the author of the exclamation. The exclamation may be favorable or unfavorable to the interests of the declarant.

In this connection, confessions, admissions, and declarations against interest are recognized exceptions to the hearsay rule, subject of course to the restrictions of the Fifth and Sixth Amendments of the U.S. Constitution in obtaining such statements. Statements made by codefendants, however, are only admissible if the material that implicates all nondeclarant codefendants can be deleted from the testimony before the court. If such deletions cannot be made and the prosecution desires to use the statement against the declaring codefendant, it must sever the cases and proceed against the codefendants in separate trials.

Similar to the spontaneous exclamation in rationale, is the policy of admitting into evidence statements that qualify as dying declarations. It is felt that a person confronting death is likely to tell the truth in his final utterances, even if it constitutes an admission against interest. To be admissible, such evidence must relate to statements made by a dying person who believes he is dying and who must, in fact, die. Of course, the declarant must have been competent at the time the statement was made.

Documentary evidence has long been held admissible under certain circumstances as exceptions to the hearsay rule. Official and business records are admissible, for example, if made in the regular course of business, at or near the time of the event recorded, under such circumstances as to indicate trustworthiness.

The "best evidence rule" generally controls the admission of such documents. Therefore, the original of a written document should be produced whenever possible and cogent reason offered for the absence of the original when duplicates or copies are sought to be admitted.

There are instances in which a witness is simply unavailable at the time of trial. If the prior testimony is given under oath, involves the same issue, and the same opportunity is provided to cross-examine said witness, such prior testimony is generally admissible. It is not admissible, however, without a clear demonstration of the impossibility of producing the absent witness in person, for the defendant's constitutional right of confrontation and cross-examination always takes precedence over procedural rules of expediency.

Corpus Delicti Evidence

No charge can be supported in a criminal trial unless the *corpus delicti* has been established. This is a term that often confuses the lay citizen and the police officer alike. Contrary to popular films and television, the *corpus delicti* does not refer to the body of the victim in a homicide case. In its simplest terms, it refers to the body of the crime. The crime may be murder, robbery, theft, and the like. The crime may have a victim (rape) or be victimless (gambling), but it must have a *corpus delicti.*

The *corpus delicti* is comprised of the elements of the offense of the particular crime in question. Every crime consists of distinctive elements, all of which must be established before a conviction of an accused may be sustained. For example, at common law, the *corpus delicti* of the crime of burglary consisted of the following elements: there was a breaking, and an entering, of the dwelling house, of another, in the nighttime, with the intent to commit a felony therein. If any one or more of these elements is missing, a conviction cannot be sustained for the crime of burglary in any jurisdiction that continues to base its criminal code upon the common law.

It might be noted that about half of the states in America still rely upon the common law. Even a state that has abolished common-law offenses and made all crimes statutory, however, may still make reference to the old common law for definitional purposes.

In any case, whether governed by common law or statutory foundations, every criminal offense is comprised of a series of elements that must be established by the prosecution before a defendant can be adjudged guilty in a criminal trial. In fact, the prosecution must prove the *corpus delicti* at trial before it can even attempt to establish the defendant's guilt.

Likewise, a police investigator should keep this requirement uppermost in mind while conducting his or her investigations. He should organize his investigation around the elements of the offense that he believes has been committed. If in the course of the investigation he determines that the elements do not exist to sustain the specific charge, he should withhold making an arrest pending further investigation. Otherwise, there may exist sufficient elements of an offense other than the one initially under investigation, and the charges to be brought against the suspect may then be duly amended. Certainly the time to make such discoveries and amendments is in the investigatory phase and not after the case has proceeded to court.

CASE PREPARATION
AND APPEARANCE IN COURT

It should not be difficult to understand why Officer Smith was having trouble managing the questioning of the defense counsel in the hypothetical cross-examination that opened this chapter. There is no more demanding phase of a criminal investigation than that of the investigator's testimony in court. No matter how commendable his performance has been up to this point, all of the fine work that has gone before can be undone by the few minutes, or hours, that the investigator spends on the witness stand.

Of course his demeanor, his attitude, and even his personal appearance, will have considerable bearing upon the value of his testimony. And in the final analysis, the value of his testimony is measured solely by the reception it receives from judge and jury. It does not matter at this point that his superiors are pleased with the way he has handled his part of the investigation, or that the prosecutor is satisfied with the manner in which the investigation has been conducted and presented to him, or that the news media has for weeks been laudatory of the department's professionalism in general and the investigator's competence in particular. What matters now is whether or not the investigator can perform as a witness with the same high degree of competence and professionalism.

Certainly he should be well prepared for his appearance. No other single factor will impress the judge and jurors more. He should review his notes of the investigation and refresh his recollection on all important details of the case. And he must have a thorough working knowledge of the complex and numerous rules of evidence that govern the testimony of all witnesses. Above all, he should prepare his testimony in anticipation of the questions that will be asked him on the stand by prosecutor and defense counsel alike.

He should make an effort to know as much about the attorneys in the case as is possible, including their general reputation in the courtroom, their techniques of cross-examination, and their personal idiosyncrasies. He should prepare to face any tactical approach—charm, skepticism, belligerency, and even personal animosity.

The best course at all times is the display of a calm, dignified effort to be helpful. The investigator must never lose his composure or his temper on the witness stand, no matter how much he is provoked. He can best achieve such equanimity by adhering scrupulously to the truth in all matters, large and small. If he does not recall the answer to a question, he should say so and request to be allowed to refresh his memory by referring to his notebook. If he does not know the answer, he should acknowledge the fact; he should never attempt to bluff his way through such an evidentiary minefield.

Nor should the investigator hesitate to acknowledge the preparation he has made in anticipation of his appearance as a witness. He would clearly have been remiss in his duties had he not prepared and should therefore offer no apologies or excuses for having done so. Certainly he should not deny having done so.

For example, one of the favorite lines of cross-examination of many astute defense attorneys is to suddenly turn on the witness and demand if he or she has been rehearsed prior to giving testimony. If the witness flusters and says no, of course not, the defense attorney will make a liar out of him in front of the jury by establishing the fact that the witness has most assuredly discussed his testimony with the prosecutor or his associates, more than likely on numerous occasions. He will then demand to know with heavy sarcasm and innuendo in his voice, why the witness has lied, why he was "coached" as to how to tell his story, how much of his testimony is his own and how much has been suggested or "planted" by his coaches, and similar such nonsense. The witness will indeed be made to look at least foolish, if not actually a liar.

On the other hand, if the witness merely smiles in response to the provocative question and simply replies that of course he rehearsed his testimony with the prosecuting attorney and that he did so in order to be sufficiently prepared for his appearance and to remove any possibility of mistake concerning the evidence he was to give, the investigator may rest assured that the astute defense attorney will instantly abandon that line of questioning and proceed on another tack.

One word of warning: In spite of the contrary advice often advanced in manuals and textbooks on the subject, the investigator should *never* attempt to match wits with the defense attorney, no matter how thoroughly prepared he believes himself to be. It will seldom be thorough enough. He is not trained for such courtroom jousting, whereas the defense attorney most likely is. In addition, it is not the best method of impressing judge and jury. It bears repeating: Calm, dignified, articulate truthfulness is the guiding rule. Professionalism is the goal.

- **DISCUSSION QUESTIONS**

1. *Name and define the two major categories of evidence.*

2. *What three requirements must be met by all evidence to be admissible in court?*

3. *What are exclusionary rules of evidence?*

4. *What is meant by the term* corpus delicti *evidence?*

Index